A METAPHYSICS OF BEING AND GOD

James V. McGlynn, S.J.
and
Sister Paul Mary Farley, R.S.M.

PRENTICE-HALL, INC. Englewood Cliffs, N.J.

Imprimi potest

Walter L. Farrell, S.J.
Provincial of the Detroit Province

Nihil obstat

Walter L. Farrell, S.J.
Censor Deputatus

Imprimatur

✠ Henry E. Donnelly, D.D.
Vicar General
Archdiocese of Detroit

Library of Congress Catalog Card Number: 66-12091

Printed in the United States of America 57854-C

Current printing (last digit):
10 9 8 7 6 5 4 3 2

PRENTICE-HALL INTERNATIONAL, INC., *London*
PRENTICE-HALL OF AUSTRALIA, PTY. LTD., *Sydney*
PRENTICE-HALL OF CANADA, LTD., *Toronto*
PRENTICE-HALL OF INDIA (PRIVATE), LTD., *New Delhi*
PRENTICE-HALL OF JAPAN, INC., *Tokyo*

ACKNOWLEDGMENTS

The authors wish to thank the various publishers who granted permission to quote from copyrighted material. These are, in every instance except those listed below, indicated in the footnotes of the chapters. Acknowledgment is here made to the following publishers for permission to quote from English translations of the works of Plato, Aristotle, and St. Thomas Aquinas.

Benziger Brothers, Inc., for St. Thomas Aquinas, *Summa Theologica,* trans. Fathers of the English Dominican Province (1947), Parts I-II and II-II.

Doubleday & Company, Inc., for St. Thomas Aquinas, *On the Truth of the Catholic Faith* (*Summa Contra Gentiles*), Books I, II, III, IV, trans. Anton C. Pegis, James F. Anderson, Vernon J. Bourke, C. J. O'Neill, reprinted by permission.

B. Herder Book Co., for St. Thomas Aquinas, *Compendium of Theology,* trans. C. Vollert (1947).

Oxford University Press, for Aristotle, *Metaphysics,* in *The Basic Works of Aristotle,* ed. R. McKeon (New York: Random House, 1941); for Plato, *Republic* and *Timaeus,* in *The Dialogues of Plato,* trans. B. Jowett (New York: Random House, 1937).

Prentice-Hall, Inc., for St. Thomas Aquinas, *Summa Theologiae,* Part I, Question 2, Article 3, in *Treatise on God,* trans. J. F. Anderson (1963), pp. 10-11.

Random House, Inc., and Burns & Oates, Ltd., for St. Thomas Aquinas, *Summa Theologiae,* Part I, in *Basic Writings of St. Thomas Aquinas,* ed. A. C. Pegis, Vol. I (1945).

Henry Regnery Company, for St. Thomas Aquinas, *Commentary on the Metaphysics of Aristotle,* trans. J. Rowan, 2 vols. (1961); for St. Thomas Aquinas, *Truth,* trans. R. W. Mulligan, J. V. McGlynn, R. W. Schmidt, 3 vols. (1952-54).

PREFACE

A German proverb says, "*Aller Anfang ist schwer.*" (Every beginning is difficult.) Perhaps this is especially true of philosophy, since it asks questions and takes a point of view which the student has encountered in no other course. There is some need, therefore, to help the beginner learn to think philosophically and to approach philosophical discussion with confidence. *A Metaphysics of Being and God* has been conceived as such an introduction to philosophy and is dedicated to the thesis that college students can gain metaphysical insight.

Our objective, consequently, has been to write a textbook for the introductory course which combines what in the past has been done separately as metaphysics and natural theology. The present text does not presuppose earlier courses in philosophy. It is meant to give the student enough help (with the essential guidance of an instructor) to learn the elements of metaphysics.

Obviously, not everyone will agree with our choice of topics. It represents, however, our considered judgment about the questions and the amount of matter which can and should be included in an introductory course combining metaphysics and natural theology. The order of our presentation may require some explanation. The discussion of a notion of being has been delayed until the ninth chapter in order to give the student some content for "being" before he is asked to look into its meaning. The proof for the existence of God comes earlier than in most textbooks but at the logical place in our plan. We begin from our experience of finite being and discover the *possibility* of God in Chapter 3. In Chapter 4 we study causality, the bridge between our knowledge of finite being and God. It is natural, then, to elaborate a proof for the existence of God in the fifth chapter. There should be no difficulty about the order of the other chapters.

Like most textbooks, ours reflects our experience in studying, discussing, and teaching metaphysics. The philosophy faculties of West Baden College and Louvain have left their mark on one of us and that of the University of Detroit has had a comparable influence on the other. We acknowledge our debt to our mentors without burdening them with the responsibility for what we have written. Almost everything in this book has been discussed at length with our colleagues at the University of Detroit and Mercy College of Detroit. We are grateful to them for the clarification of our ideas from this discussion. They will doubtless find that we have appropriated many of their ideas in the process of formulating our own positions. We hope, too, that our successes and failures with past classes will be reflected here. We have tried to use what has proved most successful in our teaching and to avoid modes of presentation which proved ineffective in the classroom.

It is never possible to acknowledge adequately the help authors receive in writing a book. We thank all those who contributed in so many ways to make our task easier. Special mention must be made, however, of Reverend Edmund W. Morton, S.J. for his careful reading of the manuscript and his many fine suggestions for improving it, and of Mrs. Eugene L. Wielock, who painstakingly transcribed the final version of the manuscript from more than a score of tapes.

JAMES V. MCGLYNN, S.J.
SISTER PAUL MARY FARLEY, R.S.M.

CONTENTS

1 INTRODUCTION

THE TASK OF METAPHYSICS

"Amid all the menacing signs that surround us in the middle of this twentieth century, perhaps the one which fills thoughtful people with the greatest foreboding is the growing general sense of meaninglessness. It is this which underlies most of the other threats. How is it that the more able man becomes to manipulate the world to his advantage, the less he can perceive any meaning in it?" [1]

Owen Barfield is expressing perhaps the most important concern of our times. For in philosophy, literature, and the social sciences, not to speak of our personal lives, we are constantly brought face to face with the problem of the meaning of our lives and of the whole world. We have reached unimagined heights in our development of scientific knowledge. Within a decade we will have men on the moon. Our computers are working problems which would have taken unaided mathematicians generations to calculate. Automation is

---

[1] Owen Barfield, "The Rediscovery of Meaning," *The Saturday Evening Post,* January 7, 1961, p. 36.

producing better products at fantastic speeds. No one can dream what the next century may bring. And yet we live in the shadow of "The Bomb"; we hold our breath in a cold war which could erupt into the bloodiest war of all history; the underdeveloped nations outside our borders and the underprivileged people within them seem like vast powder kegs ready to explode and destroy us all.

Even such a seemingly confirmed optimist as H. G. Wells wrote in 1946: "If his [Wells' own] thinking has been sound, then this world is at the end of its tether. . . . He [Wells] has come to believe that the congruence with mind, which man has attributed to the secular process, is not really there at all. . . . A remarkable queerness has come over life. It is as if the law of gravitation no longer functioned in a physical world. . . . Mankind has reached an impasse and there is no way around, or above or through this impasse. It is the end." [2]

On the European continent some of the existentialists have voiced similar despair. Jean-Paul Sartre's plays, for instance, portray man in an impossible situation, faced with problems to which there are no solutions. In *No Exit,* "Hell is other people." Their looks, their judgments of me continually freeze me into poses from which I cannot break loose. I am thief or coward or what have you, as they see me. And in the long run their viewpoint will triumph, for they will still be there after I die. For Sartre, "Man is condemned to freedom" in the sense that he is condemned to attempt to give meaning to his life, knowing all the while that he can never succeed, because the world is fundamentally absurd.

This conviction of the absurdity of the universe has been taken over by our extreme "Beats." Hazel Barnes compares French existentialist Jean Genet and Jack Kerouac, a leader of the "Beat Generation": "In the works of both there is an aggressive, wholly negative individualism, a contempt for all middle class, respectable values, and all idealism. . . . Both writers take it for granted that existence, as such, is painful and meaningless, though Genet's heroes escape

---

[2] *The Mind at the End of Its Tether* (New York: Didier Publishers, 1946), pp. 1–4, as quoted by Peter Stanlis in "The Present Impasse of the Idea of Progress," *Modern Age,* II, No. 1 (Winter 1957–58), 73.

via private myth, whereas Kerouac's characters are more inclined to try marijuana." [3]

This sense of meaninglessness is not new. Four hundred years ago Shakespeare had Macbeth cry out in a moment of despair at the loss of his wife:

> Tomorrow, and tomorrow, and tomorrow,
> Creeps in this petty pace from day to day,
> To the last syllable of recorded time;
> And all our yesterdays have lighted fools
> The way to dusty death.
> Out, out, brief candle!
> Life's but a walking shadow, a poor player
> That struts and frets his hour upon the stage
> And then is heard no more: it is a tale
> Told by an idiot, full of sound and fury,
> Signifying nothing.

There are various ways of reacting to this situation. The Beats, as we have just pointed out, rebel against all conformity in order to dramatize their rejection of what they consider to be the false values of our society. They show by their dress and their actions that they want no part of our "civilized" world. But although they reject the current social values, they have no new values to put in their place. For them the world is absurd and they can only proclaim this absurdity. We meet something like this in the "Theater of the Absurd." Thus in Samuel Beckett's *Waiting for Godot* we see the absurdity of existence portrayed in the utter futility of man's insistent search for something absolute to give meaning to his life. It is as though man is waiting for a God who is not there. Ultimately, Beckett is saying, we must forget about looking for any justification or explanation of human existence. It is absurd; there is no explanation.

At the opposite extreme from the Beats and the literature of the absurd we find the positivists. They reduce all questions about the meaning of life and of the world to purely scientific statements: "We shall set ourselves to show that insofar as statements of value are significant, they are ordinary 'scientific' statements; and that inso-

---

[3] *Humanistic Existentialism* (Lincoln: University of Nebraska Press, 1959), p. 348.

far as they are not scientific, they are not in the literal sense significant, but are simply expressions of emotions which can be neither true nor false." [4] What Ayer means here is that the only language that makes any sense is language that talks about the things we experience. We can experience desks and tables, people and animals, food and drink, and things like these. Everything that can have any meaning must in some way be reduced to these kinds of things. Thus our sense of value, if it is to have any meaning, must be described and explained in terms of physiological reactions, that is, in terms of what happens in our nervous system, especially our brain. For thinkers like Ayer, any statement which cannot be verified in the way we verify chairs and tables is a "metaphysical" statement and so is meaningless. The soul, the mind, virtue and vice, good and evil are words which we use, and which philosophers from Plato and Aristotle to our contemporaries have used, but which for men like Ayer have no real meaning. Rudolph Carnap, one of the founders of this system of philosophy, which is called logical positivism, says quite clearly: "*Metaphysical* statements are neither true nor false, because they assert nothing; they contain neither knowledge nor error; they lie completely outside the field of knowledge, of theory, outside the discussion of truth or falsehood. . . . They express . . . permanent emotional or volitional dispositions." [5] He adds that metaphysics, when it tries to discuss things beyond the range of our sense experience, is like lyric poetry. But the poet at least knows that he is a poet: "A metaphysical statement, however—as distinguished from a lyrical verse—*seems* to have some [representative function and theoretical content], and by this not only is the reader deceived, but the metaphysician himself." [6]

These are two extreme positions. Most people, including the majority of philosophers, take a stand somewhere between them. As we proceed it will become apparent that we are convinced our lives and the world we live in do have meaning and it is possible to

---

[4] A. J. Ayer, *Language, Truth, and Logic* (New York: Dover Publications, Inc., 1946), pp. 102–3.

[5] *Philosophy and Logical Syntax*, as quoted in W. Alston and G. Nakhnikian, *Readings in Twentieth-Century Philosophy* (New York: The Free Press of Glencoe, Inc., 1963), p. 432, by courtesy of The Orthological Institute, London, England. Our italics.

[6] *Ibid.*, p. 433.

construct a valid philosophy embodying this meaning. Up to this point we have been talking about philosophy in general. We have been asking whether our world and our own lives have any meaning. In the philosophical discussion of the world and ourselves we can ask either very specific questions or very general questions. Metaphysics asks the *most* general, the ultimate, questions about the meaningfulness of our world and the universe. It wants to know whether there is more to the universe than appears at first glance and whether our universe has any sort of unity. It asks where it came from, if it did come from anywhere, and where it is going. However, to the beginner, metaphysics may seem to answer these questions in a rather dull way—for it is sometimes called the study of "being as being." It will be our task in what follows to show that these general questions are important and that what we might call the question of being is important because the stand which we take regarding it influences in a radical way our ideas about the meaning of the universe. The crucial questions for every one of us, "Who am I?" and "Where am I going?" can be answered with some depth of meaning only in metaphysics. In other words, I can know my place in the universe only when I have some idea of the universe as a whole. And to give us an idea of the universe as a whole is the job of metaphysics.

METAPHYSICS AND THE WAYS OF KNOWING

Branches of Knowledge

Before we begin our formal consideration of metaphysics, it may be wise to spend a little time placing it in the general scheme of our knowledge. All knowledge implies a presence of the known to the one knowing. What distinguishes a person from a thing is that he is open to be united in knowledge and love with other beings than himself. This is put very strikingly by the phenomenologists, who talk both of man's finding himself "in the world" among objects and other persons and of man's "openness to Being." Martin Heidegger, for instance, defines truth as the unhiddenness or uncoveredness of Being. Man is the place in which Being reveals itself. Being can reveal itself in various ways and man can be united to Being in many ways. Or to put it differently, we can say that the different ways of knowing are different ways in which and by which the known can be united to the knower, different ways in which a person can both go out from himself to penetrate something other and receive into himself the being of something other.

In fact each of these ways of knowing opens up a whole world in itself. The aspect of the world opened up by physics is different from that opened up by biology and both are poles apart from that opened up for us by the novel. Each gives us its own insight into the universe and each requires its own discipline of the mind. The chemist in his laboratory thinks differently from the artist in his studio. And yet it is still one world which we know in these various ways and one self in each person who does the knowing and in each discipline one desire of a unified vision of all.

There is no limit, in a way, to what the human person can know. He never reaches the point at which he can say there is not one more thing he can know. He has therefore the capability of being united to all things by his knowledge of them. In principle there is nothing which he cannot know. On the other hand no man knows anything so perfectly that he cannot learn more about it. There is always more being than man has in his grasp; he cannot circumscribe all reality or possess it perfectly. This is a commonplace truth which we all know: the more we learn, the more we see how little we really know. Einstein's discovery of relativity led the way to a tremendous advance over Newtonian physics, but for every new answer it gave, the theory of relativity opened dozens of new fields of research—the nature of time, quantum mechanics, molecular theory, and so forth. In biology we have discovered the gene-structure of cells and so expanded our knowledge of genetics. Simultaneously, a whole battery of new questions about heredity have had to be asked. Consequently, our knowledge has always to be renewed and expanded. It is ever possible for us to take another look at the very things we have long studied and know them in the same way but more thoroughly. It is also possible for us to look at them in new ways and to know them newly. The recognition of this latter possibility is what brings us to the study of metaphysics.

If after a certain amount of educational experience we were to consider the various disciplines we had studied, and were to attempt to see how these differ from one another or are united with one another; and if we were to associate with these all our informal and unstructured ways of gaining and possessing knowledge, we might find ourselves using some of the countless adjectives which have been employed by others in describing and grouping all the ways of knowing. We might speak of personal knowledge, of humanistic or artistic knowledge, of intuitive or discursive knowledge, of concrete or abstract knowledge, of philosophic or scientific knowledge; we might talk in terms of knowledge of nature or of man or of God, in terms of quantity or quality, measurement or insight. Presumably we should end by characterizing the various human approaches in knowledge according to their objects, methods, and aims.

Whatever difficulties we might have in finding a framework, for the graphic ordering of all the ways of knowing, it is clear that knowledge through the arts is characterized differently from scientific knowledge. Humanistic or artistic [7] knowledge is not, as such, precisely the object of a logical demonstration; the abstract is incarnate in the concrete, the universal is both sensibly and intellectually encountered in an experience of the individual. The original epiphany, or intuition, of the artist—whether he is a poet, painter, or musician—is embodied with a form that expresses that intuition, renders that reality present to the mind of another. In *Hamlet* "The play's the thing"; it is not the formulation of a theory.

Scientific Knowledge

Science penetrates reality and renders it present in a way quite different from the arts. The poet and the botanist may both approach a rose. The botanist, as a man, may be poetic, and the poet, as a man, may be botanical, but as poet and botanist they will regard the rose in largely different ways. Science, in its traditional and broad sense,[8] is an organized body of knowledge, ordered in such a way that its truth is demonstrable, causal, and reasonably certain.

[7] The areas usually designated as humanistic knowledge are literature, the plastic arts, music, some approaches in philosophy, and some interpretations of history.

[8] This is in contradistinction to the contemporary use of the term in a sense limited to the area of the natural sciences—physical, biological, and behavioral sciences. Obviously, in this latter sense, which implies the subject matter and methods of the natural sciences, metaphysics could not be called a science. If the meaning is clear, there need be no unnecessary debate over terminology.

To say that a truth is demonstrable is to say that it is able to be proved and explained, and therefore able to be taught and learned. Scientific knowledge must reach to the causes or principles of the things it tries to understand; and the order of its truths, together with the order of its demonstrations, will follow from one another not merely as an accumulation of data, but in causal relationship. The certitude of science varies in degree, but it aims always to be more than mere opinion.

Metaphysics partakes in a limited way of nearly every approach in knowledge; everything that helps to understand being, insofar as it is being, is both valuable and necessary in its study. There is a sense in which metaphysics is the most abstract of all intellectual pursuits, and a sense in which it is the most concrete. It has received nourishment from existential and artistic experience and from starkly rational deduction. It has been expressed in concrete art forms, in concrete lives, and in precise and systematic treatises. Its methods have been called dialectical and intuitive, objective and subjective, existential and essential, empirical and idealistic, critical and symbolic, speculative and practical. In spite of, or even because of, this variety, for those who accept the validity of metaphysics, it is usually to be understood first as a science. Philosophy is so understood, and metaphysics is a part of philosophy.

The rather broad interpretation which this reference to philosophy as a science puts on the word "science" can be clarified somewhat by an understanding of what it means to test a metaphysical propostion. Michael Novak has said: "The testing of a metaphysical proposition, however, differs from the testing of a proposition of physics in that the data for the latter are almost entirely external to the knower, in observable experiments contrived to test the theoretical system at a given point; whereas the data of metaphysics are almost entirely internal to the knower. This does not mean that the data of metaphysics are private, incommunicable, and inaccessible to intersubjective checking. It does mean that each of us sometimes claims to know, and that therefore each of us claims to have had the requisite experience for testing the alternative reflective analyses offered by a Hume, a Kant, a Sartre. It means that each knower must test the rival hypotheses about experience for himself, in his own experience. In this way, metaphysics is just as intersubjective, just as controlled, just as empirically grounded as physics. In the interaction of knower and known, it is true, physics concentrates more on the known, unnecessarily prompting the mistake that knowing is a kind of looking outwards. In the same interaction of knower and known, metaphysics reflects more on the knower and moves back to its own unique reflection on the structure of the known things. These known things are the same as the things known by physics: bits of cobalt, oceans, falling stones. But the physicist is interested in their molecular structure, their energy, their behavior in space and time; the metaphysician, on the other hand, is interested in them as the focal points of many different kinds of awareness$_1$ [that is, direct awareness]. Thus the businessman has one kind of interest in cobalt, the scientist another, the engineer another, the poet still another, and the plain man again another; the metaphysician asks: What constitutes a thing as an intelligible unity under so many different viewpoints? The metaphysician is not interested in Platonic other worlds or uncontrolled intuitions into essences; he handles a bit of stone, and begins to reflect that he can be aware$_1$ [that is, directly] of it, relate it by science to other materials, come to be aware$_2$ [that is, reflectively] of himself in handling it and again in thinking of it. What is this thing? What is he? He begins to wonder."[9]

Branches of Science

To understand the place of philosophy and metaphysics in scientific knowledge it is helpful to consider the various branches of science. All are characterized to a greater or lesser extent by the marks of scientific knowledge already noted. The science of theology is differentiated from every other science in that it is based on supernatural revelation, on knowledge received, not merely from the natural light of reason, but from the word of God. It includes within itself everything that will aid in understanding what is necessary for salvation; however, its ultimate authority is not human understanding but divine revelation. The other sciences, which depend only on

[9] Michael Novak, "An Empirically Controlled Metaphysics," *International Philosophical Quarterly*, IV, No. 2 (May 1964), 280–81.

reason, as opposed to revelation, are distinguished among themselves just as other ways of knowing are distinguished—by their aims, objects, and methods.

Science in general can be divided into two broad categories: *speculative* science, or knowledge which is studied primarily for its value as knowledge; *practical* science, or knowledge which is studied primarily for some action which will follow from it.

All reality is the concern of science. If we use the Aristotelian classification, the universe is the subject matter or object, and God is a conclusion. The various sciences are specified by their subject matter and by the aspects of this subject matter which they study. Two sciences may concern themselves with the same general subject matter and yet constitute two different sciences if they study two different aspects of that object. Thus, for example, both the biologist and the psychologist may study man, but not under the same aspect. All sciences, of course, study being—for there is nothing else to study—but they do not study it in the same way. Some sciences study a particular kind of being—such as living beings, inanimate beings, or human beings. Some study a particular characteristic of certain beings—such as quantity, energy, or heredity.

More than one science may study not only the same object but even the same aspect of that object. Then they are differentiated by their methods. Experimental psychology and philosophy of human nature, for instance, may both be concerned with human love and may even arrive at the same conclusions, but by different methods. Because knowledge is qualified by the way in which it is gained, sciences do not thereby duplicate but rather complement one another.

Man and nature are the concern of the natural sciences, the social sciences, psychology, and philosophy. Each of these disciplines is further divided into separate sciences studying separate segments or aspects of the world and man. The philosophical study of the physical universe, the search for its ultimate constitutive principles and relationships, is called philosophy of nature, or cosmology. The philosophical approach to man, the attempt to understand the essence of man, is called philosophy of human nature. To try to understand the universe in terms of quantity is the province of mathematics. It becomes increasingly difficult, however, to separate mathematics from the natural sciences, on the one hand, and from philosophy, on the other. Science has become mathematical through its use of mathematical methods and its quantitative interpretation of the universe. The influence of symbolic logic, linguistic analysis, and questions on the nature of quantity and number seem to make mathematics and philosophy at least partially overlap.

Many sciences are concerned with being in its sensible and quantitative aspects and with certain kinds of beings. Only one science tries to understand being simply as being. This is the science of metaphysics. We find ourselves engaging in this science when we make the philosophical attempt to understand what being is, what it means "to be," what all being as being has in common.

Philosophy

The metaphysically questioning glance which seeks to understand being in its most fundamental principles, and which seeks, therefore, to push the questions "What?" and "Why?" as far as they can be pushed by the light of reason, is best understood in the whole context of philosophy, at the heart of which is metaphysics. The name "philosophy" is itself of interesting origin, deriving as it does from the Greek *philia* and *sophia*, "love" and "wisdom." The understanding of things in their ultimate causes, the unveiling of the inmost meaning of things, the deep possession of being in the presence which is knowledge—all this is what the Greeks meant by wisdom. That philosophy was called the "love of wisdom" implied not that the philosopher was a wise man, but that he was one who sought wisdom, went in pursuit of it, out of love. The Pythagoreans [10] first coined the term in the sixth century B.C., as an expression of their own approach to knowledge. Wisdom, they thought, belonged only to God; man is ever a beggar at Wisdom's door. For anyone to call himself a wise man, then, would be to presume too much. St. Thomas comments on Aristotle: "Now we must note that, while this science was first designated by the name wisdom, this was later changed to the name philosophy, since they mean the same thing. For while the

[10] A religious society in the Grecian colonies in Italy, the members of which elaborated an intricate explanation of the essence of things based on a mathematical system of numbers.

ancients who pursued the study of wisdom were called sophists, that is, wise men, Pythagoras, when asked what he professed himself to be, refused to call himself a wise man as his predecessors had done, because he thought this was presumptuous, but called himself a philosopher, that is, a lover of wisdom. And from that time the name 'wise man' was changed to 'philosopher' and 'wisdom' to 'philosophy.' "[11]

This meaning of philosophy, a loving search for perfect knowledge, is not merely a poetic description of yet one more attempt to understand being. It implies an approach to reality which all students share—not because it is part of the method of any other discipline nor because it directs the method of other disciplines, but because if we ask ourselves what it is we want to know, need to know, what it is we do know and do not know, we will sooner or later be in the realm of philosophy, sooner or later raising questions of a philosophical nature. Whether or not these questions and the answers we find transcend or inspire, are within or beyond, flow from or lead to, other disciplines is something we can know only when we have asked them and found them. Such a judgment, therefore, is better left until later.

Wisdom has recently been described as follows: "Wisdom is a basic human attitude, characterized first of all by a complete openness to transcendent Truth, Goodness, and Beauty. Hence the attitude of the wise man is essentially positive: he will not reject as one immense error the road that humanity has traveled during the course of two millennia, nor will he erase, destroy, or deny the manifold secular efforts of mankind. It is absolutely required that science and technique receive, in the framework of modern wisdom, some function, even though it be a subordinate one. (The *predominance* of science and technique must be rejected because the scientist, as scientist, and the technician, as technician, are occupationally blind with respect to transcendent values. In this sense our modern way must be opposed and remain opposed to the idolatry of science and technology.) All of this implies that the esoteric attitude of some 'Mythomaniacs'—an attitude which might be summed up in the

---

[11] *In Metaphysicam,* I, Lect. 3, n. 56; trans. J. Rowan (Chicago: Henry Regnery Co., 1961), I, 24.

famous words: '*Nous n'avons rien appris et rien oublié*' [We have learned nothing and forgotten nothing]—is the very opposite of wisdom; it is folly.

"What then is wisdom? We have already mentioned its complete openness to transcendent Truth, Goodness, and Beauty in their undivided unity. In the wise man this original unity, which precedes the distinction between a speculative, a practical, and an esoteric attitude is recovered at a very high human level.

"One whose existence is a continual listening to Transcendence feels detached from insignificant human concerns. It is from a certain distance and with a certain inner detachment that the wise man observes the claims, the ambitions, the rivalries, and the conflicts of his fellow men; hence his superior disinterestedness (ataraxia), his intangible impartiality, or, as Marcel puts it, his 'détachement.' In addition, his contact with Transcendence provides the wise man with a great degree of inner freedom and he is free precisely because he does not belong to himself, but is the servant of the *Tao*, the primal origin of all things, or herald of *ratio*, which guides the course of the universe. If his own psychic and bodily existence were in conflict with the cosmic order and harmony, he would be unfit for such service. Hence the wise man is obliged to impose a severe discipline on his emotions and passions and prescribe rules even for his instincts. And it is precisely because he knows about human passions, which he has overcome through his ascetic efforts, that he can interiorly stand at the disposal of his fellow citizens; he can assist them as an advisor, counselor, or arbiter in their needs, helping them with their problems and amidst their conflicts. He is *disponible* in their regard, to use Marcel's term." [12]

This is not naïve confidence in the world or in our ability to understand it. Wisdom is beyond both facile acceptance of the meaningfulness of the universe and the anxious fear of its senselessness. It is not the spinning of an abstract theory of being, but a grappling with the meaning of the world in all its concrete reality. To be a philosopher, to "love wisdom," is to be willing to seek this vision of the universe, to grapple with the problem of the meaningfulness or senselessness of reality.

---

[12] S. Strasser, "After Scientific Philosophy: Myth or Wisdom?" *International Philosophical Quarterly*, III, No. 1 (February 1963), 48–49.

Branches of philosophy Since philosophical questions have this range and depth, it should be clear that every kind of being yields philosophical knowledge of itself. There is a branch of philosophy corresponding to every general aim and object within the sciences. The human mind can therefore look philosophically at all things—without fearing either repetition of effort or competition of interests. This fact, coupled with the notion of philosophy as the love of wisdom, emphasizes that there can be true philosophizing in regard to all things, provided there be an earnest desire to know as much as can be known. If the truth and beauty in reality can be rendered present to the student of literature only if he reads as a way of experiencing them, and if real progress is made in the natural sciences only if one seeks to understand, control, or enjoy the universe, how much more so will the depths of being, nature and existence, source and end, remain opaque to the mind whose search does not rise out of true wonder or is not a conscious cry of the spirit for meaning in suffering and confusion.

Philosophy is a science, but its very scientific order, its efforts at precision, at causal demonstration, arise from questions which man needs to have answered. Plato, for example, wanted to know how a man should act, and whether or not there are absolute and universal moral laws. To know this he had to question the very nature of man (for as his nature is so should he act). To understand man he was obliged to question his place in the universe and the nature of the reality that surrounds him. Then he sought what ultimate explanations he could find. He was, in effect, asking questions of and studying what today would be called ethics, philosophy of man, philosophy of nature, and metaphysics. Concern for certitude led to the scientific formulation of these studies.

Today these same questions lead to these same studies. At least one philosophical bent of the mind, one approach to philosophy and its various branches, is to try to know speculatively what it means to be a being (metaphysics), what it means to be a human being (philosophy of man), and then, practically, how a human being should act in order to achieve the fullness of his nature (moral philosophy, or ethics). Other areas related to these are the study of human knowledge itself (epistemology), the study of the material universe (cosmology), the study of the principles of art (aesthetics, or philosophy of art), and so forth.

THE NATURE OF METAPHYSICAL INQUIRY

In the context, therefore, of all the ways of knowing and all the ways of philosophical knowing, metaphysics asks for the meaning of being.[13] As a formal study, metaphysics has sometimes been divided into general metaphysics and natural theology.[14] General metaphysics is concerned with finite being as being, and, more specifically, with the causes of finite being. Natural theology begins from finite being and argues to its first cause—God thus is its term, its conclusion. In our discussions we will not make a sharp division between these two parts of metaphysics. Natural theology, or the metaphysics of infinite Being, as it is sometimes called, unifies the whole of metaphysics in an ultimate search for God. We unite the two parts because metaphysics is the mind's effort to understand the limited being which man experiences and which he is, and man finds that this limited being is without meaning apart from God and finally unintelligible except in relation to God. What is a search for God, in its turn, yields also knowledge of all that is not God.

In natural theology the relation of philosophy to supernatural theology becomes most evident. Like the other sciences, philosophy differs radically from supernatural theology because it strives to know reality by the light of natural reason, not by revelation. Philosophy and theology may be concerned with some of the same truths, as for example, when both natural and supernatural theology consider the existence of God, but philosophy begins with reason, with existential experience of the effects of God, whereas theology begins with the revealed Word of God.

There is a sense in which we can say that God reveals Himself in two ways: on a natural level, through His creation, and on a supernatural level through special communications to man at given points in history. Mankind stands before God listening for the words which will express His presence and His Being, and which will unfold the meaning of human existence and the meaning of the world for man. Men listen to the words which are God's natural creation, spoken in

---

[13] "Meaning" does not here refer to the linguistic content symbolized by the word, "being." It rather refers to "what being itself, in reality, is."

[14] Natural theology is variously referred to as metaphysics of infinite being or, following Christian Wolff, as theodicy.

the universe of things and of persons; philosophy is a part of this listening. Men listen, also, to the Word of God which has been spoken in various and sundry ways in times past, and last of all by His Son; theology is a part of this listening.

Philosophy and theology bear an important relation to each other. Philosophy, no less than the other sciences, is taken up within theology, serving to lead the mind of man into the presence of mystery. Just as it is a help to theology, so theology is a help to it. Although philosophy is an autonomous science in its own right, truths known by revelation function as negative norms for philosophy; that is, they indicate that certain conclusions are false. Thus there is a saving of time, effort, and error. They also positively point to areas of truth to be explored. There is, further, a very real sense in which reason can be said to be healed by faith, to be able in the light of faith now to see what before it should have been able to see but apparently did not.[15]

METAPHYSICAL QUESTIONS AND THE POSSIBILITY OF ANSWERS

Since metaphysics begins *objectively* with the present world of existing finite beings, and *subjectively* with the mind's awareness of this world and itself, what are its possibilities of penetrating this world, of rendering the beings of experience present to the mind in a way in which they are truly united to the conscious being of man? How shall those of us who may not have raised the question even of the existence of being, let alone of how and why beings exist, look

---

[15] This explanation of the relationship between philosophy and supernatural theology touches the crux of the problem of the existence and nature of Christian philosophy. An understanding of philosophy and theology which sees them as distinct but interrelated is what makes it possible to speak of "Christian philosophy." Christian philosophy, in this sense, is genuine philosophy (based on reason), but philosophy into which supernatural revelation descends, not as a constitutive element in its texture (which would contradict the nature of philosophy), but as a regulative principle, extrinsically and intrinsically, in the work of its construction. ". . . I call Christian, every philosophy which, although keeping the two orders [philosophy and theology] distinct, nevertheless considers the Christian revelation as an indispensable auxiliary to reason." E. Gilson, *The Spirit of Mediaeval Philosophy*, trans. A. H. C. Downes (New York: Charles Scribner's Sons, 1940), p. 37.

philosophically, metaphysically, at reality? And what kind of answers can we reasonably expect as the fruit of these studies?

It may or may not be an illusion that leads us to ask what, after all, it means to exist; what the meaning of life is; what sort of thing we are, and where we are going. It may or may not be a shallow game that speaks of a conscious thirst for truth, for being, for awakening. There may or may not be any answers to the questions of why there is something and not nothing; of what it means to be a person, to choose; of why there is anything to love.[16] The least we can do is test the illusion, try the game, take a look at the answers. Whatever the claims of relativism and skepticism, the emptiness or the fullness of the meaning of being must be tested, and whatever doubts one may have as to the capability of human reason for the discovery of truth, one must at least recognize the possibility that something more can be known. If "being" *means* nothing, if its questioning is a reaching for shadows, one must wonder why it has not always seemed so.

"We shall have to ask why this fact, that for us 'being' is no more than a word or a vapor, should have arisen precisely today, or whether and why it has existed for a long time. We must learn to see that this fact is not as harmless as it seems at first sight. For ultimately what matters is not that the word 'being' remains a mere sound and its meaning a vapor, but that we have fallen away from what this word says and for the moment cannot find our way back; that it is for this and no other reason that the word 'being' no longer applies to anything; that everything, if we merely take hold of it, dissolves like a tatter of cloud in the sunlight. Because this is so—that is why we ask about being." [17]

When we ask about being, therefore, perhaps the *sine qua non* of finding answers is simply first of all to "go and see." But perhaps something more can be said to indicate the possibilities of "seeing," avoiding, on the one hand, expectation of too little, and on the other, expectation of too much.[18] The two current vogues, existentialism and analytical philosophy, err on the side of too little. For both,

---

[16] See above on existentialism and logical positivism.

[17] M. Heidegger, *An Introduction to Metaphysics*, trans. Ralph Manheim (New York: Doubleday & Company, Inc., 1961), pp. 32–33.

[18] Novak makes much of this in his article, "An Empirically Controlled Metaphysics," *International Philosophical Quarterly*, IV, No. 2 (May 1964), 279.

metaphysics as we are discussing it is impossible, either because it seeks a meaning which is not there (existentialism), or because it asks questions which are meaningless (analytical philosophy). In general the idealists and rationalists erred on the side of claiming to see too much. We will seek a middle ground between these two extremes of refusing to see any meaning and of claiming to see too much.

The Question of Certitude

The question of discovery and certitude in metaphysics is involved with the whole question of discovery and certitude in human knowledge. Is there anything in reality to be known, any absolute truth to be found, and if there is, is the human intellect able to know it?

One of the difficulties involved in discovering metaphysical truth is the belief that all truth is relative because reality is constantly changing—so that what is true today will not be true tomorrow. Whether or not there is any stability in being or any stable being —that is, whether it is change or permanence that is ultimate in being—remains to be seen. Thus, whether or not there can be discovered unchanging, absolute truths about the nature of a being is one of the things metaphysics must find out. Whatever the findings in this regard, however, the changeableness of being does not itself preclude certitude in knowledge. Even if something changes in time, so that what it was yesterday it is not today, knowledge that it was so yesterday will always remain valid, provided that we indicate its location in space and time. St. Thomas expresses this with medieval quaintness: "If an intellect is true, and it is not changed when a thing is changed, or vice versa, or if each thing is changed but not similarly, falsity results. . . ." [19] What he means is: If I know that you are sitting down and you stand up, I have false knowledge if I do not now know you as standing up; or if you remain seated and I know you as standing up, I am also wrong. Or, finally, if you stand up and I know you as walking away, I am also wrong.

The difficulty which sees all human knowledge as mere opinion,

---

[19] *De Veritate*, I, 6c.

because of the incapacity of the human intellect to know anything with certitude, is not so easily dismissed. How indeed can the student of metaphysics be sure of what he knows if there is even some question as to the truth of any of his knowledge? If man is subject to illusion and condemned to live only in terms of a world he builds for himself in an effort to find a modicum of happiness, the kind of knowledge which helps him discover this illusion will be metaphysical knowledge.

As will become readily apparent when we look at reality to find its metaphysical depths, vast areas will remain in the shadows and we will find ourselves unable to understand many questions concerning them. St. Thomas, for instance, says that the weakness of the human mind explains this: "The difficulty experienced in knowing the truth is due principally to some weakness on the part of our intellect. From this it follows that our soul's intellectual power is related to those immaterial beings, which are by nature the most knowable of all, as the eyes of owls are to the light of day." [20] Many aspects of being will not reveal themselves with absolute clarity and corresponding certitude. Many truths will be partial truths, subject to ever greater modification. This is not at all the same as to say that all metaphysical knowledge is relative, or that all the study of metaphysics is at best a collection of good opinions. The human mind seeks to know more of reality, to possess it in deeper union, to have it more truly present; and in this effort it is not without success, not without true and certain knowledge.

The very nature of consciousness makes it possible to affirm the existence of beings other than the knowing self. Awareness implies awareness of something, and even self-awareness is intelligible only in terms of relationships with other beings. This means that one who desires to know cannot begin only in terms of the world of ideas, but must be open to receive the world of real beings. Ideas are constituted as means whereby reality is united with the knower.[21] On the other hand we must not let attention to concrete reality turn into a limitation of the realm of knowledge to the observable and the

---

[20] *In Metaphysicam,* II, Lect. 1, n. 282 (ed. Cathala).
[21] *Summa Theologiae,* I, 85, 2.

measurable. The intellect is able to "see" what no sense power can see; the intellect is able to reach depths of being which no material organ can functionally penetrate. The very formation of universal concepts makes this clear. To quote St. Thomas again: "The name intellect arises from the intellect's ability to know the most profound elements of a thing; for to understand (*intelligere*) means to read what is inside a thing (*intus legere*). Sense and imagination know only external accidents, but the intellect alone penetrates to the interior and to the essence of a thing." [22]

The Tests of Certitude

First Principles

Intellectual consciousness, therefore, is meant to receive being. We attain certitude in this reception and in the assent whereby the intellect in its act of judgment places its seal on its union with reality. This derives from the necessary affirmation which the intellect makes of certain first principles, from the awareness in the intellect of its own activity, and from the verification of at least some truths by a return to experience.

The question of first principles [23] has become complicated by some recent misunderstanding of the role they play in traditional philosophy. For the present, however, we shall bypass this problem and present a brief summary of the vital role which first principles play in the achievement of metaphysical truths according to the historic realistic philosophy of Aristotle and St. Thomas.

The principles with which we are concerned are not principles from which we are able to deduce all our conclusions about reality. They are, rather, the expression which the mind gives to primordial insights given in its encounter with being. They are not judgments *about* the natures of beings, but are implicit *within* such judgments.

---

[22] *De Veritate,* I, 12c. See also *Summa Theologiae,* I, 84, 2.

[23] A principle is that from which anything proceeds in any way. There are various kinds of principles: a point may be the principle of a line; a spring may be the principle of a river. There are several principles of being, as we shall see. The first principles spoken of here in the text are principles of knowledge.

We refer to these principles as self-evident.[24] This means that they are part of the givenness of being as it unveils itself to be known, and it is in their light that the intellect is able to unveil the reality that it knows. They necessitate implicit intellectual assent, but may be explicitly recognized only in reflection or when presented to us already formulated in a verbal expression. Without at least implicit acknowledgment of these principles it would be impossible for the mind to reach any certitude in knowing.

The validity of the explanation of the role of these principles can be tested by considering two of them, the two on which a further understanding of the metaphysical depths of reality will most directly depend.

The first of these principles is called the *Principle of Contradiction.* Wherever the intellect encounters being, it recognizes that, absolutely speaking, a thing cannot be and not be at the same time in the same respect. *Respect* here means some aspect of being. The insight which this judgment expresses does not mean that the intellect is incapable of recognizing apparently divergent modes of being nor that being itself cannot manifest itself in endless nuances of being. Rather, it means that, for example, we recognize that it is impossible for someone to exist and not exist at the same time in the same respect or aspect. Such a person may not have existed some time in the past, and he may exist now, and he may lose existence in the future; or he may exist now in that he is and not exist now in that he is not fully what he is able to be. Or he may exist now as knowing something which he did not know in the past. None of these possibilities involves absolute contradiction. It is, however, contradictory to both exist and not exist at the same time in *exactly* the same respect. Thus, I cannot now know something and not know it in exactly the same way, and I cannot now at the same time be both sitting and standing. Similarly, a board cannot be both green and red at the same time and in the same respect. It can be red and then later be painted green; it can be red on one end and green on

[24] Whatever is self-evident needs no proof and indeed renders impossible any proof. If we open our eyes and see a book in front of us, we cannot prove that it is in front of us. It is directly seen, so that—with all due caution to test possible optical illusions—there is no thing by which we could prove its presence; there is no movement possible from the unknown to the known.

the other; but it cannot be both red and green all over and all at once.

The same Principle of Contradiction expressed in a different way, somewhat like the other side of a coin, is the *Principle of Identity.* In every encounter with being through knowledge we affirm positively that it must be what it is, since it is impossible not to be what it is and still be what it is.[25] We formulate this judgment simply: a thing is what it is. To affirm this validly of a thing insofar as it *is* is to affirm it validly of all being. Without such an affirmation, we can have no other judgments that are judgments.

The second principle which is of utmost importance in the continuing pursuit of metaphysical truths is the *Principle of Sufficient Reason.* Although any explicit expression of this principle comes as a conclusion rather than as a starting point in our knowledge, the openness of consciousness to being contains the implict affirmation that being as being is knowable and that every being, insofar as it is, is grounded in being. Once we are able to reach an explicit formulation of this affirmation, it can then serve as a principle of further insight into being. Explicit expressions have taken various forms, but all focus on the same insight: if a thing exists, and exists as a certain kind of being, then whatever is necessary for it to exist and to exist as that certain kind of thing must be and must be exerting its influence. A being precisely as a being and as long as it is a being has that whereby it is and is what it is. If what is necessary to it is not within it, it must be somehow outside of it. If it is not a part of the being itself, it must be something other than the being.

Corresponding to this principle is the *Principle of Intelligibility:* Every being is intelligible, able to be known. If there is for every being, in it or outside it, whatever it needs for its existence and way of existence, it is explainable, understandable, knowable, in terms of what it has or is. No thing, then, is absurd, unexplainable, un-

---

[25] It does not really matter whether priority is given to the Principle of Contradiction or the Principle of Identity, since they both point to the same self-evident truth, negatively or positively. The difficulty which many contemporary philosophers, especially those in the United States, have with the Principles of Contradiction and Identity lies in the interpretation of them to mean that two things of the same nature are exactly alike, or that one thing cannot simultaneously be characterized by contrary attributes. Neither of these interpretations, however, is the meaning given to the principles here.

knowable, in *itself*—though, of course, it is very possible that it is not yet known to a particular mind or to the mind of any man, for that matter. Metaphysical study is part of the effort to open the way to the intelligibility of being.[26]

Reflexive Awareness

Along with the necessary affirmation by the intellect of the self-evident first principles, the intellect's own awareness of itself makes certitude possible in human knowledge. A rational being by his power of intellect knows that he knows. He is conscious of his consciousness. He can reflect upon his own cognitional activity, understanding it and its relation to its object. He can know his intellect as a power whose object is *being* and whose activity is to penetrate being with insight and receive *being* in concepts. This activity involves awareness of the activity of apprehension and of assent to first principles and of consistency in proceeding from first principles. In the words of St. Thomas, "Truth is known by the intellect in view of the fact that the intellect reflects upon its own act—not merely as knowing its own act, but as knowing the proportion of its act to the thing. Now this proportion cannot be known without knowing the nature of the act; and the nature of the act cannot be known without knowing the nature of the active principle, that is, the intellect itself, to whose nature it belongs to be conformed to things. Consequently it is because the intellect reflects upon itself that it knows truth."[27]

Metaphysical questions, therefore, are answered and the truth of these answers is assured to the extent that they are derived from what is self-evident in experience,[28] from what is grasped in the light of first principles, and from what is penetrated by conscious and careful unfolding—by reasoning, by looking, by intuiting, or by whatever way the intellect uses to proceed through its own activity from what is given to what is, at first, hidden.

---

[26] See Peter Hoenen, *Reality and Judgment According to St. Thomas* (Chicago: Henry Regnery Co., 1952), p. 192.

[27] *De Veritate,* I, 9c.

[28] See J. Owens, *An Elementary Christian Metaphysics* (Milwaukee: Bruce Publishing Company, 1963), pp. 55 n., 271.

Verification in Experience

Verification of truth by return to experience is not always possible in metaphysics. Nevertheless the practical fruitfulness of a judgment can serve as a further assurance of the truth of that judgment. A renewed contemplation of the unity in beautiful things deepens the certitude that unity belongs to the fullness of being. The constant return to our experience of individual limitation as men, and of our fulfillment by union with other men helps us understand that all men participate in human nature. The translation of what one knows into the way one lives, of knowledge into being, brings to fruition any metaphysical possession of truth.

We will make an effort in the following chapters to proceed from the given in experience to a metaphysical vision of the depths of being. This, of course, will not end in a complete and perfect understanding of reality. Hopefully, however, it will help push back the dimensions of our knowledge, giving us possession of reality in a new way, possession of truths which will at least partially answer the questions we have asked and are going to ask of being.

PHILOSOPHERS AS GUIDES

In philosophy, and especially in metaphysics, possession of truth depends entirely on each individual's grasp of it. That someone else has seen it before is not so important as that each one sees it now. To accept a truth on the authority of another is not to hold it philosophically. When a student looks at the world philosophically, he attempts to understand, not to believe. This by no means constitutes a conflict with the surrender in faith to what cannot be understood by the human mind. To try to understand what can be understood is part of the reverence which faith engenders. Nevertheless, although philosophy is not built on authority, it is still helpful and sometimes absolutely necessary to have a master, a guide, who can lead us around the obstacles that keep us from seeing the truths. The fact that great minds in the past have seen great things does make a difference to minds trying to see today. Indeed, those who look out into the realm of truth in each succeeding age should be able to see further than those who went before—precisely because they have the shoulders of their predecessors on which to stand. Because they have a guide they can proceed more directly to the point of vision heretofore reached, and thus sooner begin to see what has not yet been seen even by their guides.

St. Thomas Aquinas will serve as the main guide in the efforts at understanding which follow. The choice of St. Thomas is prompted by his approach to being: his starting point in the here-and-now with what is experientially present, his search which reaches all the way to existence, the emphasis he places on existence, his philosophizing within a Christian theological commitment. St. Thomas' attitude toward reality and the central truths which he discovered will comprise his guidance. Part of his attitude is expressive of the conviction that there is always more to be known. For this reason, the doctrine of St. Thomas is not, and will not function here as, a terminal point in itself, a sterile circumscription of the realm of knowledge. Perhaps it will become clear that the gigantic work of St. Thomas is full enough, pregnant enough, to serve rather as a fountainhead, a fruit in itself ripe enough to bear new fruit. Perhaps it will be seen, also, that what is often regarded as incompatibility between St. Thomas and contemporary developments in philosophy is not only compatibility but in many cases even confirmation. We will use other authors, especially our contemporaries, to help us gain in our present-day circumstances insights which we might not discover in the medieval expression of St. Thomas. We will turn to these writers to help us with contemporary attitudes, insights, and questions, which we might otherwise either overlook or not put in their proper perspective. They should help us understand St. Thomas better and help us to formulate our own metaphysics for twentieth-century living.

PROCEDURE—STARTING POINT AND METHOD

The order of study followed in the succeeding chapters is directed by the existential circumstances and needs of the human intellect, and by the way in which reality reveals itself to that intellect. This means, first of all, that the starting point for metaphysics is the activities observable in the beings of experience. Although the ultimate goal is to understand being itself, being can be approached only through its revelation of itself, through its activities. One principle of knowledge says that "operation follows being." This means, among other things, that a being can act only according to its nature: a tulip bulb cannot produce an oak tree, a dog cannot sing like a canary, a man cannot stay underwater indefinitely like a fish. Therefore, the kind of activity a being performs will be indicative of the kind of being it is, indicative of its nature. If one detects activities of growth, nutrition, reproduction in a thing, he will conclude that it is alive. That operation follows being is a principle directive of a metaphysical approach to reality; this means that man can know *that* things are as well as *what* they are by knowing what they do.[29] That they act indicates that they are, that they exist; that they act in a certain way indicates that they have a certain way of existence, a certain nature or essence—however inadequate may be our final concept of that nature. Beginning with evident characteristics of the activity of being, the mind is led to an understanding of what in being itself accounts for these activities and their characteristics.

What is given in experience in regard to the activities of beings is first of all simply that they do act, and therefore that they do exist. The limitation of their activities, the changeableness, the nonnecessity (that is, the contingency) of them, is also in some way given. We can experience directly these characteristics of our own activities, or at least find some trace of them which might lead us to wish to investigate the underlying characteristics of being which account for them. The fact of existence, and even of apparent limitation, change, and contingency are enough to set the mind to questioning in a philosophical way.

PLAN OF THE BOOK

In the second chapter there will be the opportunity of questioning with those who first formally turned a philosophical glance at the world. To awaken with the Greeks and to wonder with them will provide the twofold advantage of feeling one's way into a philosoph-

---

[29] Although activity tells something of the nature of a thing, it is not thereby implied that it reveals fully that nature, nor that it fully unveils existence.

ical habit of mind and of concentrating one's attention so that greater precision will begin to mark the questions put to being.

Beginning with existing things, we will consider their multiplication and limitation. This is different from what is customary in many textbooks, which take change as the point of departure in metaphysical inquiry. We think that to proceed from change to a knowledge both of the structure of being and of an outside cause of change seems often to bar a final understanding of the need of a cause for existence; it becomes possible to arrive at a Prime Mover without being able to transcend that idea and discover a cause of existence itself. For this reason, our first approach to being will be from the given knowledge of multitude and limitation in being. This does not imply that we will begin with what is more difficult, for change is not necessarily the easiest phenomenon to see and experience. Indeed, we may be more readily aware of limitation in our experience than of anything else. Even apart from the limitation everywhere evident in other beings, we directly, sometimes painfully, experience the limitation of our own activity. We cannot completely transcend the limitations of our own powers, nor the limitations placed upon us by time and space, nor the limitations constantly borne witness to by our desires.

In an attempt to explain multiplicity and limitation, therefore, we will try in succeeding chapters to unfold or let be unfolded the underlying structure of limited beings; and through this effort will come the discovery of the importance of existence (Chapter 3). Finite existence itself will then open to Pure Existence as its ultimate source and end, as that which is necessary to hold its being here and now away from the abyss of absurdity and nothingness (Chapters 4 and 5). A knowledge of the existence of God can then lead to an investigation of the names of God, those names which signify the relation of His creatures to Him and those which signify what in Himself He is and is not (Chapter 6).

To look immediately to existence is not to negate that aspect of experience which is change. To understand created being without seeing it as becoming would be to fail altogether to perceive the reality of experience. Thus, having seen the structure of being and its relation to Infinite Being, an explanation of change, of becoming, must somehow be discovered within the understanding of being already achieved (Chapter 7). Contemporary concern for evolution and time must somehow reach some resolution in a further insight into finite existence. Both poles of reality, finite and infinite, infinitely apart yet intimately united, can be again brought together in understanding. Just as the meaning of finite existence is found within the context of knowledge of Pure Existence, so the meaning of becoming is to be found within the context of Being, and the meaning of time within the context of eternity. When we have achieved some explanation of limitation and change, some knowledge of being and becoming, activity itself will still remain to be understood. Where before activity was the means which led to an understanding of that from which it flows, now it will have to be considered in itself. Such a consideration leads to the discovery of the tendential aspect of being, of secondary causality, of participated and participating activity, of providence and freedom (Chapter 8). At this point a notion of being as analogical can be elaborated (Chapter 9). But to have seen all this of being is still not to have understood it in its fullness. The mind may look again and again, seeing more and more deeply, and in this effort come to know being as unity, as truth, as goodness, and as beauty, come to know activity which is correspondent to be-ing, and come to know knowledge, love, and joy (Chapters 10 and 11). When all is said and done here, we will still be beginning. It will still be possible for us to look once again at the things we have long studied and know them again in the same way more thoroughly, and also in a new way. But we will not reach that second beginning unless we begin this one, pursuing wisdom with reaffirmed expectancy.

SUGGESTED READINGS

Ayer, Alfred J., "The Elimination of Metaphysics," in *Language, Truth, and Logic*, pp. 33–45. New York: Dover Publications, Inc., 1946. Ayer gives in this chapter some of the reasons of the positivists for rejecting the validity and usefulness of metaphysical inquiry.

Gilson, Etienne, *The Spirit of Medieval Philosophy*, trans. A. H. C. Downes, Chapters 1 and 2. New York: Charles Scribner's Sons, 1936. In these chapters Gilson discusses the meaning and authenticity of "Christian philosophy."

Luijpen, William A., *Existential Phenomenology,* pp. 4–73. Pittsburgh: Duquesne University Press, 1960. Phenomenological treatment of the authenticity of philosophy, man as a metaphysical being, and the relationship of technocracy and philosophy to the life of man.

Marcel, Gabriel, *The Philosophy of Existence,* trans. M. Harari, Chapter 1. New York: The Philosophical Library, Inc., 1949. Expresses contemporary neo-Socratic concern for an approach to existence which will preserve its mystery.

Maritain, Jacques, *Science and Wisdom,* pp. 3–33. New York: Charles Scribner's Sons, 1940. Cross-cultural view of the meaning and role of wisdom and the sciences.

St. Thomas Aquinas, *On the Division and Methods of the Sciences: Questions V and VI of the Commentary on the De Trinitate of Boethius,* trans. Armand Maurer (2nd rev. ed.), Question V, Article 1. Toronto: The Pontifical Institute of Medieval Studies, 1958.

Weigel, Gustave, and Arthur G. Madden, *Knowledge, Its Values and Limits,* Chapters 3 and 4. Englewood Cliffs, N.J.: Prentice-Hall, Inc., 1961. Chapter 3 treats the possibility of certitude in human knowing. Chapter 4 discusses the various scientific disciplines and the validity of philosophy in relation to them.

2 BEING AND THE GREEKS

INTRODUCTION

Why should a twentieth-century philosopher begin his study of metaphysics with a discussion of the Greek philosophers, of men who faced the problems of an age and a civilization now twenty-five centuries behind us? The reason, of course, is the same as that of the constitutional historian, who spends much of his time reading the historical and philosophical books which he knows were in the private libraries of our Founding Fathers. An important way to study the Constitution is to study its origins, especially the origins of the ideas which inspired the Founding Fathers to write it. In metaphysics we can proceed in much the same way. For Western philosophy began with the Greeks, and their first spontaneous questions about philosophy set Western thought on a path which leads directly to our present-day contemporary systems. Existentialism, analytical philosophy, realism, idealism—all these have their roots in Greek thought. So in studying the Greeks, we are going to the wellspring of Western philosophy. Furthermore, the problems raised especially by the earlier Greek thinkers have a simplicity and straightforwardness about their formulation which make them an excellent starting point for the study of metaphysics. Aristotle says of these early days: "For it is owing to their wonder that men both now begin and at first began to philosophize; they wondered originally at the obvious difficulties, then advanced little by little and stated difficulties about greater matters, for example, about the phenomena of the moon and those of the sun and of the stars, and about the genesis of the universe. And a man who is puzzled and wonders thinks himself ignorant (whence even the lover of myth is in a sense a lover of Wisdom, for the myth is composed of wonders); therefore since they philosophized in order to escape from ignorance, evidently they were pursuing science in order to know, and not for any utilitarian end."[1]

APPROACH OF EARLY THINKERS

The wonder of these early Greek thinkers began with what many generations of philosophers have called "philosophy of nature." As they looked around them, they saw things coming into existence and dropping out of existence. Men are born and they die. The flowers bloom and wither. The sequence of day and night, the circle of the seasons, and the stages of man's existence impressed upon these thinkers the idea that change governs our world. At the same time, however, they observed that nothing drops completely out of existence. The dead, withered blossoms, the shriveled stalks and leaves remain after the flowers die. The corpses of men are still there when life is gone. Ashes remain when the fire has burned itself out.

Moved by the wonder which Aristotle calls the beginning of all philosophy, the early Greek thinkers were not satisfied with answers to the specific questions about change, but pushed their inquiries to the basic metaphysical question of the unifying explanatory principle of the world. The turn which their investigations took led these thinkers to ask whether throughout all the changes they saw

---

[1] *Metaphysics,* A, 2, 982b 13–22.

and experienced there was not something permanent, something which assumed these various shapes, sizes, and activities.

If we look beyond the various formulations of this basic question, we can see that each of the Greek thinkers is looking in his own way for that which makes our world and our universe *one* world and *one* universe. Each of them is asking in his own way, "What is being?" or "What in things makes them have being?" On the surface these questions may seem simple, but in reality they embody a whole metaphysical outlook which, as we shall see, brings the metaphysical discussion of being to an impasse. This is so because the Greeks from Thales to Plotinus all make the question of being a question about essence, that is, to a man they ask *what* it is that makes a being a being. The accent is on "what," and so inevitably the Greek thinkers were looking for "something" which made a being a being. Rather than attempt to explain this in the abstract, as it were, we will see how each of the important Greek thinkers conceived the question and how he asked it. This will give us concrete examples of the earliest formulations of what we may call the "question of being."

To ask what being is is perhaps the natural way to begin the discussion of being. In any event, it is a theme which can be traced throughout Greek philosophy and one which gives us the benefit of the Greek experience. Perhaps after we have followed the Greek thinkers through their attempts at a solution of the problem of the unity of being, we will be in a position to ask the question in terms which will provide a more successful answer. At least, if we understand what the Greeks were doing, we can save ourselves from the ever-present danger of remaking the mistakes of our predecessors. In metaphysics one of the most fundamental problems is that of asking the right questions in the right way; if we learn this from the Greeks we will have taken a giant stride ahead. A word of explanation about our procedure may be in order here. We are looking at Greek philosophy from a vantage point some two thousand years after the fact. We are therefore able to put questions in a way in which the Greeks themselves could not. We can see directions of their thought which they themselves could not discern. In this sense, we are giving an interpretation to the history of Greek philosophy and not simply presenting what the Greek thinkers wrote. It is necessary to give this word of caution because the question of being is not put with equal clarity by all the philosophers whom we will consider. But even when the question is not asked explicitly it motivates the thought of the men in question, as will appear.

THE PRE-SOCRATICS

Interestingly enough, the earliest Greek philosophers ask the question very clearly. The Ionians, who flourished from 600 to 550 B.C., asked the question quite plainly and gave answers which have a certain classic simplicity. Aristotle in the first book of his *Metaphysics* tells us: "Of the first philosophers, then, most thought the principles which were of the nature of matter were the only principles of all things. That of which all things consist, the first from which they come to be, the last into which they are resolved (the substance remaining, but changing in its modifications), this they say is the element and this the principle of things, and therefore they think nothing is generated or destroyed, since this sort of entity is always conserved." [2] Aristotle is telling us that these early Greek philosophers identified "being" with a certain type of being, that for them everything was really just this type of being under different appearances. This explanation and Aristotle's discussion of it are involved with the Greek notions of science, in which earth, air, fire, and water are the elements present in all things in various mixtures. The exact status of these elements varies with the different thinkers.[3]

The Ionians

THALES

Thales (c. 585 B.C.), for instance, the earliest of the Ionian School, is reported to have held that the primary stuff of all things is water. Aristotle reports this without elaborating.[4] He suggests that Thales might have gotten this notion "from seeing that the nutriment of all things is moist, and that heat itself is generated from the moist and

[2] *Ibid.*, A, 3, 983b 7–13. See J. Owens, *A History of Ancient Western Philosophy,* copyright © 1959, Appleton-Century-Crofts, Inc., pp. 7–12, for Aristotle's dependability as a historian of Greek philosophy.
[3] See Owens, *Ancient Western Philosophy, passim.*
[4] *Metaphysics,* A, 3, 984a 6–7.

kept alive by it."[5] It would be a mistake to make too much out of this reference of Aristotle to Thales or to use it to construct a whole cosmology or metaphysics. On the other hand, Aristotle was a careful historian; therefore, we have no reason to doubt that Thales did "open up a properly philosophical inquiry into the nature of the ultimate matter from which all sensible things are derived."[6] Consequently, without making too much of it, we can say that Thales maintained that a thing has being ultimately because it is made of water. This is to say in a simple way that the essence of being is water. Thales suggests that we can ask, "What is being?" and that the answer is, "Being is water."

ANAXIMENES

Later Ionian thinkers asked the same question, but answered it differently. Anaximenes (c. 525 B.C.), for instance, chose air as the essence of reality. One sentence of his has survived: "As our soul, being air, keeps us together, so do breath and air encompass the whole cosmos."[7] Hippolytus reports this: "Infinite air is the first principle, from which arise the things that have come and are coming into existence, and the things that will be, and gods and divine beings, while other beings are produced from these."[8] Anaximenes held, too, that condensation and rarefaction produced the different things in the universe.[9] This was probably conceived in terms of a quantitative rather than a qualitative process, so that the differences in being are really just differences in the way air is expanded or compacted.[10] In this sense, Anaximenes takes an even stronger stand than Thales, since for him all being actually is air under one form or another. The essence of being, therefore, is air. Or, to put it differently, Anaximenes' answer to the question, "What is being?" is, "Being is air."

---

[5] *Ibid.*, 983b 22–24.
[6] Owens, *Ancient Western Philosophy*, p. 12.
[7] Quoted in *ibid.*, p. 19.
[8] M. Nahm, *Selections from Early Greek Philosophy*, 4th ed. (New York: Appleton-Century-Crofts, 1964), p. 44. Copyright © 1964, Meredith Publishing Company.
[9] *Ibid.*
[10] See Owens, *Ancient Western Philosophy*, p. 20.

Hippasus and Xenophanes

One might expect that some thinkers would select the other two elements, fire and earth, as the essential stuff of the universe; however, this is not always the case. Hippasus of Metapontum, in southern Italy, did choose fire. Aristotle mentions this without going into any detail.[11] Earth was not chosen by any of the Ionians, because it was thought to be found only in the central region of the universe, and so could not act as a general first principle.[12] There is, however, a fragment from Xenophanes of Colophon (c. 500 B.C.), reputed founder of the Eleatic school, which has been interpreted as saying that earth is the first principle of all reality. Xenophanes says: "For all things come from earth, and all things end by becoming earth." [13] Aristotle and Theophrastus interpret this statement as a poetic reflection, rather than as philosophical teaching, and this is probably the best interpretation.[14] For those who take Xenophanes literally, however, the question, "What is being?" would be answered, "Being is earth." And if the fragment from Hippasus is taken literally, the question, "What is being?" would be answered, "Being is fire."

Anaximander

Anaximander of Miletus (c. 600 B.C.) took a slightly different tack from the other Ionians. As quoted by Theophrastus, he suggests that "The first principle and element of all things is infinite [or the unlimited] . . . it is neither water nor any of the other things called elements, but the infinite is something of a different nature from which came all the heavens and all the worlds in them." [15] Aristotle confirms this interpretation.[16] Anaximander, therefore, is saying that the essence of being is the infinite or unlimited. He would answer the question, "What is being?" with, "Being is the unlimited or infinite."

---

[11] *Metaphysics,* A, 3, 984a 6–7.
[12] Owens, *Ancient Western Philosophy,* pp. 21-22.
[13] Nahm, *Selections,* p. 85 No. 8; Owens, *Ancient Western Philosophy,* pp. 21–22.
[14] Owens, *ibid.*
[15] Nahm, *Selections,* p. 39.
[16] *Physics,* III, 5, 204b 22–28.

Empedocles

Empedocles of Acragas (c. 500 B.C.) avoided the unifying trend of the pre-Socratic philosophers we have been considering. He holds that the four roots of things are called, "Fire and Water and Earth, and the boundless height of air." [17] No element takes precedence, "For these are equal, all of them, and of like ancient race." [18] Furthermore, no real change takes place in the elements, "For nothing is added to them, nor yet does anything pass away from them; for if they were continually perishing they would no longer exist." [19] Two things are clear from this. First, the world is composed of the four elements, earth, air, fire, and water. Second, there is never any essential change in these elements. Empedocles, therefore, would answer our question, "What is being?" with, "Being is the four elements." He would admit of no further unity.

Anaxagoras

A similar rejection of any ultimate unity is found in Anaxagoras of Clazomenae (c. 500 B.C.). But hc speaks not only of the four elements, but of an infinite number of first principles. There are two stages to Anaxagoras' thought. First, there was a past state in which all things were together in a mixture and in it they were unlimited in number. The first fragment tells us that "All things were together, unlimited both in number and in smallness; for the small, too, was unlimited. And when all were together, none was visible on account of the smallness. For air-and-ether prevailed over all, both being unlimited. For in the sum total of things these are the greatest both in number and in size." [20] Then there is the later state, in which various things have "separated off" and become visible as in our present stage of the world. The air and ether separate off from the

---

[17] Reprinted by permission of the publishers from Kathleen Freeman, *Ancilla to the Pre-Socratic Philosophers*, Cambridge, Mass.: Harvard University Press, 1957, *Fragment 6*, p. 52. See Owens, *Ancient Western Philosophy*, p. 105.
[18] Nahm, *Selections*, p. 118 No. 87.
[19] *Ibid.*, p. 119.
[20] *Fragment 1*, quoted in Owens, *Ancient Western Philosophy*, p. 115.

rest of things, and these, unlimited in number, surround them.[21] Because of this, Anaxagoras adds, "It is necessary to believe that there are many things of all kinds in all composites, and the seeds of all things, seeds that have all kinds of shapes and surface characteristics and pleasant sensations." [22] There is in each thing an individual mixture with an unlimited number of "shares" or "seeds" of all things. As with Empedocles, there is no possibility of essential change. Nor does the "separating off" increase the number of things in the universe, for "These things having been separated in this manner, it is necessary to know that all things are in no way less or more (for it is not possible to be more than all) but all are always equal." [23] If, then, we were to ask Anaxagoras, "What is being?" his answer would be: "Being is an infinity of things." And there is no way of surpassing this multitude to reach any unity.

The Atomists: Leucippus and Democritus

The atomists Leucippus (fifth century B.C.) and Democritus (c. 450 B.C.) believed that being was composed of an unlimited number of elements, the atoms, to which they added a kind of negative reality, the void. Theophrastus summarizes Leucippus' doctrine: "He assumed elements unlimited (in number) and ever moving, the atoms; and in them an unlimited number of shapes, because there was no reason why any should be of one shape rather than another and because he saw an unceasing becoming and change in things. He assumed further that what is is no more real than what is not, and that both are equally causes of the things that come into being. For assuming that the substance of the atoms was compact and full, he said that they were what is and that they moved about in a void, which is called what is not and said that it existed no less than what is." [24] We need not delay over the details of this atomic conception of being. Democritus believed essentially what Leucippus did. Their answer to our question, "What is being?" would be, "Be-

[21] *Fragment 2,* quoted *ibid.,* p. 117.
[22] *Fragment 4,* quoted *ibid.*
[23] *Fragment 5,* quoted *ibid.,* p. 119.
[24] *Fragment 8,* quoted *ibid.,* p. 133.

ing is part of reality, it is the unlimited number of atoms." But this escapes the intent of our question, since by "being" we mean the whole of reality. Leucippus and Democritus are saying that their predecessors had too narrow a concept of reality in their idea of "being." [25]

The Pythagoreans

The Pythagoreans (fifth century B.C.) took a different tack. Enamored of their newly discovered mathematics, they thought that it gave them the key to the nature of reality. As Aristotle says of them, "because they saw many attributes of numbers belonging to sensible bodies, [they] supposed real things to be numbers." [26] He adds, "they saw that the modifications and ratios of the musical scale were expressible in numbers, . . . all other things seemed in their whole nature to be modeled after numbers, and numbers seemed to be the first things." [27] And again, "the so-called Pythagoreans, who were the first to take up mathematics, not only advanced this study but also having been brought up in it, they thought that its principles were the principles of all things." [28] They were impressed by the unlimited and the finite, the unit and the infinite multitude of things discussed by their predecessors, and so concluded that "infinity itself and unity itself were the substance of the things of which they are predicated. This is why number was the substance of all things." [29] One of the unanswered questions of this concept of reality is how the spatially extended units of our visible world could be constructed out of numbers. Aristotle found no answer to this question in the Pythagoreans.[30] But this need not detain us since their conception of reality is quite clear, as far as it goes. To our question, "What is being?" the Pythagoreans would answer, "Being is number."

---

[25] For a discussion of the contention of Leucippus and Democritus that the void is real see Owens, *ibid.*, pp. 132 ff.
[26] *Metaphysics*, N, 2, 1090a 20–23.
[27] *Ibid.*, A, 5, 985b 31–986a 1.
[28] *Ibid.*, A, 5, 985b 23–26.
[29] *Ibid.*, 987a 17–19.
[30] *Ibid.*, M, 6, 1080b 18–21.

Parmenides

The answers which we have seen so far have put the question of being in a fairly simple and straightforward manner. They have identified being with one or more of the elements, with an infinity of things, or, finally, with numbers. In each case the thinkers have been looking for "something" which is the principle of our world, the essence of being or reality. Parmenides (c. 485 B.C.) and Heraclitus (c. 500 B.C.), although historically they precede the atomists and Pythagoreans, put the question differently.[31] They do not seek the essence of being in some particular kind of being, but identify it with unity and multiplicity, respectively.

Parmenides seems to think that that which is and its being are identical.[32] Looking at being in this way, he defines being as "That which is." For him this obviously encompasses the whole of reality. Its opposite is "That which is not," or nonbeing, and this has no reality whatsoever. Between these opposites there is no real middle ground. If we follow the "Way of Truth," we understand this.[33] We see, according to Parmenides, "that Being has no coming into being, and no destruction, for it is whole of limb, without motion, and without end." [34] "It is now, a Whole altogether, One, continuous." [35] Consequently, there is no real multiplicity, no "beings," only Being. There is no movement or change, only stable Being. However, in addition to the Way of Truth or Reason, there is the Way of Opinion, that is, the "opinions of mortals" [36] which attempt to mix Being and nonbeing. It is these false opinions which mislead us into believing that there are many beings which are created and which perish, which are in motion and which come to rest.[37] The truth, however, is that "Being is," alone in its solitary splendor. To have many beings, Being would have to be diversified, but diversification

---

[31] Or at least Heraclitus as described by Plato and Aristotle. See Owens, *Ancient Western Philosophy,* p. 52.
[32] *Ibid.*
[33] *Fragment* 2, trans. Freeman, *Ancilla,* p. 42.
[34] *Fragments* 7 and 8, *ibid.,* p. 43.
[35] *Ibid.*
[36] *Ibid.,* p. 44.
[37] *Fragment* 19, *ibid.,* p. 46.

can come only from Being or from nonbeing; there is no third alternative. But Being cannot diversify Being, since it already is Being. In other words, Being adds nothing to Being; we have instead perfect identity. On the other hand, nonbeing cannot diversify Being because nonbeing has no reality and so it adds nothing to Being. Parmenides reiterates his conclusion, "Being is that which is."

There is a positive and a negative aspect to Parmenides' conclusion. Positively, he defined the content of being independently of the particular limitations of beings. As Father Owens points out, "Parmenides saw vividly and expressed forcefully the implications of what it means for a thing to be, when the aspect of Being is viewed as a real and meaningful form." [38] That is, Parmenides considered being to be "something," an essence or a form, which would somehow be different from the other individual things of our ordinary experience. Parmenides saw that if Being is something different from the beings which we meet in our everyday world, then only one of the two can be real. Either Being is really such a form, and then it is one and immutable, or the individual beings are real and changeable, and so Being does not exist. Parmenides sided with Being. Parmenides is thus the first of the Greeks to reach a truly metaphysical insight into things from the viewpoint of their being. He is the first to become aware of the problem of being, that is, of how different beings can still have or be Being. Negatively, however, by conceiving being as a form, he had to give it a content which would leave room for nothing else. As Father Owens continues, "Because it was being, it included everything. Because it was a form, it was finite. Complete and perfect in itself it allowed no possibility of motion or change." [39]

Heraclitus

As we have seen, the earlier Greeks asked, "What is being?" in a rather naïve way. They were, however, asking about the essence of being, or to put it the other way around, about being considered as an essence. Parmenides does the same thing in a more sophisticated

---

[38] *Ancient Western Philosophy*, p. 72.
[39] *Ibid.*

way. He conceives of being as a form, that is as an essence, and so makes the question of being a question of essence. It will be our contention that this way of putting the question of being dominated Greek thought from the pre-Socratics down to Plotinus.[40] For all the Greek thinkers being is considered as a form or essence. Heraclitus was impressed more by the mobility of reality than by its permanence. Thus, "It is not possible to step twice into the same river,"[41] since Heraclitus claims that there is no fixed object called "a river" for him to step into. Instead there are only ever-flowing, ever-changing waters.[42] The same holds for objects; they are always changing, therefore we cannot grasp one because it changes as we touch it. Heraclitus, therefore, is saying that being is really a flux and nothing stable. His famous *panta rhei*, "all things are in a flux,"[43] is the answer to the question, "What is being?" and says, "Being is the flux." Heraclitus is talking, like his fellows, about the form or essence of being, and says that it is the "flux." His answer has not proved satisfactory to many thinkers, but it is an answer to the question of being, and it is conceived in terms of form and essence.

Part of the importance of Parmenides and Heraclitus is that they realized that being could not be conceived of in terms of the elements, as their predecessors had conceived of it. Being, they saw, must be thought of in a different way. As we have seen, they still conceived of it as a form, but as a unique form, which thus really excluded all other forms. In this way they were able to grasp the real question of being, but looking for an answer in the same mold, of form and essence, were unable to answer it.

PLATO

The next important step in our discussion of the Greek treatment of the question of being brings us to the golden age of Greek philosophy. About two generations after Parmenides Plato became the

---

[40] *Ibid.*

[41] *Fragment 91,* trans. Freeman, *Ancilla,* p. 31.

[42] K. Freeman, *The Pre-Socratic Philosophers* (Oxford: Basil Blackwell, Ltd., 1949), p. 114.

[43] Reported by Plato, Cratylus, 439C, trans. B. Jowett, in *The Dialogues of Plato* (New York: Random House, 1937), I, 228.

outstanding Greek thinker. The beauty of his literary style has made his writings classics of the Western world. His thought, too, has won him perhaps the highest rung on the ladder of Western philosophy. Whitehead, for instance, thinks that Plato stands so far superior to his successors that all of Western philosophical writing after Plato has been a series of footnotes to his work. Burnet, the British historian of Greek thought, is just as emphatic: "Plato has been the source of all that is best and of most importance in our civilization."[44]

Plato has much to say on the whole range of philosophical problems; however, for the present, we have but one question to put to him: "What is being?" Plato accepts the question as legitimate, and in his answer includes the problematic of his predecessors. He is keenly aware of the force of the arguments of both Parmenides and Heraclitus. Ultimately, he agrees with Parmenides that being is that which is, and like Parmenides he takes "that which is" in a formal, essential sense, rather than in any existential sense. Perhaps another way of putting this is to say that being is the "real," and that things can have "reality" without existing. Accepting this meaning of real being, Plato's problem is to show how the "real" can escape the unity, immobility, and total lack of differentiation of Parmenides' being.[45]

Plato answers Parmenides first by distinguishing between two worlds, the really real (*ontos on*) spiritual world of forms or ideas, which are permanent and unchanging, and the not-so-real material world of our sense experience, in which things are always in movement and undergoing change. These are never fully what they are, but are always in the process of becoming. They are "appearances," which somehow participate in the forms without possessing their full being. One of the ways in which Plato arrives at this double type of reality is through his analysis of human knowing. He is convinced that there are two kinds of knowing, one by means of *knowledge*, the other by way of *opinion*. Knowledge puts us in touch with

---

[44] *Platonism,* p. 1, quoted in Owens, *Ancient Western Philosophy,* p. 196.
[45] Most commentators think that Plato finally admitted, in the dialogue *Parmenides,* that he could not answer Parmenides. In this, then, his metaphysics reached an impasse.

the stable, spiritual Being, whereas opinion connects us with the changing material appearances. Plato illustrates the difference between the objects of these two types of knowledge in his analogy of the cave in the dialogue, *The Republic.* There he tells us that in our present life we are like men chained in an underground cave in such a way that we can see only the back wall of the cavern. Behind us is a ledge with a wall along its edge. On the ledge, behind the wall, a fire burns and casts its light on the back wall which we are facing. Along the ledge, between the fire and the wall, people walk carrying all kinds of sensible objects, the shadows of which move along the back wall of the cave. These shadows are what we see in this mortal life of ours. Unless we are able to free ourselves and climb out of the cave into the sunlight, we never see the real objects themselves, nor do we see the light of the sun in which and by which real objects are seen. Actually what we see is two steps from reality. It is as though we were looking at the shadows of cardboard cutout representations of real things. Plato applies the analogy of the cave in this way: "The prison-house is the world of sight, the light of the fire is the sun, and you will not misapprehend me if you interpret the journey upwards to be the ascent of the soul into the intellectual world." [46] What he is saying is that the seeming reality of the things in the cave is illusory. The illusions correspond to the material things which we experience. The really real beings, which exist outside the cave, correspond to the spiritual realities which Plato calls the forms or ideas. Put most simply, in the world of appearances we have individual men, individual dogs, individual houses, and so on, each existing in the material world with what Plato calls a kind of shadow existence. In the world of forms, the spiritual world, we have man as such, dog as such, house as such, the immaterial spiritual realities (forms or ideas), which exist in an unchanging spiritual world.

Thus far the picture of Plato's double world is fairly easy to grasp. Provided that we do not ask too many questions, we can understand fairly well what it means to have material individual men in this world of change, and an idea or form of man as such, house as such, and so forth in a kind of spiritual world. The big difficulty arises, of

---

[46] *Republic,* VII, 517B, trans. Jowett, in *The Dialogues of Plato,* I, 776.

course, when we try to discover the exact relation between these two worlds. Ultimately, one chooses either the spiritual world or the material world; it is difficult to see why one needs both.

Plato, however, was never quite satisfied with this obvious duality of the world of forms and of appearances. Consequently, he tried to unify the two worlds by raising one of the forms, that of the Good, into a place of primacy, so that it would in some way be the source of all the other forms. Thus in *The Republic* he says, "You would say, would you not, that the sun is not only the author of visibility in all things visible, but of generation and nourishment and growth, though he himself is not generation? Certainly. In like manner the Good may be said to be not only the author of knowledge to all things known, but of their being and essence, and yet the Good is not essence, but far exceeds essence in dignity and power." [47] In this passage Plato is giving the Good the role and place of a super-form, somehow beyond essence. Nowhere does he clarify what he means by this, although frequently enough he refers to the Good as the highest of the forms. Therefore, we can interpret Plato's doctrine of being in two ways. Either the Good is beyond essence and is a source of everything else, or the Good is a form like the others, but simply the highest of the forms. In either case, however, Plato conceives the Good after the manner of a form. And so in both cases he faces the problem which Parmenides found insoluble, that of giving being a formal unity without destroying the multiplicity of beings. Plato's idea of the Good as a source of unity of being also fails to solve the problem. For if the Good is a separate form or super-form, it must not overlap with the others. However, if the Good is really the Good, it must be one. Otherwise it would also be something else.[48] Therefore it must be one, and so share in the essence of the One. The same holds for the relation of the Good to the other forms. Again we are saying that if being is a form or if whatever is the equivalent of being, here the Good, is a form, it must be *something* and if it is something, only that something is being, and everything else is nonbeing. And so there can really only be one being, which brings us back to Parmenides.

---

[47] *Ibid.*, VI, 509B, I, 770.

[48] See E. Gilson, *Being and Some Philosophers* (Toronto: Pontifical Institute of Mediaeval Studies, 1952), pp. 17 f.

When we look at Plato's discussion of being in this way, we see that in him we find another example of what happens to a philosopher when he tries to work out a conception of being in terms of essence. Ultimately to our question, "What is being?" Plato answers, "Being is form." And once he says this, he cannot explain how there can be more than one form. This is the lesson of his dialogue, *Parmenides.*

ARISTOTLE

The name always associated with Plato's is that of Aristotle, whom the Medievals called The Philosopher because of the breadth and depth of his work. In fact for many centuries of the Christian era, to be a philosopher in the Western world was to be either a Platonist or an Aristotelian. The range of Aristotle's philosophy is immense. His writings cover logic, psychology, metaphysics, politics, natural science, and even natural history. Basically a natural scientist, Aristotle was attracted more to the concrete reality around us than to any Platonic separated forms. The substantial things we meet every day were the real beings for Aristotle. Emphasizing this empirical outlook, Aristotle was the first to work out an explanation of the four causes: material, formal, efficient, and final. These we will examine in detail in a later chapter. He, too, is responsible for the doctrine of matter and form (*hylemorphism,* from the Greek *hylē* = matter and *morphē* = form), which also will engage us in a subsequent chapter.

However, to the extent that Aristotle asked the question of being, he asked it in surprisingly Platonic terms. If we were to ask him, "What is being?" Aristotle would have answered, "Being is substance." Thus, at the beginning of Book Z of the *Metaphysics* he writes, "While 'being' has all these senses, obviously that which 'is' primarily is the 'what,' which indicates the substance of the thing." [49] In Aristotle the key element of substance is form, for form makes the substance actually be what it is. Matter, the correlative of form, may explain the multiplicity of forms in a given species, since the form, man, for example, may be received into many "matters." Fur-

---

[49] *Metaphysics,* Z, 1, 1028a 13-15.

thermore, it helps explain change. It is the form, however, which makes a thing be what it is. For Aristotle there can be many substances because there can be many kinds of things, each kind having its own form, such as man, dog, rose, oak tree, and so forth; and there can be many individuals belonging to each of these kinds of substance. Thus there can be many men, as we have said, because each individual man has the form, man, existing in his particular matter; this holds, too, for the various individual dogs, roses, oak trees, and so on.

To understand these ideas about substance, matter, and form in Aristotle, it will be well for us to take a quick look at his theory of act and potency. We will have to discuss this in greater detail later, but for the moment we can see that Aristotle claimed that the trouble with Parmenides, Heraclitus, and even Plato was that for them being was only actual, so that they lived in a frozen world of unchanging act, as with Parmenides, or in a completely fluid world, such as that of Heraclitus. The mistake in this viewpoint, according to Aristotle, is that for them whatever is is fully what it is and nothing more. However, in reality at any given time the things around us are really more than they actually are. This sounds paradoxical, but it is really quite simple. In a world such as ours, in which there is change, the food we eat, for instance, is actually food, but it is also potentially part of us. After we eat it, it loses its character of being food and becomes part of our flesh and bones. The nutrition which the flower takes from the soil ceases to be soil and becomes part of the flower. Or on another level, the block of stone becomes a statue and the pile of bricks and mortar becomes a house. Aristotle concluded from all this that when we speak of being, we must talk both of what being actually is and what it is in potency to become. This is a powerful theory, as far as it goes. As we have pointed out, it explains change and the multiplication of individuals within a species. However, it puts form at the apex of reality; form is the highest actuality. As Etienne Gilson says, "If anyone posits above the form, an act of that act, he may well use the technical terminology of Aristotle, but on that point at least he is not an Aristotelian." [50] Gilson means that when Aristotle says that being is substance and

[50] *Being and Some Philosophers,* p. 47.

in substance form is the highest act, he is saying all that he has to say about the definition of being.

We can say, then, that for Aristotle being is substance and form, so that in the long run Aristotle will have to face Plato's problem about the multiplicity of essences. For Aristotle's substance is just as universal as are Plato's forms and ideas. And Aristotle ultimately will have to choose between substance as the true reality and the individual things which exist in our experience. These latter individuals exist; substance as such does not. It has, then, the strange function of not existing, but at the same time of guaranteeing the being of the individuals which are the only things which do exist, for they are being because they are substance. For Aristotle, therefore, being means substance, and substance is essence, which is primarily universal. Had he pressed on further in his investigations, he would have had to face the Platonic dilemma of the two worlds: the individual, concrete, material world and the spiritual, universal world of forms.[51] As we proceed, we shall see that Aristotle has furnished many of the elements needed for a successful theory of being but that since he has left out of consideration the one thing which makes beings real, their existence, he has not really formulated the question differently from Parmenides and Plato.

PLOTINUS

The last Greek philosopher whom we shall consider is Plotinus (c. A.D. 250), the greatest of the so-called Neoplatonists. We need not delay long on his thought, since his main contribution to the question of being is to draw a conclusion which Plato perhaps should have drawn. Plotinus took very seriously Plato's statement that the Good is not a form or essence. If the source of being, which the Good was for Plato, is not a form or essence, it must be, Plotinus concluded, somehow outside of being and beyond it. In order to

---

[51] It is interesting to note that G. Martin (*An Introduction to General Metaphysics* [London: George Allen & Unwin Ltd., 1961], p. 152) is forced to conclude that there is no answer to the question, "What is being?" His difficulty in the twentieth century is exactly Aristotle's. B. Lonergan (*Insight* [New York: Philosophical Library, 1956], p. 367) notes, as we do, that Aristotle was asking, "What is being?"

reach this source of being, which is not being, Plotinus argued along Platonic lines to a highest being, a supreme intelligence (*nous*), in which the whole intelligibility of the world is summed up. This supreme intelligence includes the whole intelligibility of being. As Plotinus says, "The intelligence is identical with being." [52] Plotinus conceived of being and intelligence as forms, just as Plato did, and so he faced the difficulty which Plato encountered. For although he claimed that intelligence and being are identical, nevertheless they do not mean the same thing, and so there is still a duality in being and not the fundamental unity which Plato sought in the Good. Plotinus was aware of this problem and thought he had an answer to it. There must be unity; there must be a "One." But this One must be, according to Plotinus, beyond being and intelligibility. It is nonbeing, nonintelligibility, which is the source of all being and intelligibility. Since the One is beyond being and intelligibility, obviously we cannot understand it. Plotinus, however, would say that it must be postulated as the source of all being and intelligibility.

If we put this in a theistic context, we see that the One corresponds to some modern ideas of God. The One is not Being; it is wholly other than Being, and yet is somehow the source of Being. For Plotinus, Being comes from the One by way of *emanation;* it *emanates* (flows out) from the One. Some modern theologians, mainly Protestant, without accepting Plotinus' idea of the One, speak of God in a similar way as wholly other, as totally inconceivable by men. Thus, Rudolf Otto speaks of God as the "Numinous," as fear-inspiring mystery (*tremendum mysterium*).[53] Such a God is not Being, but is still the source of Being, a God unknown and unnamed, in whom we believe with a kind of blind faith. In both these theories, of Plotinus and of the modern theologians, we have something beyond Being which accounts for Being. We can say, too, that we have in both an attempt to get beyond form and essence for the "explanation" of reality.

In one sense, therefore, Plotinus answers our question, "What is being?" He says that being is intelligibility and that being and intel-

---

[52] *Enneads,* V, 4, 2. See Gilson, *Being and Some Philosophers,* p. 28.
[53] "The Idea of the Holy," Chapter 5, in J. Hick, *Classical and Contemporary Readings in the Philosophy of Religion* (Englewood Cliffs, N.J.: Prentice-Hall, Inc., 1964), pp. 256 ff.

ligibility, as identical, are the limit which human understanding can reach. He also says, however, that beyond being and intelligibility there is the unexplainable unity of the One. There is no ultimate human explanation, according to Plotinus. This is so because explanation means intelligibility and the source of being is beyond intelligibility in the inexpressible, inconceivable One. In one sense, of course, this is an explanation, but one which we cannot understand. The One can properly be referred to only negatively: it is not substance, not something, not attainable by an act of our understanding. Obviously, Plotinus makes no attempt to expand the notion of being to include the One and so he says that the question of being as posed by the Greeks is insoluble. The Greeks were looking for a form or essence which would explain all reality. Plotinus says there is no such form or essence but only the One which is beyond all explanation.[54]

Plotinus, therefore, draws our conclusion for us. He tells us that the Greek approach to the question of being is self-defeating. It looks for a definition of being in terms of form and essence, and no such definition can be found. Historically, the Greek thinkers are extremely important to metaphysics because they have tried all the possible ways of analyzing being into terms of essence. Philosophically they influenced the approach of all subsequent thinkers by focusing on the most fundamental questions and by seeking ultimate answers. Plotinus comes closest to giving an answer. At least he tells us that we will be wasting our time if we try to solve the question of being in terms of essence.

CONCLUSION

It is important to understand the Greek experiment. Etienne Gilson, in *Being and Some Philosophers* and in *The Unity of Philosophical Experience,* has given important examples of attempts over the years to solve the question of being in terms of essence. Gottfried Martin [55] is a perfect instance in point; for him the problems of metaphysics are essentially insoluble precisely because he con-

---

[54] See Gilson, *Being and Some Philosophers,* p. 28; Owens, *Ancient Western Philosophy,* p. 405.

[55] See note 51 above.

ceives of being in terms of essence. Many of our contemporaries, especially the existentialists, attack metaphysics because they, too, conceive of being as necessarily essentialistic. Martin Heidegger, perhaps the most famous of present-day European philosophers, says at the beginning of his monumental *Being and Time* that the metaphysics of Plato and Aristotle has simply been altered and retouched by subsequent thinkers. In view of all this, we will have to be alert to distinguish between the approach of the Greeks and the approach which we will take in the succeeding chapters. If metaphysics is to be meaningful, it must raise the problem of being in terms of existing reality, and not in terms of essence. We shall try to keep this clear as we proceed. That the approach taken today by many contemporary American and European philosophers is really the essentialism of Plato and Aristotle will become clearer as we proceed.

SUGGESTED READINGS

Aristotle, *Metaphysics,* in *Basic Works,* ed. Richard McKeon. New York: Random House, 1941.

Burnet, John, *Early Greek Philosophy* (4th ed.). London: Adam & Charles Black, Ltd., 1930. Treatment of the pre-Socratic philosophers, including translations of fragments.

Copleston, Frederick, *A History of Philosophy,* Vol. I, Chapters 2–10 (on the pre-Socratics), 19–20 (Plato's theory of knowledge and of forms), 29 (Aristotle's metaphysics), 45 (Plotinus). Westminster: The Newman Press, 1955.

Freeman, Kathleen, *Ancilla to the Pre-Socratic Philosophers.* Cambridge, Mass.: Harvard University Press, 1957.

Gilson, Etienne, *God and Philosophy,* Chapter 1. New Haven, Conn.: Yale University Press, 1941. Consideration of Greek conception of being.

Katz, J., *The Philosophy of Plotinus.* New York: Appleton-Century-Crofts, 1950. Includes translations of selections.

Nahm, Milton C., ed., *Selections from Early Greek Philosophy* (4th ed.). New York: Appleton-Century-Crofts, 1964. Includes selections from the Ionians, Pythagoreans, Heraclitus, Parmenides, and atomists.

Owens, Joseph, *A History of Ancient Western Philosophy*. New York: Appleton-Century-Crofts, 1959. Treatments of the pre-Socratics, Plato, Aristotle, and Neoplatonists.

Plato, *The Dialogues of Plato*, ed. B. Jowett, revised by D. J. Allan and H. E. Dale, 4 vols. Oxford: Clarendon Press, Ltd., 1953.

Stevans, Edward, "The Perfection of Being in Aristotle," *The Modern Schoolman*, XLI (March 1964), 227–50.

3 THE DISCOVERY OF EXISTENCE AND THE RELEVANCE OF ACT AND POTENCY

PLACING THE QUESTION

The lesson which we have learned from the Greeks is that we cannot successfully understand reality if we investigate it in terms of essence. From them we learn too that the answer to the question "What is being?" must be "Being is not a 'what,'" and so no answer in terms of what being is can be satisfactory. Implicit in this discovery of the inadequacy of an explanation of being in terms of what it is is the importance of the other aspect of being, namely, "*that* it is." In this chapter we will want to investigate this aspect of being to see if it will lead us to a solution which the Greeks were unable to find.

We need a few warnings, however, before we begin our discussion of the existence, or the "that it is," of beings. The first caution is not to pass over the "that it is" too quickly. This is a stronger temptation than many realize, for as soon as we become interested in knowing about something, we tend to forget about its existence. Thus the physicist is not really interested in the actual acceleration of a given particle speeding from his cyclotron toward its target. He wants to know the *law* of the movement of such particles. The chemist does not care particularly about the existence or nonexistence of the compound which he is analyzing. He is looking for the properties of this kind of compound. The psychologist, as scientist, is not concerned with the peculiarities of an individual person. He may be investigating the symptoms of the manic-depressive type, for instance. As scientists, they are all interested in general knowledge, for which the existence of this or that individual being has no particular importance.

The second warning is that we must be wary of the little word "is." It has two basic meanings, which we must not confuse. "Is" can be used simply to show the relationship between a subject and a predicate in a statement. Thus, "Man is a rational animal" tells us that "rational animal" is a definition of man. It says nothing about the actual existence or nonexistence of human beings. Similarly, in "The unicorn is a one-horned animal," the "is" does not tell us that there are or are not real unicorns. Again, the "is" simply tells us that the predicate goes with the subject. The second meaning of "is" can be called "existential." In this usage "is" tells us that the subject referred to is a real existing thing. For example, when I say, "John Jones is in this room," I mean that there is a real human being, John Jones, who is in this room. And when I say, "Sir Walter Scott was the author of *Waverly*," I mean that there existed a man, named Sir Walter Scott, who wrote *Waverly*.[1] Sometimes we use "is" in this second sense without a predicate, as when we say, "John is," to mean "John exists." Heidegger points out the many ways in which we can

[1] We will omit consideration of the logical discussions of these two uses, especially the complications in which G. E. Moore and B. Russell get involved in their attempt to distinguish between statements with real subjects and those with nonreal subjects, for example, Sir Walter Scott vs. the present king of France. Moore, for instance, says that "Though in one sense of the word there certainly are no unicorns—that sense, namely, in which to assert that there are would be equivalent to asserting that unicorns are real—yet there must be some other sense in which there *are* such things; since if there were not, we could not think of them." (*Philosophical Studies* [London: Routledge & Kegan Paul, Ltd., 1922], p. 215). This points up the need for clarifying the distinction between the logical and existential uses of "is." See M. Charlesworth, *Philosophy and Linguistic Analysis* (Pittsburgh: Duquesne University, 1959), pp. 59 ff. for a discussion of "is" as a nonpredicate.

use this existential "is": " 'God is'; i.e., He is *really present.* 'The earth is'; i.e., we experience it and believe it to be *permanently there.* 'The lecture is in the auditorium'; i.e., it *takes place.* 'The man is from Swabia'; i.e., he *comes from there.* 'The cup is of silver'; i.e., it is *made of. . . .* 'The peasant is to the fields'; i.e., he has gone to the field and *is staying there.* 'The book is mine'; i.e., it *belongs to* me. 'Red is the port side'; i.e., it *stands* for port. 'The dog is in the garden'; i.e., he is *running around* in the garden." [2] And there are others, for they include all the ways in which things can exist.

Our interest in the "that is" aspect of being is a concern with the existential use of "is." We are not forced to look at "is" in this way. We could turn our backs on the whole discussion and say, as many contemporary empiricists do, that existence is a bare fact which cannot be investigated except empirically. That is, we can make the various tests to find out whether there is a burglar in the basement, or a watermelon in the refrigerator, or whether water boils at 212° Fahrenheit at sea-level barometric pressure, and so forth. This approach assumes that "is" does no more than state the fact of existence, so that there is no point in discussing the matter further. Some thinkers, however, have believed that the subject is more complex than this, as we saw from Heidegger. We agree that there is more and therefore we will investigate further the existential meaning of "is."

It might be useful to begin our discussion of the existential "is" from a very personal point of view and ask ourselves, "What difference does it make that anything at all is?" Or, to put it another way, what do we find when we interrogate existence? One of the first things we discover is that each of us shares something with every other person or thing in our experience: we *are,* and they, too, *are.* Each of us may turn to himself and ask of himself, "What am I?" If we do this, we produce a series of answers which describe what we are. At the end of this investigation we can ask ourselves again, "Am I this and no more?" For instance when we say, "I am a student; I am a human being; I am six feet tall; I am the son of my father and the brother of my sister and a friend of my friend," do we say less

---

[2] *An Introduction to Metaphysics,* trans. Ralph Manheim (New York: Doubleday & Company, Inc., 1961), p. 75.

or more than when we say only, "I am"? When we look up from the book we are reading at whatever confronts us—at the table beneath the book, at the wall beyond, at the pencil beside us—we see that they are, too. They exist. They are in contrast to David Copperfield, Superman, and the people who will live in the next century. The things around us exist; these other things do not exist. And there is all the difference in the world and more between what exists and what does not exist.

Ordinarily, however, we do not advert to this difference; it escapes our usual awareness. Although it is most fundamental of all, most often it solicits only an implicit nod. And yet there are times when existence becomes momentarily crucial; times when there is a possibility of nonexistence. For example, let there be a brush with death—an automobile crash avoided by inches, the discovery of escaping gas minutes before a threatened explosion, the terror of realization that the plane one should have taken has crashed—and the "I am," which seemed so close to extinction, breaks in on our consciousness. We become sharply, sometimes painfully, aware of the existence which was almost snatched away from us. There are less vital cases, such as the panic of hunting for our driver's license when the patrol car has waved us to the side of the road. The very existence of the license takes on new importance. Or, again, the search for food when a man is starving. Then the bare existence of any kind of food becomes essential. In such cases hope and despair are ultimately manifestations of existence and of the fullness of existence.

But still, what does it mean to exist? Is it so basic that all we can do is affirm it, "I am," "It is," and "You are"? Is it only a "state" of being or of being-there, a given, brute fact which cannot be questioned, so that it would be absurd to ask for a meaning of being beyond this?

We have seen that the Greeks never really undertook an investigation of this side of being. But the question must be asked. "That someone is" and "what he is" seem somehow not reducible to the same explanation. "That he is" he shares in common with everything else that is. Furthermore, "what he is" is shared with various other beings. But the way that he is what he is, is unique and peculiar to him. This is an aspect of the age-old problem of "the one and the many": beings are one in that they all exist and one in that they fall into various classifications, that is, belong to given genera and species, but many in that they are multiplied in existence and diversified in their manner of existence. We are faced with two problems here, the multiplication of beings and the multiplication of beings within a particular classification. For the moment, we will discuss only the former. In terms of this problem we see that *to exist* is not precisely the same as *to-exist-as-man* or *to-exist-as-tree* or *to-exist-as-stone* (because a man and a tree and a stone all exist, but a man is not thereby a tree nor a tree thereby a stone). If, therefore, *to exist* and *to-exist-as-this-kind-of-being* are not the same, something must explain both existence and kind of existence which is manifested in each thing. The same principle cannot account for both, just as the same constitutive element cannot explain why one thing is alive and another dead.

At this point we must be careful not to panic, for although we are studying reality in a new way and attempting to see its ultimate structure, the principles which account for its existence, and the particular kinds of existence in reality, our investigation is much less complicated than many think. Half the job is getting a grasp of the question. This is not too difficult, although it may take a bit of readjustment in our thinking. For although we understand easily enough what it means to ask about the chemical, biological, or psychological structure of a being, we do not often push on to ask about its metaphysical structure. We seldom ask, "What, after all, does it mean for this thing to be?" We are asking whether an answer similar to that given by the chemist, biologist, or psychologist can be given to the question of the metaphysical structure of being. Obviously we are not asking the same question as the chemist, physicist, or psychologist. We may not know what the answer will be, but we know that the question is of a different type, since it asks why something *is* rather than why something *is such* as it is.

Once we understand that this is a new kind of question, we realize that we have already discussed it, at least under one aspect, in our treatment of the Greeks, who asked the question of being in terms of essence. Our contemporaries take various approaches. Some, such as Gabriel Marcel, think that the problem can be solved by taking the difficult path which lies between giving a dogmatic an-

swer and despairing of any answer. "Between these two there exists a middle way—a narrow, difficult and dangerous path which I have tried to discover. . . . I can only proceed in this kind of country by calling out to other travelers. If, as it occasionally happens, certain minds respond . . . then there is a way. But, as I believe Plato perceived with incomparable clarity, it is a way which is undiscoverable except through love, to which alone it is visible, and this brings us to what is perhaps the deepest characteristic of that realm of the meta-problematical [the area between rationally solvable *problems* and insoluble *mystery*] of which I have tried to explore certain regions."[3] Jacques Maritain and Louis De Raeymaeker seem to use the same intuition in different ways.[4] At the opposite extreme there is A. J. Ayer, who holds that even if there is such a thing as a "vision" of being, it is useless to us. For although most metaphysics is "merely the embodiment of humdrum errors, there remain a number of metaphysical passages which are the work of genuine mystical feeling. . . . But, as far as we are concerned, the distinction between the kind of metaphysics that is produced by a philosopher who has been duped by grammar, and the kind that is produced by a mystic who is trying to express the inexpressible, is of no great importance: what is important to us is to realize that even the utterances of the metaphysician who is attempting to expound a vision are literally senseless; so that henceforth we may pursue our philosophical researches with as little regard for them as for the more inglorious kind of metaphysics which comes from a failure to understand the workings of our language."[5]

At this point we need not affirm or deny the intuition of being based on love. That being is encountered in such an intuition is not essential to our discussion. However it is experienced, we may still subject it to carefully reasoned, concentrated search. Ayer's attitude denies the possibility of such a search. Perhaps the best answer to his limitation of meaning to empirically verifiable meaning is simply

---

[3] *The Philosophy of Existence,* trans. M. Harari (New York: The Citadel Press, 1961), p. 44.

[4] L. De Raeymaeker, *The Philosophy of Being,* trans. E. Ziegelmeyer (St. Louis: B. Herder Book Co., 1954), p. 37. J. Maritain, *A Preface to Metaphysics* (New York: Sheed & Ward, 1948), pp. 3–12.

[5] *Language, Truth, and Logic* (New York: Dover Publications, Inc., 1946), p. 45.

to let our empirically unverifiable meanings manifest themselves and speak for themselves. They are their own best justification. Ayer in fact gives up the search before it begins. We should be more brave, and go as far as our minds will lead us. We should grapple at each stage with the opaqueness of the reality we seek to understand. If our search finally brings us to that point at which we cannot see clearly and yet can see enough to know that there is more to be seen—or cannot hear, and yet hear enough to know that there is a further sounding which indeed we may someday break through to hear—it will be a search worth making. It is up to us now to look and to listen.

THE DISCOVERY OF ACT AND POTENCY

The choice of a starting point is really rather simple. We must begin with the self-evident fact: there are many beings that exist. Countless existents make up the world for each of us. Our own existence simply cannot be experienced without relation to the existence of a myriad of other persons and things.[6] If we know anything, we know that we are not alone in the universe. Some may be tempted by solipsism, the doctrine that the thinker alone exists; in-

---

[6] This seems to be generally accepted today. The phenomenologists, the recent logical positivists, and the linguistic analysts—to mention the most popular trends—agree that we begin philosophy in a world, the existence of which we cannot doubt. There is no such agreement, however, about the *metaphysical significance* of this fact. An interesting recent discussion of experience as the starting point of metaphysics is Michael Novak's, "An Empirically Controlled Metaphysics," *International Philosophical Quarterly*, IV, No. 2, 265–82. Using Father Lonergan's, *Insight*, he suggests: "The first problem for metaphysicians, in our generation at least, is to block rationalistic excesses by putting the starting-place of metaphysics under the control of experience. The experience on which metaphysics cannot be grounded, as a survey of recent attempts makes clear, is that of sensation, observation, or taking a look—not even the spiritual look of rationalist intuition. It is rather the experience of that special but multiform awareness, which accompanies sensation, observation, taking a look, thinking, deciding, and the like, and constitutes them as conscious acts. The second problem of metaphysicians, however, is to *maintain* the control of experience over metaphysics, by submitting the several methods of reflective analysis (I have given only some examples) to the test of awareness. A purported reflective analysis, after all, must at least be faithful to the experience it claims to be analyzing; until confirmed by such experience, it is only an hypothesis. In this way, metaphysics, too, is subject to testing by experience" (p. 280).

deed, some have adopted this view. But such a temptation is exorcised by the pangs of hunger, by the awareness that one is in the path of a speeding automobile, by the chill of loneliness, and by the warmth of human comfort. We experience the reality of the world, and we should not let the "*a prioris* of the positivists and the rationalists" [7] stampede us into a denial of this experience. We are not rationalist or empiricist "observers" of sensations and ideas, who can know nothing of their reality. The metaphysician experiences the same world as the physicist. He is "not interested in the Platonic other worlds or uncontrolled intuition into essences; he handles a bit of stone, and begins to reflect that he can be aware [that is, directly] of it, related by science to other materials, come to be aware [that is, reflexively] of himself in handling it and again in thinking of it. What is this thing? What is he? He begins to wonder." [8]

There are several ways one can go from here. Many contemporary Thomists prefer to work through our act of knowing to a "critical" metaphysics. Joseph Maréchal and Bernard Lonergan are the spearheads of this movement. Emerich Coreth explains this approach in a recent article: "[Metaphysics] has now at last become aware that ultimately its only function is to take possession reflectively of the knowledge of being which every mind already possesses and exercises even in the simplest act of inquiring and knowing. This shows that man is by nature the metaphysical being and that human knowledge is always implicitly metaphysical knowledge, moving against the open horizon of being, steadily reaching out beyond the first existent towards the infinity of absolute being." [9]

Father Owens presents what has been a more popular Thomistic view when he suggests that we begin metaphysics by doing it: "The soundest method in approaching metaphysics today, accordingly, is to arouse that disposition [to do metaphysics], set it in motion, and observe where it leads. In particular, one may watch whether or not it succeeds in formulating meaningful statements, whether it develops a properly scientific procedure in the traditional sense of knowledge through causes, and finally whether the knowledge it provides

---

[7] *Ibid.*, p. 278.
[8] *Ibid.*, p. 281.
[9] E. Coreth, "The Problem and Method of Metaphysics," *International Philosophical Quarterly*, III, No. 3 (September 1963), 416–17.

is really worthwhile for the enrichment of human living and able to repay the tremendous and concentrated efforts demanded for its pursuit." [10] Our approach will be closer to that of Father Owens than to that of Maréchal, Lonergan, and Coreth. We shall begin by examining the multiplicity of the beings of our experience, for although the finite and the multiple may ultimately have meaning only by opening into unity and infinity, they serve as a concrete point of departure directly presented to the questioning glance which we turn upon reality.

We see that this multiplicity of beings immediately implies another aspect of being given in experience: difference. By the very fact that these beings are many, they must be different. No two beings, if they are really two, can be exactly alike; if they were so, they would be one. Take two pearls as perfectly matched as possible. Make them as indistinguishable as possible. Yet each has its own material and one is here, the other there. There is always at least this difference. One of the tasks of the scientist is to discover these variations in the minutest of beings. Psychologists, too, have discovered much about individual human differences. These commonsense conclusions about multiplicity and difference are tested again and again as novelty is discovered in repetition. Nor is this surprising, since this is the way things have to be. To have two or more beings alike in every respect would be self-contradictory. Even if it were possible (despite what the geneticists tell us is so) to find twins truly identical in all physical, emotional, and intellectual characteristics, they would still be different beings whose difference could be seen, if only by their difference in place—one in one chair and one in another—and by the difference in the material which they embody—*A*'s matter is not *B*'s matter.

This difference in being seems commonplace, but what explains it? How can we account for the fact that existence, which presents a totality, can be diversified in many different beings, that the perfection or actuality of being appears in this one and in that one, in the reader and in the book, in the earth and in the water? How is it that all have being in common, all are alike in a community of be-

[10] J. Owens, *An Elementary Christian Metaphysics* (Milwaukee: Bruce Publishing Co., 1963), p. 13.

ing, if they are all radically different? This is the old question of the Greeks: how is it possible for many beings to exist and yet not be totally one? to be the same and yet different?

As we look at the difference which is necessarily connected with multiplicity, another feature appears. If beings are different, one has the perfection or actuality which the others do not. Or to take a different point of view, we can see that the total perfection of the beings of our experience is not in any one of these beings. Beings do not present themselves as totally sealed off from one another, and yet each of the things we meet is what it is and is not the other beings. Therefore each has its share of the perfection of being, and lacks the share of perfection of being of every other being. John Jones has the individual perfections of his human nature, for instance, but he does not have all the perfection of humanity. For if he did, there could be no other men. Similarly, John Jones does not have the total perfection of being, since the being he possesses is only one *kind* of being. Each of these beings is therefore limited. We could, of course, have begun with limitation, given as it is in the immediate experience of the activities of a man's self and of the beings around him. Nevertheless, to begin with multiplicity and difference allows the reduction of the problem of multiplicity to the problem of limitation, and it thereby deepens the implications of the limitation of being.

To recapitulate, if beings are many and different, they must somehow be limited; they must not possess the fullness of being, the fullness of existence. Each is limited to its own particular share because it has not what another has; it has not all of being, because another has some of it. If, however, there is one unlimited being, which is the fullness of existence, it is differentiated from all other beings in that it has all of what they share in. How this is so will be explored later. What is important now is to see that multiplicity and difference in being demand limitation in being—so that if there are only two beings, one of them must still be limited.[11] As a matter of fact, there are many beings, and all but one of them must therefore be limited. This is readily visible in the beings of experience.

[11] St. Thomas, *Summa Contra Gentiles,* II, 52, n. 4. How there can be a second being at all if there is an infinite being is something which we will have to discuss later.

Passing mention must be made at this point of the extent of this correlation of difference-multiplicity-limitation. The correlation does not apply only to "being" but to every "order." Whether we are talking about being, or humanity, or treeness, or color, or shape, or sound, wherever there is multiplicity, there is limitation. Each man has a limited share of humanity; each tree a limited share of treeness; each white thing a limited share of whiteness, and so on.

But to proceed with our analysis of the beings of our experience, we see now that a resolution of the problem of the one and the many and an understanding of the structure of the limited beings we meet in our experience will be rooted in an explanation of their limitation. This we can now follow a step further. St. Thomas points out: "If a common nature [for example, humanity] is understood as being separate [that is, not in a subject], it can be only one, although it is possible to find many possessing the same nature. For if the nature, *animal,* existed substantially of itself, there would not be humans or animals." [12] When we have different animals, rather than just animal in itself, so to speak, there is something which *has* the nature, animal, without *being* that nature. It is easy to see that this entails that the particular being, here the type of animal, limits the *animality* to that particular type of animality. And if this is so, there must be something besides animality in the particular man or dog or cat. From this it follows that there is some composition, for if it were purely and simply animal, it would have the perfection of animal and nothing else. Another conclusion can also be drawn from this: the composition must be between something limited (in St. Thomas' example, the perfection humanity) and something limiting (in his example, something in the individual man). This limiting element is a capacity for perfection. The individual man, therefore, has a capacity for a certain share of human perfection.[13] To give a very crude example, the perfection is like water and the limitation is like a drinking glass. If water is poured into the glass, when the glass is full something accounts for the perfection it holds and something accounts for the limitation of that perfection—the

---

[12] *Ibid.,* n. 3.

[13] At this point we will not attempt to ascertain in detail the exact nature of this composition. We will see later that it is a composition of "matter" and "form." See below pages 70–71.

water is the perfection and the capacity of the glass is the limitation on that perfection.

Following St. Thomas, we have taken our examples of multiplication-limitation from the realm of specific essences. However, once the principle is established that such multiplication-limitation involves composition, we must further conclude that all limited beings have some sort of composition. Here we see that the perfection which is multiplied and limited is their "being," and so there must be some capacity for this perfection which receives it. The example of the Greeks has shown us the futility of trying to find an essence, *being,* which is received into a specific type of being, for example, man, and is thereby limited. Parmenides has shown once and for all that the added perfection of man is either included in being, or is nothing and so no capacity for anything at all. What, then, is the perfection of being? Plainly, it is that which makes it real, its existence. The perfection of being is that it "is," or exists. The limitation is that it is this or that kind of being.

As we proceed in this chapter, we will follow this argumentation to its conclusion. Here, however, we must insert a warning. When one is considering an individual, existing being, and its perfection and limitation, one is obviously not going to find two "things" composing that being (which would make it two beings, held together in some way). Rather, whatever composition there is must be a composition of "principles of being." [14] Thus, the example of the limited and limiting factors in the glass of water cannot be applied to the structure of being without important modifications. Nevertheless what remains clear is that whenever any perfection is limited, the same principle cannot account for both the perfection and its limitation. And the limiting factor is always some kind of capacity for that perfection. Perfection in itself carries no notion of imperfection; in itself it is unlimited and unique. It contains the fullness of whatever it is. Consequently, whenever it is found limited, and so

[14] A "principle of being" is something which goes to make up that being, but which cannot itself exist as a being. The most easily comprehended examples of this are "accidents" such as whiteness, warmth, and so forth. Whiteness cannot exist by itself as a being but only as a quality of some being which is white. Similarly, warmth cannot exist by itself as a being, but only as a characteristic of something which is warm.

lacking the fullness it expresses, this must be so precisely because it is received in some capacity which limits it.[15]

In the study of metaphysics, every principle of perfection (which may be limited) is in the scholastic tradition called "act," and every principle which is a capacity for perfection (which therefore limits) is called "potency." Limitation is explained, therefore, by composition—composition of a limited and a limiting principle, composition of act and potency.

Summary

DISCOVERY OF ACT AND POTENCY IN STRUCTURE OF FINITE BEING

Multiplicity posits difference.

Difference posits limitation.

Limitation posits composition of:
limited principle (perfection) = *act*
limiting principle (capacity for perfection) = *potency*

Act here means not an activity performed (though activity is one kind of act), but perfection or actuality. It is the perfecting principle intrinsic to being, the actuating principle. As such, it of course implies no limitation of itself, no difference, no multiplicity. Wherever it is found limited, differentiated, multiplied, it is so because it is joined to some potency. As St. Thomas says: "Every act inhering in another is terminated by that in which it inheres, since what is in another is in it according the mode of the receiver. Hence an act that exists in nothing is terminated by nothing." [16] Thus, although every act in the beings of experience is limited because it has a corresponding potency, unlimited act is not thereby precluded.

A constitutive principle of being which is a capacity for act and which exerts a limiting influence cannot be nothing. On the other hand, if it is not actual save by reason of its act, of itself it cannot be called being. This is why potency has been described as "relative nonbeing." It has no reality apart from some relation to act; pure potency alone cannot be. It is true that potency, potentiality, can

[15] Limitation is a negation of perfection; to call limit a mere negation is insufficient, for every negation supposes something real, something positive.
[16] *Summa Contra Gentiles,* I, 43, n. 5.

exist in a being without being actualized, as, for example, the potency to become a great musician may lie dormant forever in a man. Yet even this potency, unactualized, is given reality by the actual being of the man in which it is. When potency has been actualized, it is not substituted for by its act; rather it continues to limit the act which it receives, continues to differentiate the perfection whereby it has been made actual. Thus, for example, an acorn has the potency to become an oak tree. If that potency is actualized, the tree must continue to be a tree, not a man, and an oak tree, not a maple—and this because the perfection of treeness is limited in it by its potency to become an oak, as the perfection of life in it is limited by its potency for vegetative life only. Or, as another example, if the capacity to be a great musician is actualized in a man, he will be no greater, in the last analysis, than that capacity allows him to be.

Potency and act are, therefore, metaphysical principles of being. They constitute finite beings, not as physical parts, but as ultimate intrinsic principles. They are not "things" in themselves, but principles of things, incapable (except in the unique instance of pure act) of existing apart, yet truly distinct from one another, two truly distinct principles of being.[17] Their relationship is that of a potential principle limiting an actual principle, a capacity for perfection re-

[17] It will be helpful in understanding the distinction between potency and act, between every corresponding potential and actual principle, to see it in context with the general kinds of distinction:

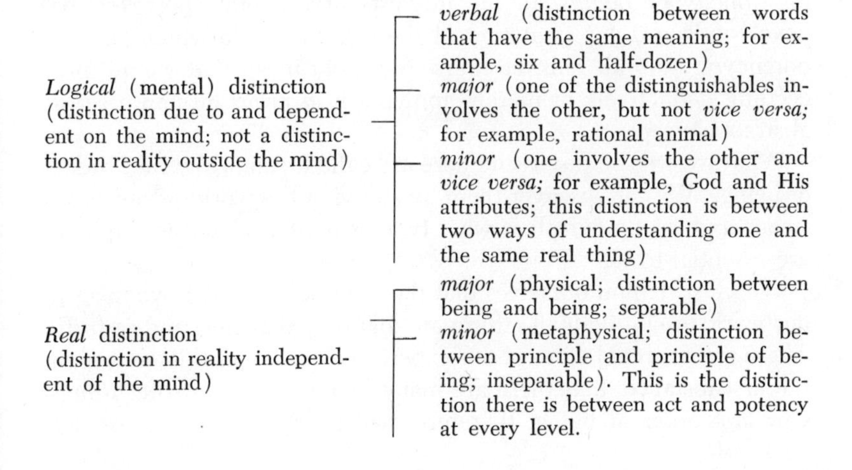

ceiving perfection, and an actual principle making real a potential principle, a perfective principle perfecting a capacity for perfection.

Before we try to see how the principles of act and potency may be found in the several "orders of being," it may be worthwhile to recapitulate a bit. Let us remind ourselves that we have not engaged in anything very mysterious. What we have done has been no more than to follow the common-sense logic of the relationships between multiplicity, limitation, and composition. We have required no more than close attention to the meaning of these terms in our experience, and careful analysis of the implications of real multiplicity and limitation in our world. Such attention and analysis demand a certain concentration, which perhaps calls for dealing with concepts somewhat more general and more abstract than most of us are accustomed to; but, we repeat, there is nothing complicated or mysterious about the procedure or its conclusions. We are simply interrogating the facts and determining where the answers lead us.

Now that we have seen act and potency in the multiplication of finite beings, we must look at other aspects of being to see if act and potency appear in any other contexts. Since we have discovered that the act-potency composition is an explanation of limitation, we must now investigate the several levels of being at which limitation is found, in order to see how multiplication and limitation may be found there. It would be possible to approach each level of being inductively and repeat the analysis which we have given of the multiplicity of *beings.* In the interests of economy, however, we have condensed our treatment of the other areas in which act and potency are found. This, of course, does not mean that we are proceeding deductively or merely applying in *a priori* fashion a set of abstract concepts.

What we will be discussing here are called technically the "orders of being." We can discover them by studying the world of our experience and asking ourselves what type of limitation and multiplicity are essential to it.

We must remind ourselves that the only beings which we meet in our world are individuals: this man, that dog, that tree, and so forth. These are the real beings of our experience. Aware of this, we see, in the first instance, that there are many *beings*, many *existing things.* Our first order of being, therefore, will be the *order of existence.*

Further investigation shows that these beings fall into natural classes or species: man, elm trees, fruit flies, the chemical elements, each of which has many members sharing the same nature of essence. When we speak of multiplicity within these groups, we are talking about many real individuals which share a common essence; many men each of whom has human nature. This we call the *order of essence*. Third, in our changing world we see real individuals continuing to exist for a longer or shorter period of time, but, while remaining the same individuals, still changing in many ways. The child grows, and so changes his quantity. He plays in the sun and becomes tanned, changing his color. In the course of the years he learns many things which he had not known before. None of these changes make him a different being or different person. We say that he remains *substantially* the same, but changes *accidentally*. The quantity, color, knowledge, and so forth, which change are called *accidents*. To apply this to our discussion, these "accidents" are shared by many individuals and so are multiplied. All material beings have quantity. Many human beings go out in the sun and get tanned. All men acquire some knowledge. Hence quantity, suntan, knowledge, and so forth exist in many individuals, and we will have to face the problem of the multiplicity and limitation of these accidental perfections. In technical language we say that they are accidents which inhere in substances. This gives us the third order of being: the *order of substance-accident*. Finally, we see that the beings of our experience not only exist but are *active*. Men move about and talk and think. Fire burns. Chemical elements react, sometimes violently. Our world is not a dead, motionless place, but an arena of constant activity. Motion and change derive from the actually existing beings themselves. Therefore, we have another kind of multiplicity. Each of us thinks, walks, feels joyous or sad. Fire burns in fireplaces, in furnaces, in trash heaps, in buildings, in forests. Here again the same activity is characteristic of many subjects. This activity has been called "operation," and it constitutes the fourth order of being, the *order of operation*. These are the four basic orders of being, each of which we shall study in some detail.

Before examining the several orders of being, perhaps we should forestall a difficulty or two. Of necessity we will have to proceed somewhat in the manner of the anatomist, dissecting being as he dissects the human body. Hence, although we may seem to treat the "members" in isolation from each other, we have not forgotten their interrelation or lost sight of the meaning of being as a whole. We will take the occasion, as the opportunity arises, to put the pieces back together.

A second source of confusion for modern students arises from the seemingly static nature of the world of act and potency. The theory was conceived by Aristotle and used by St. Thomas long before our contemporary concept of evolution was formulated. Consequently, to show how the doctrine of act and potency is consistent with evolution, it will be necessary to make explicit certain insights which are only implicit in the tradition. We will do this as we proceed with our discussion.

ACT AND POTENCY IN THE ORDER OF EXISTENCE

The first order of being to be examined is the order of existence. There are various reasons for beginning with it, the most cogent being that it is the most basic and the most obvious order. It is the most basic because it posits the most fundamental question of metaphysics: how are there many beings? It is most obvious because one of the clearest experiences we have is that of the multiplicity of beings in the world.

If beings are multiplied, that is, if many beings exist, as they obviously do, their perfection as beings must somehow be limited. From what we have seen about such multiplicity, we can conclude that beings can only be so limited by some capacity for this perfection of being. The perfection, to recall our previous discussion, will be called *act,* and the capacity will be called *potency.* Again, as part of our general discussion and of our introduction to this section, we pointed out that the perfection shared by all real beings is *existence.* Consequently, *existence* will be called act in the order of existence. Its correlative capacity is not hard to find. If we ask ourselves what it is that keeps John Jones from possessing the whole perfection of being, the answer is simple: He does not exist as being; he exists as a *human* being. His humanness limits his existence to that of a human being. Therefore since each being is *what it is* and is not anything else, the *what it is,* or in other words its *essence,* is the capacity for existence, is called *potency* in the order of existence.

Existence, therefore, is the act of being, limited and multiplied by essence, the potential element. Existence, consequently, is the most fundamental actual principle in being. It is *that by which a thing is.* It is what makes "all the difference in the world and more" between being and nothing. It is, therefore, the "perfection of perfections," ultimately giving reality to a being and to everything in a being.[18] Like any act, it is not a "thing," or merely a "state"; it is a real principle of being, that on which everything else depends. The soul gives life to the body, but the act of existing gives reality to soul and body. If the soul ceases to inform the body, the body becomes dead, but if the act of existing ceases to actualize the being, the being becomes nothing. If the soul ceases to enliven even one tip of one finger, the finger dies and must be cut off, but if the act of existing were to cease to make real the tip of that finger, it would not die—it would not be.

Existence, as act, is unrestricted in itself. It would be infinite and unique, if it were not limited by being joined to its potential principle, to essence. Essence, by limiting existence, determines it to be a certain kind of existence, determines the being to be a certain kind of being. Existence therefore actuates; essence specifies and limits. Essence is therefore *that by which a thing is what it is.* The essence of a stone limits and determines the stone to be a stone, differentiated from plant or animal or human existents. The essence of a human being limits and determines a man to be neither a stone nor an animal nor an angel, but a man. Essence, therefore, explains why many beings may share in the perfection of existence and yet be different, distinct—for essence differentiates, limits, and distinguishes existence and enables it thereby to be multiplied and yet one, the same perfection in many subjects of perfection.

Before we turn from the order of existence, one caution may be noted. When we discover essence as a principle limiting existence, the danger arises of conceiving existents as sealed off from one another, as beings isolated from one another, restricted by essence to complete separation in being. To avoid this danger it is enough to recall that beings share in existence, communicate in being, and are

[18] See St. Thomas, *Summa Theologiae,* I, 4, 1 ad 3.

thereby irrevocably united in the community and totality of being. This will become clearer when we turn our attention to the unity of being and to the participation of beings in being. For now, we may retain this all-important perspective by reflecting on our own conscious-being-in-the-world. We are aware that as human persons we are neither angels nor things; our essence, our mode of existing, is human and personal. But we are no less aware that as human persons we do not exist sealed off from one another or from the world. Our essence opens us to being, specifies our existence as relative, as existence dynamically oriented to all human beings and to all being through, above all, the conscious openness of knowledge and love.

ACT AND POTENCY IN THE ORDER OF ESSENCE

The problem of the one and the many seems resolved. When a student says, "I am," he means that he shares existence with every other being, and yet he himself is by his own active existence, existing, be-ing. Further, the "I" that speaks out of its existence is of a certain kind, a certain essence—so that he who is not alone as a being is yet unique in his being.

But the problem is not resolved. On one end it steps into the presence of mystery, for the full meaning of the act of existing finally escapes reason's vision. This "end" refers to God and our knowledge of God as a source of all being.[19] At the other end there are loose threads, shadows still inviting to reason. If there can be many beings, all of which exist distinct from one another by reason of a distinct essence, what of the many beings that have the same essence? If a dog is distinguished in existence from a man because its existence is received into the canine essence and not into the human, how will Fido be distinguished from Spot, or for that matter, James be distinguished from John? The one and the many seen in the order of existence reappear in the order of essence. The problem of the multiplication of existents becomes the problem of the multiplication of individuals within a species. But the same pattern of

---

[19] In Chapter 5 we will explain what for the moment must remain a cryptic statement.

reasoning may bring a solution here even as it did in the order of existence.

Multiplication posits difference: as men, sharers in humanity, James and John are alike (even as a man and a tree and a stone were seen before to be alike in that they exist); but because they are two, they must be different, else they would be one. As individuals, they are unlike. Difference posits limitation: neither James nor John has all there is of humanity; each one has not the share in the perfection of human nature which the other has. Even as their share in existence is limited, so their share in the human essence is limited. There can be, again, only one explanation for limitation: composition of a limited and a limiting, an actual and a potential principle, this time within essence itself.

We must ask ourselves, "What is act in essence?", which is to ask about the perfection which is multiplied. Aristotle hit upon the answer when he compared the humanity in men to the shape of a coin which is imprinted on the bronze from which the coin is made. The shape he called "form," and the bronze, "matter." [20] The former shape can be reproduced in various materials. Coins of the same denomination are stamped out of the same kind of metal. They could be stamped out of other metals or clay or any suitable material. The form remains the same; the material varies. So with men, Aristotle says, we all have the same form (human nature), which is embodied in matter. There are as many men as there are matters to receive the form. The form Aristotle is talking about in man, however, is not just his external shape; it is rather that which makes man to be man and not just material being or animal. It gives the essential or substantial act of man, as man, and so is called *substantial form*.[21]

Just as the substantial form is not like the form which is only shape, so the "matter" which Aristotle refers to as the potential element is not like the matter out of which the coin is made. The matter in the coin has existence and qualities of itself and carries these

[20] The Greek word for "matter" is *hylē* and for "form" *morphē*. Hence Aristotle's theory is called hylemorphism.

[21] It might be clearer to the student to call this actual principle "essential form," rather than "substantial form." However, the latter is the traditional name for it, and it will be understood relative to the explanation given of essence, substance, and nature here below. It is important, also, that the philosophical use of the term "form" be not confused with a notion of figure.

through its various configurations. The bronze from which the coin is stamped continues to have the characteristics of bronze; the silver from which a coin is stamped continues to have the qualities of silver, and so on. The matter which is correlative to substantial form does not have this independent existence and possession of qualities. The individual man is one substantial being, hence form is not an independently existing thing, nor is primary matter an independently existing thing. They are principles of being (similar in this respect to essence and existence), which we cannot imagine. Aristotle says of matter that "in itself [it] is neither a particular thing, nor of a certain quantity, nor assigned to any of the other categories by which being is determined." [22] Since this "matter" is something we cannot picture, we have to restrain our imaginations to keep from destroying the unity of the individual being. If we imagine matter, we turn it into a distinct and separate being. As long as we keep this caution in mind, we can diagram the orders of existence and essence in a being in the following way:

Existence (act)	Essence (potency)	Substantial Form (act)
		Primary Matter (potency)

Essence, therefore, determines what kind of being a thing is, but it is the individual which exists and it is the substantial form in the individual which communicates the essential perfection to the individual. This perfection, however, is limited to this thing by the primary matter into which the form is received. We should point out, however, that the relation of essence to existence in the "order of being" or the "order of existence" differs from the relation of form to matter in the "order of essence." Essence limits absolute, unlimited being to a particular kind of being. In this sense essence determines, in the sense of putting specific limits on existence, making it the

[22] *Metaphysics*, E, 3, 1029a 20.

existence of man rather than the existence of tree, and so on. Primary matter does not determine substantial form in this way. The substantial form determines what kind of being the individual will have; primary matter limits the form to this particular individual, without in any way restricting the *kind* of being in the individual. It multiplies by thus *limiting* without actually *determining* the substantial form. And this limitation is essential to all potency, as we have already indicated.[23]

Primary matter, consequently, is simply a capacity to receive form.[24] It is not matter in the ordinary sense of the term, as has been indicated, for matter in the ordinary sense, "secondary matter," is matter actualized in some sensibly discernible way, real to the sight and touch—a physical, not a metaphysical, reality. Primary matter, on the other hand, is the ultimate potential principle in material being, known only by reason (not by sense or imagination). It is in itself simple, not composite.[25]

The matter-form composition in essence, explained in a somewhat

---

[23] St. Thomas says this explicitly: "No act is found to be limited except through the potency which receives it; thus we find forms limited according to the potency of matter." *Compendium Theologiae,* 18, 35.

[24] The problem of the individuation of forms, and therefore of the differentiation of individual beings within a species, cannot be wholly dismissed by pointing to the reception of substantial form into primary matter. This is not the last word in the solution of this problem precisely because primary matter is purely determinable; that is, it is difficult to see how it can even serve as a foundation for multiplication unless it is first quantified, which would be to have it already determined in some way. Some explanations point to the possibility of form bestowing "corporeity" on matter, then matter individuating form, and form conferring a specific nature on quantified, "signate" or "marked," matter. Signate matter thus understood is referred to as the Principle of Individuation. *Summa Contra Gentiles,* I, 21, n. 4; *Quaestiones Quodlibetales,* IX, 2, 2.

[25] This is to say that primary matter is not composed of matter and form. As a simple principle, therefore, it is interesting to note that it is in itself not corruptible. Corporeal beings, whose composition of matter and form is always subject to decomposition, are subject thus to corruption. They are not, however, subject to annihilation, to a return to nothingness; for although beings disintegrate when matter loses its form, matter itself remains, with as great a metaphysical tenacity as marks the hold of self-subsistent forms on immortality. This truth forms the foundation for the philosophical and theological position which holds that this world will not in the end disappear, but be transformed. St. Thomas implies this when he argues that nothing will be annihilated; not even the material world will be reduced to nothingness. See *Summa Theologiae,* I, 104, 4.

compressed manner here, should not be assented to casually without regard for the many subtle and serious implications it entails. Indeed, even if we proceed carefully through the same reasoning process taken when considering the order of existence, it is very likely that in the end we will need further elucidation of the problem. This is perhaps why the conclusion to matter and form *via* the study of change will have an important bolstering role to play. Nevertheless, that each of us engages in his own reasoned search here and now, with regard to the problem of limitation within a species, is vital to our understanding of the reasoned explanation given here, and it is ultimately vital to proceed in this way to the examination of essence which leads us to affirm substantial form and primary matter. Multiplication, difference, limitation, composition—these are the milestones to be passed: if indeed there are many men, how are they each perfectly human yet none of them possessing all the perfection of humanity? How is it that they partake of the solidarity of the human race and yet are in themselves each unique, individual, somehow whole?

The theory of substantial form and primary matter is, in a way, diametrically opposed to the various monistic philosophies of materialism. To conclude that the ultimate principle of reality is matter, to say that a thing is being because it is material, leaves one with all the unsolved issues of multiplication and limitation, the one and the many.[26] Implied in our discussion has been the fact that the hylemorphic (matter and form) explanation of essence applies only to material beings. It is required to explain multiplication within a species, and St. Thomas holds that such multiplication is not possible except in material beings. For him, therefore, each purely spiritual being, for example, each angel, is the only one of its kind; it exhausts the possibilities of its species and is specifically unlike any other angel, even as man is specifically unlike chicken. Among the medievals, others such as St. Bonaventure extended the matter-form composition to purely spiritual beings, claiming for them a "spiritual matter" as potential principle in their essence.[27]

---

[26] As shall be seen later in regard to essential change, it is also possible to see that if matter receives forms, the same principle cannot account for what perfects and what is perfected.

[27] For St. Thomas' reasons for rejecting spiritual matter, see *Summa Theologiae,* I, 50, 2.

To avoid a possible confusion about the role of primary matter, it may be well to point out that to consider primary matter as the root of multiplicity and difference among material beings is not to give it precedence over substantial form. Although it is true to say, for example, that a man is individualized by his material principle, it nevertheless remains that what is individualized is his spiritual principle; and it is his spiritual principle that informs the material, that determines him to be what he is. We can ask ourselves what such a form must be that, charged with existence in the depths of man's being, makes man to be himself.

ACT AND POTENCY IN THE ORDER OF ACCIDENTS

An investigation of the relationships between the one and the many can lead to yet another insight into the structure of the beings of our experience. There are other perfections in a being in addition to its existence and its substantial form—perfections such as height and depth and color and power and activity. We find these also multiplied in many subjects. The same perfection can be found in a multitude of different individuals, and yet in no two individuals is that perfection just the same. The whiteness of the page in a book is not the whiteness of a man's shirt, though for all practical purposes they may be considered as the same shade. The genius in any two artists is not exactly the same. Nor is the courage of any two men identical. Since these qualities or perfections are multiplied, their multiplicity posits a difference, and the difference posits limitation. All the whiteness in the world cannot be in the page of the book because some of it is in the man's shirt. Again we can apply our correlation: multiplicity-limitation-composition. The composition, as we have seen for existence and essence, will be of principles of act and potency. The act, the perfection which is multiplied, is the perfection of whiteness, genius, courage, and so forth. What is it that limits these perfections as it multiplies them? The answer is quite simple; the whiteness is limited by being the whiteness of this page or that shirt; the courage is limited because it is the courage of this man or that man. Therefore it is the very person or thing, the subject of these perfections, which limits them. The thing itself, considered apart from further determinations of color, size, and so forth, is, then, the subject of these perfections. For centuries this subject has been called *substance*.[28] The perfections themselves, the whiteness, the courage, and so forth, are added to the thing itself. As Aristotle and the medievals put it they "happen to" (*accidere*) the thing and so are called *accidents*. As substantial form is the perfection, and so the act, of primary matter, so accidental form is the further act of substance. It gives substance an added determination.

Substance limits accidental form by making it the form of this particular thing and not the total perfection of that accident. One might therefore ask whether, for example, the artist limits his ability or his ability limits the artist. We can answer this by looking at the essence of the being and noting that it sets essential limits to any accidental perfection it can receive. Thus, for instance, a dog will never develop the power of intellectual intuition, since it simply has not by nature the capacity for such a perfection. The individualized essence sets further individual limits to any accidental perfection a thing can receive. Thus, for example, an artist can be perfected in his art to the extent that, first a man as man can be so actualized, and then furthermore, to the extent that he as an individual shares in the perfection of man. His substantial form makes of him a man, determining his essence and the accidental perfections which it can receive; and this substantial form, limited and individualized in being joined to primary matter, constitutes together with primary matter a limited individual capacity for those accidental perfections.

It would be a mistake to think of accidental forms as actualiza-

---

[28] When we speak of substance as the subject of accidents, we are speaking of *essence* under a different aspect. It may be helpful here to point out the differences between *essence, substance,* and *nature*. All three terms refer to the same reality, but with varying relational emphasis. Essence has already been seen to be the potential principle corresponding to the act of existence. Substance is that same principle looked at under the aspect of its ability to receive accidents. Thus, substance could be defined in this usage as essence relative to its accidents. Nature, finally, is essence under its aspect as source of activity.

The use of the term "substance" is, however, further complicated by the fact that it does not always refer to essence; it may refer to the whole being insofar as it is able to exist in itself and not in another (as opposed to accident, which cannot exist in itself, but must exist in another which is its subject). In this sense, substance has been called "first substance," and substance as essence has been called "second substance."

tions somehow superadded to the substance of a being, in the way a pin might be stuck into a pincushion or a coat of paint put on a house. The act-potency relation which obtains between substance and accident is deeply significant in this regard. If substance is truly potency with regard to its accidental forms, each accidental form truly actualizes the substance, truly fills it out, modifies it, changes it in a way sometimes so profound that it would be difficult to exaggerate its importance. Thus the adult is substantially the same being as the newborn babe but has undergone vast accidental change. Then, too, the degree to which this potency is not actualized would, in its turn, constitute a limitation of the being, a failure to become what it might be. The artist might thus be said both to limit and to be limited by his skill as an artist, and a man both to limit and to be limited by his lack of courage.

ACT AND POTENCY IN THE ORDER OF ACTIVITY

Another area of multiplicity remains for us to investigate. As we pointed out earlier, individual real beings not only exist but also have individualized essences and various accidental perfections. Our world is not a static world but a world vital with movement and activity. Man not only exists; he thinks and talks and reads and writes. These activities are not part of the essential being of the individual; otherwise they would continue unchanged and unchanging. Consequently, they are in some sense to be called accidental. And yet it does not seem correct to say that an activity is merely an accidental form. We say that a thing *is* white, but that a man *thinks*. We may sometimes try to disguise this by changing it to a man *is thinking*, but even here we know that thinking is not a state of being in the way that being white is a state of being.

Our experience of activity as one of the fundamental structures of being stands in rather strange contrast to many philosophical attempts to explain it, and, what is equally important, to many philosophical *refusals* to explain it. Such refusals are common in the various materialistic philosophies and also in the newer logic-oriented philosophies such as logical positivism and analytical philosophy. To go back to the Greeks, the atomists read activity out of the universe with their conception of reality as a shower of inert pellets falling through the void. Bertrand Russell's "logical atomism" takes a similar turn when he dissolves objects into "sense data" [29] which can go together or drift apart, but which cannot have any "activity" in our ordinary sense of the word. The "facts" of Ludwig Wittgenstein's *Tractatus*, which are "pictured" by true propositions, seem to be objectivized "sense data" which are subject to the same incapacity for activity. Finally, it is interesting to note that the whole movement of contemporary "logical empiricism," from G. E. Moore and Bertrand Russell through A. J. Ayer and the Vienna Circle to the present-day proponents of the Oxford- and Cambridge-inspired "linguistic analysis," concentrates on the logical and linguistic analysis of *statements*, and so, with what is almost a psychological necessity, focuses on the relation of subject and predicate in static terms.[30] Hence, whatever contribution linguistic analysis makes to philosophy (and its proponents have offered many penetrating insights, especially into our use of language), their whole orientation is conceptual and antimetaphysical. It is not surprising, therefore, that they have little to offer to the discussion of metaphysics.

But whether philosophers want to admit it or not, we do experience our own activities and we witness the activity of others. We see, too, that different individuals perform the same activity. Many men think and talk and read and write. Thinking, talking, reading, and writing, therefore, are perfections which are multiplied. We have suggested that these activities are not accidental forms. The *ability* to think, to talk, to read, or to write may be an accidental

---

[29] "Sense data" are perhaps the most elusive data of contemporary philosophical discussion. About the best way to identify them is to say that they are what an experimental psychologist says I see when I think I see something. He says that I don't see the egg lying on the table but one colored patch against the background of another colored patch. Other sense data would be detached sounds, smells, tactile sensations, and so forth. See Charlesworth, *Philosophy and Linguistic Analysis*, pp. 36ff for a discussion of sense data.

[30] It is interesting to one acquainted with the history of philosophy to see the interest of contemporary "empiricists," whose main interest is supposed to be in ways to root philosophy in experience, tend more and more towards an analysis of concepts and an almost complete neglect of existence. Questions such as, "Are there objects?" are discussed purely in terms of the content of the concept, "object," and are not related to the vital problems of existence.

form, but the *actual activity* is not itself a form. For to have a form is to be in a certain *state,* whereas to exercise an activity is to be *doing* something. From this it would seem to follow that activity is not in the order of accident, although it may come and go as some accidents do. Rather it is in what we might call the order of accidental existence; it is an existential, not an essential, act. St. Thomas suggests that it is the act of a power, for example, the power to think, to read, and so forth. Hence, we can make a comparison and say that as existence is the act of essence, so activity is the act of its corresponding power.[31] Activity is, therefore, an accidental existential act. It is multiplied by being received into the corresponding power of the individual who performs the activity. This power multiplies and limits it. Because there are many minds, there are many thoughts, and no one mind has the whole perfection of thought. Beyond this, since thinking is an activity which can begin and end, and which can have different objects (I can thing about man, physics, dogs, chemistry, and so forth), each act of a given mind is further limited. Consequently, our act-potency correlation holds here between the power (for example, my mind) and the particular activity at any given moment (for example, my thinking about what I am now writing). One more thing should be pointed out: the operative powers (the mind, and so forth) are accidents. Man thinks with his mind, and the mind is a quality which is permanent and in this case spiritual. We can say that as existence is to essence in the substantial order, activity is to power in the accidental order.[32]

Before we conclude this discussion of activity, we might warn ourselves that we have the same problem in conceiving of activity as in conceiving of existence. By nature we think in terms of essence; the mistake of the Greeks is the constant temptation of the human mind. Even many followers of St. Thomas seem to think that activity is merely having a form.[33] St. Thomas' words on this are clear,

---

[31] We will not enter into the question of the distinction of powers. Human powers, which interest us most, are studied in the philosophy of man.

[32] This will be discussed more fully in Chapter 7.

[33] For a discussion of this problem, see J. de Finance, *Etre et Agir* (Rome: Librairie Editrice de l'Université Grégorienne, 1960), especially Chapter 3. See also Owens, *Christian Metaphysics,* p. 194 n. 5 and pp. 196–98.

especially when he distinguishes between existence as first act and activity as second act: "Just as being itself is a certain actuality of essence, so operating [activity] is an actuality of operative potency. In this regard both of them are in act: essence by way of being, potency by way of operating."[34] Although St. Thomas' position on this problem is clear, the application of act and potency to activity and operative power is perhaps the most difficult of all the orders of act and potency.

SUMMARY OF THE STRUCTURE OF FINITE BEINGS: THE PRIMACY OF EXISTENCE

We began this chapter by changing our perspective with regard to being. We discovered that existence is the key to reality. Existence is the act which makes being be. It is the perfection without which no other perfection is possible, for we have reality only where there is existence. We saw, furthermore, that existence is limited and multiplied by essence, and this opened to us the whole range of the orders of act and potency. We saw that in the beings of our experience we have four types of act-potency combinations:

Order	*Act*	*Potency*
Order of Existence	Existence	Essence
Order of Essence	Substantial Form	Primary Matter
Order of Accidents	Accidental Form	Substance
Order of Activity	Activity	Operative Power

We also came to realize in our discussions that existence and activity are on the existential, nonformal side of being and that substantial form, primary matter and operative power are on the essential side. Consequently, we can use the following diagram to show the four orders of act and potency in a given being. Each arrow from Ⓟ to Ⓐ indicates an order of act and potency.

[34] *De Spiritualibus Creaturis,* 11c. See Owens, *Christian Metaphysics,* p. 197, n. 16.

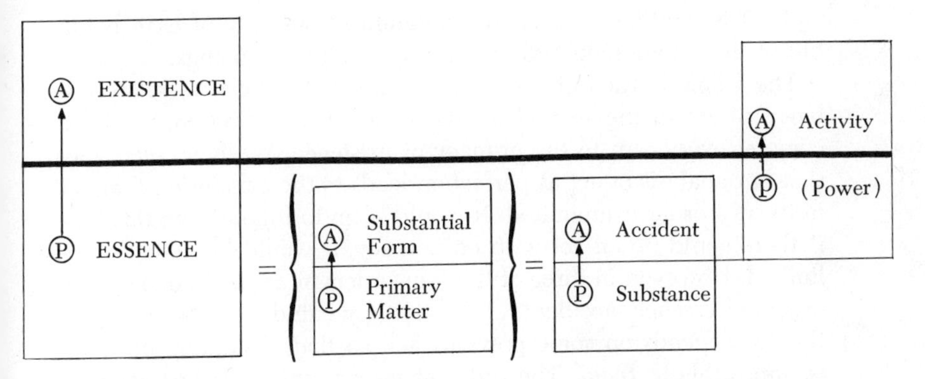

The chart can be read as follows: In the order of existence, existence is act and essence is potency. But essence in material beings is composed, and so in the order of essence substantial form is act and primary matter is potency. Substance is another name for essence, and in the order of accidents substance is potency and accident is act. Finally, some accidents are operative powers, and so in the order of activity, operative power is potency and activity is act.

As we ponder the meaning of these act-potency relationships, the primacy of the act of existing becomes more and more apparent. Accidents depend on the substance in which they inhere for their reality; the substance, or essence, is constituted by the actualization of primary matter by substantial form; the whole essence depends entirely on the act of existing for all its reality. In every being the actuality of all acts, the perfection of every potency, is ultimately dependent on the act of existing. Anything outside the range of existence is nonbeing. To quote St. Thomas, "Existence . . . signifies the highest perfection of all: and the proof is that act is always more perfect than potentiality. Now no signate form is understood to be an act unless it be supposed to have existence. . . . Existence . . . is the actuality of all acts, and therefore the perfection of all perfections." [35] Existence can no longer be thought of as a mere state of being; it is the act of all acts, the source of all perfection, the deepest reality at the heart of every being. Not a thing, but a prin-

[35] *De Potentia,* 7, 2 ad 9.

ciple, it is the foundation and fountainhead not only of each being but of the communion and community of all finite beings.

The whole burden of the present chapter has been to relate potency to act in the several orders of being. In doing so, we have come at every turn to the primacy of existence. We have seen, too, that our analysis of act as perfection leads to the conclusion that act in its own order is unlimited. It would seem to follow from this that if there could be an act with no potency, it would be actually unlimited. However, in three of the four orders of act and potency, the orders of essence, accident, and activity, we find that the reality of the act depends on some previous act, so that absolutely pure act is impossible in them. The order of essence might at first seem to have the possibility of act without potency. Purely spiritual beings, such as the angels, would be pure forms without matter.[36] But such forms, although pure act in their order of essence, would be doubly limited, first because they contain only the perfection of their species, and second because they are still in potency to existence, limiting existence to their kind of existence. In the order of accident and activity, we simply cannot have pure act absolutely, because both accident and activity make sense only as determinations of an already existing being. Consequently, they cannot exist without a subject or, in other words, as pure act even in their own orders.

Existence, however, is different. It is the act of acts. There is no contradiction in having the act of existing, which would then contain the fullness of being, as the pure act of being. At this point we can point to this only as a possibility. In a following chapter we will examine the arguments for the existence of such a pure act of being and see where they lead us. There we will see that this pure act is identified with God.[37]

---

[36] We say "would be" forms without matter because in philosophy we cannot prove the existence of purely spiritual beings. They are possible beings, who, if they exist, fit into our picture of being but whose actual existence we know only from revelation.

[37] In reality, what we have done in this analysis is to extend the meaning of being beyond the range of the beings of our experience. We have seen that a thing is a being in virtue of its existence, and so we can conclude that "to be" is not identical with or limited to material being. For a fuller treatment of this point see G. Klubertanz, *Introduction to the Philosophy of Being* (New York: Appleton-Century-Crofts, 1955), Chapter 2, "The Meaning of 'Being,'" pp. 24–44.

In the context of our present discussion, namely, that of the beings of our experience, we have been able to analyze the metaphysical structure of material beings. We have seen the various compositions of act and potency in these beings. Finally, we have indicated how the analysis of act and potency could be extended to spiritual beings and to the pure act of existence, God. In view of this it might be worthwhile to make explicit some of the general characteristics of act and potency:

1. Act is act with respect to its correlative potency, and potency is potency with respect to its correlative act.

   Comment: The existence of John Jones is act with reference to his essence. It is not the act of anything else. The substantial form of John Jones is act with respect to his primary matter, but as part of his essence it is potency to his existence. Similarly my mind as a permanent accident is act with respect to my substance, but this same mind, as power, is potency with respect to my activity of thinking.

2. Act and potency in each case are proportioned to each other.

   Comment: In John Jones the act of existence is *his* existence, tailored, so to speak, to his essence, and his essence is *his* essence which can be actuated only by his existence. Similarly in the order of essence the substantial form is *his* form and is tailored, so to speak, to his primary matter and his primary matter is *his* primary matter which, here and now, is part of the reality of his essence. The same holds for the orders of accidents and activity.

3. Act is distinct from its correlative potency and potency from its correlative act.

   Comment: The existence of John Jones is distinct from his essence, his matter is distinct from his form; his accidents are distinct from his substance; and his powers from his activity. This does not mean that his form is distinct from his essence or his accidents from his powers. In fact, we know that these overlap.

4. Act and potency in finite beings are not complete beings but are rather principles of being.

   Comment: The complete being is the individual composed of the four orders of act and potency: existence-essence, form-matter, accident-substance, activity-power. No one of these is a complete being and no one or pair can exist in and by themselves.

5. Act is perfection and in its own order is limited only by the potency into which it is received.

   Comment: If it is possible to have an act without its correlative potency, the act will have the full perfection of its order. The two possibilities of this are spiritual creatures, whose forms would have the full perfection of their species, and Pure Act, which would include the fullness of being with no limitation. In the beings of our experience act is always conjoined to potency and so is limited by it.

6. Every being and principle of being will be act, potency, or a combination of act and potency.

   Comment: We are talking of real beings, and to be real a being must have actual existence and whatever other acts are necessary for it. However since the beings of our experience are limited beings they must contain potency. Together act and potency give us the whole reality of the beings. There is nothing real which is not act or potency.

We are now in a position to ask ourselves whether the possible pure act which we have uncovered in our analysis of the beings of our experience is a reality or not. To answer this question we will have to study the nature of the argument from existing, finite, material reality to a spiritual, infinite reality. This quest will be the subject of our next chapter.

Before we enter into this discussion, however, it may be useful to discuss briefly the relationship between the theory of act and potency just described and our contemporary view of the universe as having evolved from lower levels of being into its present complex state. It is true, of course, that the theory of act and potency was elaborated in a nonevolutionary context. However, if we look at the nature of act at the various levels and if we note that on every level act means perfection and denies limitation in its order, we can see a dynamism in act which can serve as a solid metaphysical basis for an evolutionary view of the universe.

If act of itself means only perfection, we can consider each act as straining at the seams, as it were, to be pure act in its order. It is only potency which prevents this. Thus, in the essence of each man form is striving to make its subject the fullness of man. This can explain the wide variation in the development of man. Similarly, each activity of thinking tends to incorporate the fullness of its act of thought. And each existence stretches out to actualize all being.

When we conceive of act in this way, and when we see existence at every level as an act which is always trying to leap to another level, we find a world in which the highest form and the highest existence possible will appear. Early in the history of the universe, when there was no life, the only forms were those of nonliving things. When in time these things had so developed that it was possible for them to sustain life, it was perfectly natural for living forms to appear among the nonliving forms. The thrust of existence made the new forms appear. Subsequently, when under similar modifications it became possible for higher forms to appear, they did appear. Thus in the natural course of events all forms of life below man appeared at the appropriate stages of evolution.

It is necessary to differentiate between man and the lower forms of life because man's soul cannot be "educed from the potency of matter," as the lower nonspiritual forms can.[38] These latter can appear whenever the matter has proper organization. And the whole point of evolutionary theory is that over the ages matter has had the organization needed for higher forms to appear.

This is an extremely brief and condensed explanation of how act and potency can fit into a theory of evolution. It is not our purpose to give a full explanation of the problem here, but merely to suggest a few guidelines. Having done this, we may return to the quest for transcendence.

SUGGESTED READINGS

Aristotle, *Physics,* Book I, Chapter 8, 191a and b. Aristotle's treatment of act and potency in the order of essence.

Clarke, W. N., "The Limitation of Act by Potency: Aristotelianism or Neo-Platonism?," *The New Scholasticism,* XXVI (April 1952), 167–194. Questions origin of Thomistic doc-

[38] This explanation of a basis for evolution does not conflict with Teilhard de Chardin's theory of the upward sweep of being toward the noosphere. We differ in that we would locate the source of power for the upward sweep of being in existence rather than in matter. We also differ when we suggest that the creation of each human soul requires divine intervention. The arguments for the opposite opinion do not seem strong enough to warrant our abandoning the more traditional position.

trine of act and potency, with emphasis on its role in explanation of change or participation.

Gilson, Etienne, *The Christian Philosophy of St. Thomas Aquinas,* trans. L. K. Shook, Chapter 1. New York: Random House, 1956. Overview of Thomistic understanding of act and potency on the various levels of limited being, with ultimate emphasis on existence.

Heidegger, Martin, *An Introduction to Metaphysics,* Chapter 1. New Haven: Yale University Press, Inc., 1959. Heidegger places the fundamental question of metaphysics in terms of existence.

Marcel, Gabriel, *The Philosophy of Existence,* trans. M. Harari. New York: The Philosophical Library, Inc., 1949.

Peters, John A., *Metaphysics, A Systematic Survey,* Chapter 18. Pittsburgh: Duquesne University Press, 1963. Summary of the meaning of potency and act in limited being, with special relevance to powers and activity.

St. Thomas Aquinas, *Commentary on the Metaphysics of Aristotle,* Book IX. St. Thomas comments on Aristotle's explanation of act and potency in the various orders.

———, *Concerning Being and Essence,* Chapter 2. Treats of the matter-form composition within essence in corporeal being.

———, *Summa Contra Gentiles,* II, 52 and 54.

Strasser, Stephen, *The Soul in Metaphysical and Empirical Psychology,* pp. 126–30. Pittsburgh: Duquesne University Press, 1957. The method of matter-form philosophy utilized in relation to the development of a phenomenology of unity and multiplicity.

Van Melsen, Andrew G., *The Philosophy of Nature* (2nd ed.), Chapter 4. Pittsburgh: Duquesne University Press, 1954. Analysis of the essence of material being, using the problem of species-individuals as a point of departure.

Wetter, Gustav A., *Dialectical Materialism,* trans. Peter Heath, pp. 280–304. New York: Frederick A. Praeger, 1958. Succinct explanation of the theory of matter as it has developed in Marxist doctrine.

4 CAUSALITY: THE KEY TO TRANSCENDENCE

INTRODUCTION

Thus far we have investigated the structure and the principles of the beings of our experience. Toward the end of the last chapter we expanded our idea of being, and so opened the way to the possibility of other kinds of beings. In particular we raised the question of the existence of Pure Act or pure existence as infinite, absolute being. Our next step will be to examine the proofs for the existence of Pure Act. However, before we can do this, it will be necessary to examine causality, which is the way we will follow in our quest for Pure Act. This procedure is based on the conviction that in philosophy we do not have available to us an immediate experience of Pure Act. Consequently, if we are to go from the beings of our experience to Pure Act, we will have to do so by showing that the former do not explain their existence and so must depend on Pure Act to explain them. This sort of explaining is "explaining in fact," that is, something in reality which accounts for something else. This kind of "explaining in fact" is the function of *cause*.

As we pursue this investigation, we will discover that in our discussion of existence and of act and potency we have already engaged in a discussion of cause, since what we uncovered there were "explanations in fact," in this case the various principles of act and potency. For to ask what makes a being be and be the kind of being it is is to ask for its causes. This is why metaphysics is said to search for an understanding of beings in their ultimate causes. We have seen that a being is constituted by certain principles, all ultimately dependent upon existence. It may now be asked whether these constitutive principles alone cause a being, or whether there are causes outside a being which also contribute to its being.

If one were to ask for the causes of a pencil, for example, it would be possible to point to the wood and lead which compose it materially, and to the visible form whereby it is recognizable as a pencil.[1] It would be possible, moreover, to know that primary matter and substantial form underlie what is sensible and observable, and that essence and existence ultimately constitute this being.[2] But suppose that the pencil is just now being made; at this moment it is coming into being. Then it is clear that other causes are at work besides the constitutive principles which together are the being. A man, using a machine, is making the pencil. He is making it so that there will be an instrument with which to write, and no doubt also so that he may earn a living through the sale of the pencil. Without lead and wood there would be no pencil. Without the form that makes it to be a pencil, this pencil also would not be. Without the man or the machine, it also could not under these circumstances be. Without some purpose, this man would not act and so again, the pencil would not be. There are, therefore, both intrinsic and extrinsic causes of this pencil. And the pencil is not fully known until it is revealed in its causes. To know that this is a piece of wood with lead

---

[1] We use this example for purposes of clarification. However, a pencil is not one being, with one act of existence and one essence, but rather a conglomeration of things which we treat as one thing. It does not have one form and the correlative primary matter. We must bear this in mind when we use examples such as this.

[2] We have already explained the nature of matter and form to some extent in Chapter 3, where we discussed the order of essence.

in the middle of it and not to know that it is a pencil is not to know very much about it. To know that it is a pencil and not to know that it was something manufactured is also to have very limited knowledge of it. And, of course, it is not really possible to know that it is a pencil without knowing that it is to be used for writing. Similarly, to know that here is wood and form without knowing that the wood and the form ultimately are real by reason of the act of existence, or to know that here is a hand laboring at making a pencil without knowing that this hand belongs to a man, simply does not give adequate knowledge of the pencil. And if there is any other cause besides the ones already seen, the pencil will still not be fully known until it is known in relation to that cause, too.

KINDS OF CAUSES

Perhaps the nature of causality can be clarified by studying the traditional definition of cause and by examining the various kinds of causes. The definition of cause and the division into kinds of causes, however, are not formulated apart from experience and then imposed upon reality as explanations. Rather they are formulated as a result of an examination of the causal influences given in experience.

A principle has been defined above [3] as that from which anything proceeds in any way. A cause is a principle from which anything proceeds in a *dependent* way. It is therefore whatever contributes positively to the being of a thing. From our previous discussion we have seen the intrinsic principles of being in the several orders of act and potency. For our present discussion two sets of these principles are important: substantial form and primary matter in the order of essence, and accident and substance in their order. If we recall Aristotle's use of matter and form as the determinable and the determining elements in the static order of being, we can see that accident and substantial form are principles of being which *perfect, actuate, specify,* and *determine* beings in which they are found. They are forms, acts in the act-potency disjunction, and they

[3] Chapter 1, note 23, and Chapter 3, note 14.

cause by *informing*, that is, by communicating themselves to the beings to which they belong. From Aristotle on these have been called *formal causes.*[4] Primary matter and substance, on the other hand, are not active but passive in their causation. They receive their forms, substantial or accidental; *they are that out of which the things are made.* Like the bronze from which Aristotle's statue is made, primary matter *receives* the substantial form and substance *receives* the accidental form. Beginning with Aristotle these have been called *material causes.* Both formal and material causes are *intrinsic* causes, working their effect within the being of which they are part. If we apply this discussion of formal and material causes to the example of the pencil given earlier, we can see that the lead and wood of the pencil, which are its secondary matter, and ultimately the primary matter of the materials of the pencil, are material causes. The substantial forms in the pencil and its accidental forms are formal causes.

Besides the causes within beings, which we have just seen, there are causes (principles from which something proceeds in a dependent way) outside these things. The most obvious of these, and the one we usually mean when we speak of "cause" without any qualification, is the agent, or efficient cause, *by whose activity the effect is produced.*[5] In our example of the pencil the man who made it and the machine he used would be the "efficient causes" of the pencil. The man who builds a house, the sprinkler which waters the grass, the acid which etches a plate, all these are efficient causes, each in its own way producing its effect by its own activity. A second kind of extrinsic cause is the "final cause," the end or goal for which something is caused, *that on account of which something is made*

[4] Since existence and activity are not forms but existential acts rather than essential acts, they are not called formal causes. However, since in some other respects they act like forms, they are sometimes referred to as quasi-formal causes or causes which act "after the manner of forms."

[5] Father Owens points out that we do not experience efficient causality as such except in our internal acts of cognition and volition (*An Elementary Christian Metaphysics,* [Milwaukee: Bruce Publishing Co., 1963], p. 73, n. 13). He says elsewhere, however, that the ideas obtained from internal experience "are generalized by an easy and habitual process, which becomes, as it were, second nature, and so are extended to all contingent things" ("The Causal Proposition —Principle or Conclusion?" *Modern Schoolman,* XXXII, No. 4 [May 1955], p. 336).

or done.[6] The man's purpose in making the pencil is the final cause.[7] The final cause is sometimes referred to as the "cause of causes," since it moves the agent to act and is therefore the first activating cause of the resulting effect. Because it is an end, purpose, or motive, it causes by being loved.

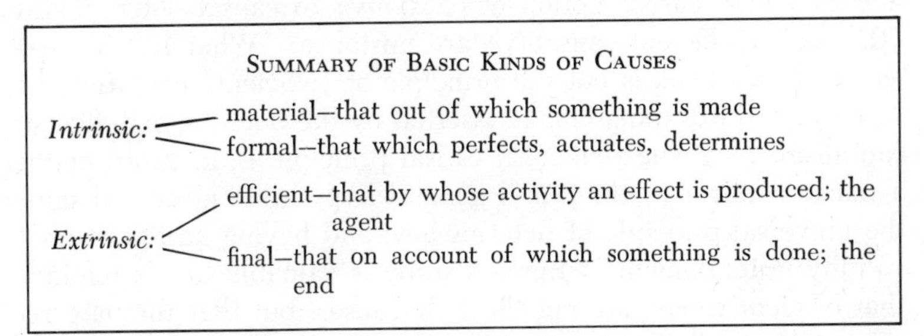

There is a fifth kind of cause which is difficult to fit into this framework because of its various meanings. This is the "exemplary cause," the *form in imitation of which something is made or done.* It is a kind of model. In the example above, it is the idea which the maker has in his mind and in accordance with which he makes the pencil, or the model or blueprint which he follows in fashioning the pencil. The exemplary cause is variously included in formal causality (as an "extrinsic formal cause"), in efficient causality (since it is one aspect of the agent's activity), and in final causality (since it gives direction as the end does).

What we have just given is an analysis of *cause* in Aristotelian terms. We should be aware, however, that much of the contemporary discussion of causality, especially in modern science and philosophy of science, limits "causality" to what earlier philosophers called "efficient causality." Mario Bunge, in his book, *Causality*, interprets causality in this way. For our broader meaning of cause he uses

---

[6] When the end is considered as an "end-in-execution," that is, as the completed effect-correspondent-to-the-end-intended, then the final cause is an intrinsic cause.

[7] A distinction may be made between the end of the work (purpose of the thing made in itself) and the end of the worker (which may be other than to produce the thing for its own sake). In the example the end of the work is the end of the pencil; the end of the worker is to produce an instrument for writing, but also to earn a living.

"determination." Among other kinds of determination he lists *"causal determination,* or *causation,"* our efficient cause; *"structural* (or *wholistic*) *determination,"* something like formal cause; and *"teleological determination,"* our final cause.[8] The basic argument of his book is that modern and contemporary attempts to limit all determination (the earlier notion of causality) to causal determination (the earlier efficient causality) are mistaken: "What has been rejected in this book is not the principle of [efficient] causation, but its unlimited extrapolation, as asserted by the doctrine of [efficient] causalism. . . . The [efficient] causal principle is, in short, neither a panacea nor a myth; it is a general hypothesis subsumed under the universal principle of determinacy, and having an approximate validity in its domain." [9] Bunge's study is valuable for its reminder that efficient causes are not the only causes, but that they are real causes. We will see that the causal principle, clearly understood, has more than "an approximate validity."

EFFICIENT CAUSALITY

Our concern in the preceding chapter centered on the structure of being, hence on intrinsic causes of finite beings. It now becomes imperative to consider the role of extrinsic causes, and in particular here, of efficient causality. Furthermore, in an effort to clear the way for a deeper understanding of existence, it is necessary to have some understanding of the different kinds of efficient causes: causes of being and causes of becoming, *per se* and accidental causes, instrumental and principal causes, and primary and secondary causes. A grasp of the kind of causality involved in each of these will facilitate later efforts at an adequate and reasonable explanation of limited existence. As in our previous discussions, we will study these causes as they appear in our experience and attempt to understand them in the context of this experience.

---

[8] Reprinted by permission of the publishers from Mario Bunge, *Causality*, Cambridge, Mass.: Harvard University Press, copyright, 1959, by the President and Fellows of Harvard College.
[9] *Ibid.*, p. 353.

Kinds of Efficient Causes

Cause of Being vs. Cause of Becoming

The most obvious experiences we have of efficient causality at work are of what are technically called causes of becoming. Ordinarily when we use the transitive verb we want to indicate that someone or something effected a change. I write a book; you build a house; the fire heats the water. In all these cases we are talking about bringing something into being or into a new state of being. Through the action of the writer the book *becomes* a reality; through the action of the builder the house *becomes* a reality; through the action of the fire, the water *becomes* warmer. In each instance the cause is a *cause of becoming,* of coming to be. This coming to be can be *substantial,* if the result is a new being which did not exist before, or *accidental,* if the result is a new mode of being for something already in existence.

This is simple enough. What is more difficult for us to understand is a cause of *being.* We experience this in fewer cases and have to argue to it in most cases. If we are to contrast cause of being with cause of becoming, it would seem logical to say that as the cause of becoming effects the *passage to being,* the cause of being effects the actual, continued *existence* of the effect. Perhaps an example or two may clarify this. If I lift a book off my desk and raise it in mid-air, I am acting as a cause of becoming. The book is changed to a new position. However, unless I continue to exert a causal influence on the book, it will immediately fall back to the desk. So as I hold it in mid-air, I am a cause of its continued *being* where it is. Clearly the *being* which is caused here is an accidental determination of being, one of position. But this accidental determination depends on a continued influx of my causal activity, which is necessary if the book is to keep its position in mid-air. We experience causes of being, therefore, when we or someone else must exert a continued influx to retain the effect achieved. Actually, this causing of the being of accidental perfections is the extent of causality of being in our experience.

Perhaps something more of the nature of causality itself must be seen before the radical difference between a cause of being and a cause of becoming can be further clarified. Every cause is, strictly speaking, simultaneous with its effect. That is, an effect is an effect only while it is being caused. When a cause stops causing, its effect also ceases. Thus, for example, when a hand stops holding a book in mid-air, the book drops to the floor; when a boy stops pushing his wagon, the wagon stands still; when a lamp stops lighting a room, the room returns to darkness. In each of these instances, the cessation of causing means the cessation of the effect. Now, of course, the terms "cause" and "effect" are often applied to two things that were once so related but are no longer so, as, for example, when a chair is referred to as the effect of a carpenter long after the carpenter has finished his work, has discontinued his causing. In the strict sense, however (that is, in that sense which applies to cause as truly cause), it is not his *effect*. There is a sense, of course, in which it can be validly referred to as a "result" of his activity—which is to indicate that at one time he was the cause of the chair's coming to be. The terms "cause" and "effect," however, will be reserved here to refer only to that aspect of reality which is a strict causal relationship: a cause is a cause only while it is causing, and an effect is an effect only while it is being caused.

A clarification of the true nature of causality should help the clarification of the difference between a cause of being and a cause of becoming, because it enables us to see this difference in concrete examples. The carpenter is not the cause of the being of the chair. He is only a cause of its becoming. To see that this is so we need only watch the carpenter finish his work on the chair, put away his tools, and walk out of the shop where the completed chair still stands. If the carpenter were the cause of the being of the chair, the cause of its very existence, then once he stopped exerting his causality the chair would go out of existence. Once again, if his effect were the being of the chair, and an effect is an effect only while it is being caused, then the cessation of his causing would mean the cessation of that effect—the cessation of the being of the chair. However, since he walks away from the chair, and the chair continues to exist, he is obviously not the cause of its existence. He may even die, and the chair may continue to be; it is not dependent upon the carpenter for its being.

Nevertheless, the carpenter does exert some causality relative to the chair. It is in some way, if not in regard to its very existence, dependent on him. What he causes is its coming to be, its becoming. The proper effect of his causality is that the chair begins to be. Cause and effect here both regard becoming, not being. If the carpenter stops causing, his effect ceases; but his effect is the coming into being of the chair.[10] Thus, the chair would not stop be-ing, but it would stop becoming. If the carpenter packs up his tools before he finishes the chair, what being it has remains, but it ceases to come to be; it remains incomplete. The point of all this is to show that just as there is a difference between being and becoming, so there is a difference between a cause of being and a cause of becoming. The proper effect of a cause of being is the act of existing. The proper effect of a cause of becoming is the coming into being of a new existent or a new modification of an existent.

What has not yet been clarified is whether or not the chair in the example used is, in its being, an effect at all. It may have needed a cause only to come-to-be, not to continue to be. It may be that, in regard to its existence, it is neither the effect of the carpenter nor, for that matter, the effect of any other cause. It may simply be no longer an effect, no longer being caused. It may simply be. On the other hand, if it does reveal itself as an effect, as caused here and now to be, there must be a cause that accounts for it as an effect, a cause that continues to exert causality as long as the chair continues to exist. Obviously, there are material and formal causes of its being, but is there here and now an efficient cause of its being? This remains to be seen.

"Per Se" Cause vs. Accidental Cause

There is a difference in the causal relationships between a man and a statue when the man breaks the statue by flinging it down in disgust and when he breaks it thoughtlessly by knocking it off its

---

[10] There is no intention here to imply that the carpenter is the sole or primary cause of the chair's beginning to be, just as there is no intention above to imply either that the chair does or does not have any cause of its being. It is too soon to determine the latter, so the chair is not here considered as an effect or not an effect in its being, only as not the effect of the carpenter in this regard.

pedestal. There is a difference in the causality which one's great-grandfather exerts on one's coming-to-be and that which one's father exerts. The carpenter who makes a chair may also be an amateur photographer, but that he is such has something quite different to do with his causing the chair than his carpentership has to do with it. The differences in all these relationships are differences which we can express as two kinds of causal influences. We note three characteristics which can combine in one kind of cause, and we can call this a *per se* cause. A cause which lacks one or more of these characteristics we can call an accidental cause. The three characteristics we note in a *per se* cause are: acting for an end, acting here and now, and in some way producing its like. Examples will show better than anything else what these characteristics mean.

In the instance of the man and the statue, in either case the effect might be said to be the same: the breaking of the statue. However, when a man intends to break the statue, acts for that end, the effect follows from his exertion of *per se* causality. When he breaks it unintentionally, the effect follows accidentally. What is missing in the latter case is the characteristic of acting for an end. The effect is accidental to the directed activity of the cause.

That one's great-grandfather begot one's grandfather, who in turn begot one's father, certainly has some influence on one's own conception. Nevertheless, a man comes into being by the generative activity of his father.[11] His coming into being is not an effect of his grandfather or great-grandfather. An effect is simultaneous with its cause. Neither the grandfather nor the great-grandfather is here and now exerting causality; indeed, they may both be dead. The causality of the father, therefore, cannot be here and now dependent upon the causality of any ancestors. Strictly speaking, only the father is a cause here. To indicate some relationship, however, between great-grandfather (and grandfather) and father, the causality of the father is called *per se* and the one-time causality of the great-grandfather is called "accidental," accidental now to the present cause-effect relationship between father and son.

That a carpenter happens also to be a photographer is only inci-

[11] The question of divine causality, whether of soul or body, is not the issue here. There is no intent to imply that the creation of a human soul is effected by a man.

dentally connected with his production of a chair. The perfection in him as carpenter, not as photographer, is what appears in his effect. As carpenter, it is *per se* causality that is exerted; as photographer, only accidental causality. From all this it may be clear that an accidental cause is not a true cause, for a cause strictly speaking always produces its like, acts for an end, and is acting here and now simultaneously with its effect.[12]

Instrumental Cause vs. Principal Cause

If a carpenter in making a chair uses a hammer, both carpenter and hammer are efficient causes. Nevertheless, their manner of exercising efficient causality is obviously not exactly the same. The hammer is not the source of its own activity; it cannot move itself to act. In other words, it contributes to the effect of the chair by reason of the power of the man who wields it, who moves it to action. The carpenter, on the other hand, is at least in some sense the source of his own activity. In a way at least different from the hammer he moves himself to action.

The distinction between the types of causality exerted by the hammer and by the carpenter is what has been called the distinction between an instrumental cause and a principal cause. An instrumental cause produces its effect only when it is moved to activity by some principal cause. It has indeed some causality proper to itself, determined precisely as an instrument to produce a certain kind of effect, but it cannot exercise this power except under the influence of a principal cause. The power of causing which belongs to it by nature is dependent upon a further power which does not belong to it permanently by nature, but which is, rather, received by it temporarily from a principal cause. Thus, for example, the hammer by nature is made to pound a nail into wood, but it can be actually pounding only when and so long as it is picked up and so used by the carpenter. On the contrary, a principal cause produces an effect by a proper power which belongs to it permanently. It is the source of a causality of its own, a power of causing which is not applied extrinsically to it by another, but which proceeds from an intrinsic principle.

[12] See page 94.

There are two observations to be made in regard to the distinction between instrumental and principal causality. One is that the meaning given to the instrumental cause here applies to instrumental causes in a strict sense. It is not uncommon that the term "instrumental cause" is used in a broader sense, referring not to the meaning noted here but simply to any secondary or subordinate cause.[13] However, it will be used herein always in its strict sense. The second observation to be made is that a principal cause need not be the first or sole source of its causality. It is not opposed to the notion of principal causality that there be secondary principal causes; that is, principal causes which are only secondarily the source of their own causality. What follows immediately concerning primary and secondary causes will clarify this.[14]

Primary vs. Secondary Principal Causes

A primary efficient cause is a principal cause which is in no way a patient, that is, is in no way influenced by another cause, and so is a cause that is the first and sole source of its causality. Many interesting questions about the nature of the primary efficient cause will also have to be discussed, when we raise the question of its existence.

A secondary principal cause is an efficient cause which receives its power of causing from another. Any of the kinds of causes referred to above might be secondary causes—whether *per se* or accidental, principal or instrumental—but the term has traditionally been used to indicate in particular a secondary principal cause. As such, it points to a cause which is dependent upon a prior cause for its causality, but which receives its power of causing as a permanent

---

[13] See this and following pages.

[14] It must be remembered throughout this discussion of the kinds of efficient causes that there is the danger of taking labels or terms and then applying them *a priori* to concrete causes. All kinds of problems arise, therefore, in attempting to categorize each instance of causality within the defined terminological framework. This is why it cannot be stressed too much that we must simply examine the nature of the causality exerted by each cause given in experience, give it a name for the sake of communication and classification (if the latter is possible), and then take care not to apply that name to any cause with a nature other than the one intended by the name. Thus, there is little point in quibbling over terms; there is much point in understanding the kind of causality involved in any given causal relationship.

possession intrinsic to its nature. It is precisely because such a cause receives its causality, but receives it as something that flows from its own nature, that it is most important to distinguish it from an instrumental cause. All this will become more crucial, and at the same time clearer, when secondary causality is considered in itself as a kind of activity.

All the kinds of efficient causes are not mutually exclusive. It is true, of course, that one and the same cause may not in the same respect be both *per se* and accidental or both instrumental and principal, or both primary and secondary. On the other hand, a *per se* efficient cause, for example, will be either instrumental or principal, and it will also be either primary or secondary. Thus there are various possible combinations among the kinds of efficient causes.

Series of Efficient Causes

Efficient causes are not necessarily completely independent of each other. A group of efficient causes may combine to produce one and the same effect. If these causes are themselves causally related, they form what is called a causal series. If, for example, someone lights a wood fire by striking a match which in turn ignites some paper which finally makes the wood burn, the person, the match, and the paper form a causal series which effects burning wood. If in a series of causes each cause is a *per se* cause, the whole is referred to as a *per se* series. If on the other hand, the causes are accidental causes, the series is an accidental series.

"Per Se" Series

We said that a *per se* cause is one that is acting here and now and so is entirely correlative and therefore simultaneous with its effect. A *series* of *per se* causes, therefore, is one in which each cause in the series is acting here and now. This means that each cause in the series is at once being caused by the one before it in the series and is producing its effect on the cause following it. Thus all the causes and all the effects are taking place simultaneously. Furthermore, every cause except the first one in the series is simultaneously an effect, an effect of the preceding causes which are all operating on it here and now. An example will clarify this. If a small boy moves a stone by pushing it with a stick, a causal series is involved which includes the stick moved by the boy's hand and arm, which in turn are moved by an impulse from his central nervous system. In this series each cause is a *per se* cause; each is here and now a cause which makes another cause operate and finally produces, together with the other causes, the effect of the stone being moved. Since each succeeding cause is an effect of the preceding one, and since there can be an effect only so long as its cause is acting, if the preceding cause stops acting, the succeeding cause will also cease to produce any effect. Thus, if the boy stops moving his hand, the hand will cease to move the stick, and the stick will not then move the stone. As a consequence, in such a series all the members must exist and act simultaneously. It follows, also, that a simultaneous grasp of the series as a whole is necessary for its intelligibility, that is, for an understanding of the effect there must be an understanding of the combined causes of this effect.[15] Thus, for example, when we see something turned by a series of cogwheels, we do not understand the effect unless we see the whole causal series, complete with the motor power which is its source.

Accidental Series

In an accidental series of causes one cause follows the other in time or space, but there is no dependence of one upon the other for its very causality here and now. Since there is not such dependence, there is no need for the members of such a series to be either acting or existing simultaneously. Two examples will perhaps make this clear. A carpenter who makes a chair may use several hammers in the process; that he discards one in favor of another gives only an accidental connection between the hammers. One hammer is not dependent upon the other for its actual causality while it is being used. The hammers would thus form an accidental series of causes. Similarly, the great-grandfather, grandfather, and father of a boy form only an accidental series of causes in relation to the boy. None of them are more than accidental causes of the being of the boy,

[15] This does not imply that it is necessary to know each individual member of the series or even the exact number of members which comprise the series.

and even in regard to his coming to be, the action of his father is not here and now an effect of the action of his grandfather or, indeed, of his great-grandfather.

Question of an Infinite Series of Causes

In an investigation of the various causal series, a question which comes up almost immediately is that of the possibility of a series of causes which would have an infinite number of members. Since many causes can coalesce to bring about an effect, each cause depending on the previous cause in the series, could such a series have an infinite number of such causes all contributing to the one effect, a chain of causality stretching to infinity? Or must there be as a source of every series a first cause, a primary cause that is its own sole source of its own causality, a cause that is in no way an effect, an uncaused cause? And if there is such an infinite series, would it contain an *actual* infinity of members or would it be a series with a *potentially* infinite, indefinite number of members?

We may approach the question of an actually infinite causal series, one in which there is an infinite number of causes all here and now actual, in one of two ways. The first way would be to follow St. Thomas and say that there seems to be a contradiction involved in the notion of an infinite number.[16] He holds that as soon as any multitude of things is wholly actual, the number in that multitude may be counted. There are only so many, however great the number, and no more. And if more are added to the multitude, these, too, may be added to the count, but there is still at any given moment an actual specific number. It is contradictory, he claims, to the very notion of specific number, whether of causes or anything else, to speak of infinity. From this it is possible to conclude that in every actual causal series there must be a first cause. If, as in a *per se* series, each succeeding cause derives its causality from the preceding cause, the first in the series can derive its causality from none. The first cause must be an uncaused cause, an absolute source of its own causality and of the causality of each of the other causes which ultimately derive from it.

---

[16] See *Summa Theologiae,* I, 7, 4.

A second approach would suppose that the contradiction implicit in "infinite number" is only apparent and would allow for the possibility in reality of an infinite number of things. In such a case both an infinite *per se* series and an infinite accidental series of causes would be possible. The puzzle in such an infinite series is that every cause in the series is at once a cause and an effect, an effect of the members of the series preceding it and a cause of the members of the series following it. But if every cause in the series is a caused cause, nothing in the series explains the actuality and activity of the whole infinite series. Consequently, there must be an uncaused cause outside of the series to explain the existence of the series. This is so because if all the causes are caused causes (dependent on another for their causality), it makes no difference whether there be one or a million or an infinite number of members in the series. Indeed, to say that there is an infinite number does not answer the problem of causality involved; it only pushes the problem further back. Thus, for example, to say that a wire stretches to infinity in no way explains why a light at a particular point on the wire is burning. The infinite coil must receive its electricity from some source of electricity which, if it is not at the end of a finite coil, must be outside the coil completely but causing the electricity in the whole coil.

Thus, a series of causes extending to actual infinity is either not possible, or if it is possible, still requires a first uncaused cause outside of the series to account for its effect. In either case, the effect as an effect is not intelligible save by reason of an ultimate uncaused cause.

If an infinite series is considered in the sense of a potentially infinite number of causes, a number to which one more may always be added, an infinite accidental series is possible, but an infinite *per se* series is not. The basis for this is that a potentially infinite multitude is possible. As St. Thomas says, "A potentially infinite multitude is possible, because the increase of multitude depends upon the division of a magnitude, since the more a thing is divided, the greater number of things result. Hence, just as the infinite is to be found potentially in the division of the continuous . . . in the same way the infinite can also be found potentially in the addition of multitude."[17] We can speak of a potentially infinite number, too, and this is what mathematicians seem to mean when they speak of an "infinite number" as a number to which one more may always be added.[18]

A *per se* series of causes may not be potentially infinite simply because each member of the series must be here and now existent and acting. There cannot, then, be a potential *per se* series in any sense, infinite or otherwise. An accidental series, on the contrary, may be potential in the sense that more members may always be added, since all the members of the accidental series need not be existing or acting simultaneously.

The only kind of infinite series of causes that is possible, therefore, is a potentially infinite accidental series. An infinite *per se* series is not possible in any sense, unless the noncontradiction of "infinite number" is allowed, in which case a first uncaused cause is still needed, outside the series, to account for the causality of each member of the series and of the series as a whole.

Principles Associated with Efficient Causality

If the nature of efficient causality is examined still more carefully, certain necessary aspects of it become evident. These can be listed as a series of principles concerning efficient causality.

1. *Transitive action, the action which passes from cause to effect, really takes place in the patient, in the one receiving the effect.*[19]

A few examples will make this clear. A flashlight by itself merely shines; it illuminates, performs transitive action, causes, only when there is something for it to light up. Its action of illuminating takes

[17] *Ibid.*

[18] Mathematicians speak usually in terms of infinite sequences or infinite series, implying an unending succession of numbers. There is general agreement that an actual specific number, or a sum in the ordinary sense of the word, always means some limit-value—and hence always refers to the finite. See M. Richardson, *Fundamentals of Mathematics* (New York: The Macmillan Company, 1941), pp. 329–32, 409; Eric Temple Bell, *Mathematics, Queen and Servant of Science* (New York: McGraw-Hill Book Company, 1951), p. 396; Friedrich Waismann, *Introduction to Mathematical Thinking* (New York: Harper & Row, Publishers, Inc. [Torchbook ed.], 1959), pp. 125–28, 139.

[19] See *Summa Contra Gentiles,* II, 16; *Summa Theologiae,* I–II, 90, 3.

place in the object illuminated. A teacher without students only talks, expresses himself, perhaps comes to new insight for himself, but does not teach. Only when a student receives the action of the teacher does the latter really teach. And the teaching takes place in the student. Again, a doctor without patients cannot heal. When he does heal, his action takes place in the patient. It is in the one being healed that the healing takes place. This is not at all to say that in the first instance the object is doing the illuminating, or that in the second instance the student is doing the teaching, or that in the third instance the patient is practicing medicine. It is to say, rather, that the flashlight is doing the illuminating *in* the object, and the teacher is teaching *in* the student, and the doctor is healing *in* his patient. This is why the causality involved in change (which is, of course, not the only kind of causality) is called action relative to the source from which it comes, and passion relative to the object which receives it. The implications of this principle in regard to efficient causality will be most apparent when we attempt to understand the all-presence of God.

2. *An agent as agent does not necessarily lose something in causing an effect.*

While it is true that if something purely material is given in the effect, as for example, if one gives his glass of water to another, then the agent no longer has that material thing given, efficient causality itself does not imply a loss of something on the part of the agent. The counselor who encourages is not thereby weakened. The artist who paints does not lose the beauty he incarnates. The teacher who teaches does not lose the knowledge he imparts.

3. *The agent in some way produces its like.*[20]

Every efficient cause must possess at least virtually[21] that perfection which it causes in the effect. Because this is so, there is some proportion, some similarity, between every cause and its effect. That this is so will have great bearing on a later consideration of the analogy of being and of the knowledge of God possible to human reason.

That a cause somehow produces an effect similar to itself does

---

[20] See *Summa Contra Gentiles,* II, 16, n. 6.

[21] The term "virtually" here means that the cause possesses the perfection it causes insofar as it possesses the power to cause it.

not imply that every effect has the same essence as its cause. Experience would immediately gainsay such a conclusion. There are, on the contrary, various ways in which the perfection of the agent is caused to be in the patient. The agent may cause a being to come to be with its same nature, as when apple trees produce apple trees and men beget men. On the other hand, cause and effect may not share the same exact nature for various reasons, such as several causes contributing to one effect or an agent causing something, the form of which he has by knowledge but not as its own form.[22]

4. *Wherever there is something that cannot account for itself, there must be an extrinsic cause, an efficient cause, to account for it.*

This is an expression of the "principle of efficient causality" and the "principle of sufficient reason." The significance of both of these principles is their implication that finite beings, since they do not exist by their nature (their nature is to be their particular kind of being, not simply to exist) need something outside of them (an efficient cause) to explain why they actually do exist. Since this is such an important aspect of the question of efficient causality, we will treat it separately.

The Principle of Efficient Causality

The principle of efficient causality, frequently called simply the principle of causality, is expressed in various ways. Plato said, "Again, all that becomes must needs become by the agency of some cause; for without a cause nothing can come to be."[23] St. Thomas, although not using the principle as such, has several statements which could pass as expressions of it: "Every composite has a cause."[24] "Whatever does not belong to a thing as such [that is, by virtue of its nature (*quod ipsum est*)] belongs to it through some cause."[25]

---

[22] When cause and effect share the same nature, the causality is said to be "univocal." When they are not of the same nature, the causality is termed "analogous." Sometimes the term "equivocal" is used, but strictly speaking, no cause and effect are totally unlike and so equivocal; some proportion always obtains between them, as explained above.

[23] *Timaeus,* 28A, trans. B. Jowett, *Dialogues of Plato,* II, 112.

[24] *Summa Theologiae,* I, 3, 7.

[25] *Summa Contra Gentiles,* II, 15, n. 2.

"For whatever is found in anything by participation must be caused in it by that to which it belongs essentially."[26] Some modern expressions of the principle are: "There is no effect without a cause."[27] "Whatever comes to be has a cause."[28] "The existence of a contingent being demands a cause."[29]

Principle or Conclusion?

Among modern scholastic philosophers there is no dispute over the validity of these statements of the principle, but there has been some rather heated discussion concerning its status as a "principle," and concerning the reasons why it is true. Etienne Gilson and Father Owens maintain that it is not really a "principle," or beginning point, but rather a conclusion reached from our experience of finite beings and an application of the principle of contradiction.[30] It is true, they say, as a conclusion, but it is of no particular value as a principle in a Thomistic system.

We need not become involved in this controversy. The principle does state an important aspect of causality, and so it will be worthwhile to examine what is involved in the fact that finite beings do not explain themselves. We can do this best by following the various clues about finite being implied in the principle of causality. This we can do without deciding whether the principle of causality is, strictly speaking, a principle or a conclusion. One clue to our investigation

---

[26] *Summa Theologiae,* I, 44, 1.
[27] Owens, *Modern Schoolman,* XXXII, No. 2 (January 1955), p. 160, n. 2.
[28] *Ibid.*
[29] Cardinal Mercier, *A Manual of Modern Scholastic Philosophy,* trans. T. L. and S. A. Parker (London: Routledge & Kegan Paul, Ltd., 1916), I, 375.
[30] See Owens, *Modern Schoolman,* XXXII, Nos. 2–4, pp. 159–71, 257–70, 323–39. Owens and Gilson (*Revue Thomiste,* 1952) have four main points: (1) the principle of causality is not derived from the principle of sufficient reason (which Leibniz first formulated: No fact can be true or existent which does not have a sufficient reason why it is so and not otherwise [*Monadologie,* Nos. 31–32]), for the latter principle is merely a restatement of the former principle (Gilson, p. 58); (2) the principle of causality is a principle which is valuable only in essentialistic systems (Gilson, p. 61); (3) it is of no particular help in setting up proofs for the existence of God (Owens, p. 339); and (4) it is not analytic in any significant sense of the word and so is of no real help in any demonstration (Owens, pp. 337–38).

may be found in an alternate statement of the principle: "Every effect has a cause." Since an effect, in the strict sense, is simultaneous with its cause (because it is an effect only insofar and so long as it is caused), to be an effect means to be caused. It is thus self-evident that an existing effect implies an existing cause. This, of course, is mere tautology if the essential question is whether or not something is an effect. It is precisely this question which is at stake in any attempt to explain the existence of beings given in experience. We can ask, therefore, whether there are any indications that these beings are effects.

Change as an Effect

The answer is clear when we experience change and see that it is an effect of an efficient cause. When we generalize from these experiences we can formulate the universal statements: nothing is educed from potency to act except by a being in act; whatever is moved [31] is moved by another; nothing can be both patient and agent in one and the same respect; nothing can give what it does not have. Put differently, all this says that if a thing is in potency for act, it is in that respect not yet actualized—it does not yet possess the perfection to which it is in potency. If it could actualize itself, be its own sole cause of its change, it would somehow have the perfection which it does not yet have. And this is contradictory. A thing cannot at the same time in the same respect be in both potency and act.[32] These conclusions follow on an analysis of change in real beings.

---

[31] The term "notion" here refers to every kind of change, of reduction of potency to act.

[32] Even living beings whose motion derives from an intrinsic principle are no exception. If a being reduces itself from potency to act, it does so by reason of an act other than the one to which it is in potency. Thus, when a man stands up, he does so by an active power, not a mere passive potency. His body is moved by his legs, which are moved by muscles moved by nerves moved by his will; and his will as an efficient cause moves itself not by giving itself a perfection it does not have, but by using the perfection it has; even free will is moved by another insofar as it is dependent upon the substance in which it inheres, which is in turn dependent upon the act of existing which makes it real, which is in turn dependent, as shall be seen, upon an outside efficient cause that is uncaused, unchanging, pure act.

Limited Being as an Effect

It is more difficult to see in the beings of experience that their very existence is an effect of an outside efficient cause, that not just as becoming but as being they are caused. The principle of efficient causality, as a conclusion which expresses this, may be stated thus: A finite being requires an efficient cause distinct from itself to account for it because its existence does not belong to it by its nature, but "accidentally." [33] This is to say, as we have seen, that no finite being has existence as its nature. This truth, once seen, provides the metaphysical basis for the demonstration of the existence of God. In other words, if it is seen to be necessary that a being, simply because it is not its own existence, must be an effect, the road is open to the discovery of a being which is pure existence. If the beings of experience reveal themselves as effects, then they reveal the existence of their cause.[34]

This explanation can be worked out in greater detail. We can accomplish this by studying the structure of limited being. We need only ask ourselves whether within limited being can be found all that is required for it to be and to be as it is. If the answer is affirmative, it is not an effect here and now of a cause other than itself. If, in other words, the reason for its being can be found in its intrinsic causes alone, it is wholly independent. It exists of and by itself. On the other hand, if what is found within a being does not account for its existing rather than not existing, some other cause must be discovered which ultimately accounts for this being.

Experience shows being to be multiplied, differentiated, limited. Limited beings have been seen to be composed of act and potency,

---

[33] "Accidentally" here does not, of course, mean "as an accident inhering in a substance," but as following upon a nature rather than as identical with the nature. See St. Thomas, *De Ente et Essentia,* Chapter 5; and Owens, *Modern Schoolman,* XXXII, No. 4, pp. 338–39.

[34] Sometimes this proof is put in terms of the composition of being. If a being is composed, it cannot be pure act but must be composed of act and potency. Since any being so composed cannot be its own existence, it requires something outside of it to explain its existence. Owens suggests that although this argument is valid, it is valid because existence is "accidental" to the composite being, not simply because the being is composite. *Modern Schoolman,* XXXII, No. 4, pp. 338–39.

a limited perfection and a limiting capacity for perfection. Existence itself, in the beings of experience, is limited by being received into an essence. It is a limited existence, therefore, which must either account for itself or be dependent upon a cause other than itself.

In a given being, matter has been seen to depend upon form, accidents upon substance, and essence upon existence, for their actuality. The act of existing thus ultimately accounts for the actuality of the being and of everything in the being. What, then, accounts for the act of existing? Does it need any accounting for by anything outside itself?

Perhaps a being is because it exists, and existence is existence and therefore is, and nothing more need be said. There is the problem, of course, of some beings beginning to exist which did not exist before, and of some beings ceasing to exist which at one time existed. If existence accounts for itself, how can it either begin or end with no explanation other than itself? There are, on the other hand, many beings in experience whose beginning or end has never been observed. But whether a being begins to be or does not begin to be, whether its beginning is observable or not, there is always the question: Does a being here and now explain itself, or does it here and now require a cause in order to exist and to continue existing? While it is—whether for all time or for some time—what ultimately makes it be?

As already seen, all beings of experience are limited, and this is clear whether they begin to be or not. A limited act of existing, since it is, must be accounted for either by something else within a being, or by itself, or by something outside the being. Some things are clear: This act of existing cannot be unless it is limited by something other than itself. Act as act is unlimited. Within the being, essence is the potential principle which limits the act of existing; thus without being joined to this essence, this act of existing cannot be. Perhaps, therefore, the act of existing is accounted for here and now by the essence which receives it. But then essence must either be existence or be the cause of existence. It cannot be identical with existence (in other words, it cannot be the nature of this being to be), else there would be no composition and so no limitation. Essence is related to existence as potency is to act; it is therefore impossible that it should actuate itself. It has no reality and so no possibility of causing prior to existing.[35] Hence, in order to cause its existence, essence would have to exist prior to existence, which is contradictory.

On the other hand, we cannot have only the act of existing, independent of essence, causing essence. An existence independent of essence would be existence without any limiting principle, and in order to produce an essence and join itself to it, it would have to destroy its own unlimited existence, which again is contradictory. This way of speaking tends, moreover, to make both existence and essence appear as things in themselves, and not as the metaphysical principles of being.

What remains is to conclude that nothing in a limited being accounts for its act of existing and that the act of existing does not account for itself, and therefore the only adequate explanation of the existence of this being is a cause outside itself upon which it is radically dependent. However, since this conclusion embraces something extremely difficult to understand, namely, the utter contingency of the beings of experience, and since its understanding is the *sine qua non* for a full understanding of the beings of experience as well as for any valid demonstration of the existence of God, it may not be superfluous to take a second look at the reasoning process just attempted.

Once again, the problem is not whether or not a limited being needs a cause in order to come into being.[36] The problem is, rather, whether or not a limited being here and now is caused or uncaused, is an effect or not an effect. We have said that every limited being is here and now an effect because within the beings of experience existence reveals itself as caused. This can be known because in beings that are multiplied, diversified, and limited in existence, existence and essence are distinct. Everything in the being depends for reality upon the first actuating principle within the being, upon the act of existing. The act of existing, in turn, cannot be unless it is limited by being joined to its essence. There is nothing about existence itself which gives rise to limitation. Hence, an act of exist-

---

[35] The priority here is one of nature, not of time.

[36] Of course, if it did begin to be at one time, it did need a cause to bring it into being, since potency cannot actuate itself. However, to look only to the cause of its beginning to be would be not to arrive at any cause here and now of its being. A cause that caused only its becoming might long since have itself ceased to exist.

ing cannot limit itself, cannot join to itself the potential principle which is actualized in the receiving of existence. The act of existing is, therefore, dependent upon something else to limit it. If it is dependent, it does not wholly account for itself. It cannot be said that it just "is." But on what can the act of existing be said to be dependent? Upon its essence, to be sure, as its limiting potential correlate. And yet the essence cannot account for the act of existing. It would involve only a vicious circle to say that the essence accounts for existence and the existence accounts for essence. Essence and existence cannot simply be mutually dependent, for essence depends upon its actualizing principle for all that it has of reality. Essence, in other words, has no actual reality save what it receives from existence. It cannot be thought of as a limiting principle which has any kind of existence before receiving existence.

Moreover, it cannot be said that once an essence is actualized by existence it then has a claim on that existence. The actualization of essence is not analogous to putting a rocket in orbit, which, once it is in orbit, continues to remain there. It cannot be said that although in the beginning it was not the nature of this being to exist, now that it has been brought into existence it is its nature to exist. To say that it is the nature of a thing to exist is to say that essence is existence. But essence cannot be identical with existence, since their duality and composition is required for the limitation of the being. As long as the being is limited, it must be so by reason of essence limiting and existence limited.

Nor can the essence be said to cause existence here and now, to have a claim on existence, as though to exist were an essential property of the essence in the way that intelligence is the property of human beings. Such properties are in the order of essence and to make existence such a property would be to make it dependent upon essence and give essence in some way a kind of priority to existence. This cannot be, since everything in a being depends for its actuality upon existence. This would be true, too, if the existence were conceived as following upon some essential property of the essence, as though the whole essence did not demand existence, but only one corner of the essence, some property of the essence did so. This too is incompatible with the fact that existence is the source of all actuality.

"To be," therefore, never becomes essence or part of essence.

Existence of itself has no necessary relation to essence. Its only relation is one of contingent possession. St. Thomas uses the analogy of the sun enlightening the air. The light of the sun permeates the air completely, but does not mix with it. It is in it but does not belong to it, so much so that as soon as the light ceases to shine the air falls back into the nothingness of light which is called darkness. In St. Thomas' own words, ". . . as the becoming of a thing cannot continue when the action of the agent, which causes the becoming of the effect, ceases, so neither can the being of a thing continue after the action of the agent which is the cause of the effect not only in becoming but also in being, has ceased. This is why hot water retains heat after the cessation of the fire's action; while, on the contrary, the air does not continue to be lit up, even for a moment, when the sun ceases to act upon it. For water is a matter susceptive of the fire's heat in the same way as it exists in the fire [that is, water receives fire as an accident to its nature]. Therefore, if it were to be reduced to the perfect form of fire, it would retain that form always; whereas if it has the form of fire, imperfectly and inchoately, the heat will remain for a time only, by reason of the imperfect participation in the principle of heat. On the other hand, air is not of such a nature as to receive the form of the sun, which is the principle of light. Therefore, since it has no root in the air, the light ceases with the action of the sun.

"Now every creature may be compared to God as the air is to the sun which illumines it. For as the sun possesses light by its nature, and as the air is illumined by sharing light from the sun, though not sharing in the sun's nature, so God alone is Being by virtue of His own essence (since His essence is His being), whereas, every creature has being by participation, so that its essence is not its being."[37]

There remains, therefore, limited being whose existence is dependent upon essence as upon a condition[38] but not as upon a

[37] *Summa Theologiae,* I, 104, 1c. Modern physics has a different explanation of the propagation of light. The light already transmitted does continue to shine, so that the light which has traveled thousands of light-years from distant stars may reach us long after the stars have disintegrated. This does not affect the argument, however, since light is used only as an example, not as a proof.

[38] A condition is that which is required for an effect to be produced, but does not itself positively influence the effect.

cause. Consequently, we have existence which must be joined to essence in order to be but which is joined to essence neither by reason of itself nor by reason of its essence. Something else is needed then to explain it. When existence is thus seen as necessarily received in an essence which is posterior to it, it is not accounted for within the limited being itself (by essence or existence) but is dependent on another as an effect upon a cause. This is why "a finite being requires an efficient cause distinct from the being to account for it." In St. Thomas' Latin, ". . . *illud cuius esse est aliud ab essentia sua habeat esse causatum ab alio.*" [39] And since it is the very act of existence which is caused, and it is the act of existence which gives whatever reality there is in a being, it follows that every being in experience is radically contingent at every level of its being.

The importance of seeing the beings of experience as effects which are here and now being caused cannot be overemphasized. This is not a matter of reaching back in time for a temporal contingency, a once-upon-a-time dependency for coming-to-be. It is a matter of causality which continues simultaneously with its effect. At every moment, so long as a thing is, it needs a cause for its being. Just as the act of existing must at every moment be actualizing every aspect of a being, so at every moment an efficient cause must be actualizing the act of existing.

To quote St. Thomas again, "The impression of an agent does not continue in the product if the agent's action ceases, unless the impression be converted into the nature of the product. Indeed, the forms of things generated, and their properties, remain in them after generation until the end, since they become natural to them. . . . Now whatever belongs to the nature of a higher type of being does not last at all after the action of the agent; light, for instance, does not continue in a diaphanous body when the source of light has gone away. Now, *to be* is not the nature or essence of any created thing . . . therefore, no thing can remain in being if divine operation ceases." [40]

In experience it is easy to see that when the causality of coming-to-be ceases in regard to anything, the effect ceases. Examples of this have already been noted. One does not see so readily the same

---

[39] *Summa Theologiae,* I, 3, 4c.
[40] *Summa Contra Gentiles,* III, 65, n. 7.

kind of utter contingency of a being in its being. Perhaps this can be seen only through understanding what has arduously been exposed above, and relating this in experience with the examples of coming-to-be, on the one hand, and examples of material and formal causes of being, on the other. For instance, when the nails which hold a desk together corrode and fall apart, the desk falls apart and is no more a desk. When the hand that presses a buzzer releases its pressure, the buzzer no longer makes a sound. When the soul that informs a body ceases to inform that body, the body dies. So, too, if the act of existing in any given limited being is fully dependent for its actuality on another cause, its relation to it is such that should the cause stop causing, the being would be no more.

CONCLUSION

It is undoubtedly very evident that the foregoing consideration of causality in general and efficient causality in particular has not issued merely in a preliminary step toward placing the question of transcendent being referred to in the beginning of this chapter. Indeed, with the principle of efficient causality and its application to the act of existence of the beings of experience, the question is already posed and largely answered. It is now clear that knowledge of a limited act of existence leads to knowledge of an efficient cause of that existence. This brings us to the heart of realistic metaphysics, but the discussion is far from completed. To know that the existence of the beings of experience is caused is not yet to discover anything more than that they are caused. Reaching this conclusion is an important accomplishment, but we must now investigate the implications of this important conclusion.

SUGGESTED READINGS

Bunge, Mario, *Causality, the Place of the Causal Principle in Modern Science.* Cambridge, Mass.: Harvard University Press, 1959.

Frank, Phillip, *Philosophy of Science: The Link Between Science and Philosophy,* Chapters 11 and 12. Englewood Cliffs, N.J.: Prentice-Hall, Inc., 1957.

Gilson, Etienne, *Elements of Christian Philosophy,* Chapter 8. Garden City, N.Y.: Doubleday & Company, Inc., 1960.

Hawkins, D. J. B., "Causality in Aristotle and Hume," in *Being and Becoming,* Chapter 10. New York: Sheed & Ward, 1954.

Owens, J., "The Causal Proposition–Principle or Conclusion?" *Modern Schoolman,* XXXII, Nos. 2–4 (1955), 159–71, 257–70, 323–39.

St. Thomas Aquinas, *Summa Contra Gentiles,* II, 21, No. 4; III, 65–67 (66, Nos. 6–7 are particularly helpful in regard to the need for a cause of the being of finite existents).

———, *Summa Theologiae,* I, 105, 5 (for general kinds of causes); I, 104, 1 (regarding cause of being); I, 7, 4 (concerning question of infinite number, applicable to question of infinite number of members in a series); I, 46, 2 ad 7 (distinction between possibility of *per se* and accidental series to infinity).

5

THE DISCOVERY OF PURE EXISTENCE

What is finally at stake, of course, in all these considerations is the revelation by the beings of experience of the existence of God. It cannot yet be concluded that God, an unlimited uncaused cause of existence, is. Such an understanding will require an integration of some of the clarifications of efficient causality seen above. If a conclusion is drawn too soon, it will not be valid; and there is not much point in a demonstration of the existence of God which does not really arrive at a knowledge of God's existence.

QUESTIONS OF DEMONSTRATION

It might be interesting to note briefly some of the peripheral questions which have long been attached to the attempts of human reason to approach God. This will serve also to focus our own attempt to reach God. Not every man has recognized the possibility of reasoning to God's existence and the consequent possibility of demonstrating the progress of reason to that conclusion. Some have thought that because the existence of God is self-evident, it need not and indeed cannot be demonstrated. Such a position has very few followers in the twentieth century, probably because the "general belief" is not so self-evident, and widespread skepticism, agnosticism, and atheism easily give the lie to the claim that there is immediate sensible or intellectual evidence for the existence of God. So many things thought so long to be true because they have had universal affirmation have been proved untrue, that no one is eager to call anything self-evident. Our own experience of the attempt to reach some metaphysical understanding about the beings of experience in the preceding chapters tells us best that it is not self-evident that God exists.[1]

But if the existence of God is not immediately self-evident, the human mind, to know it at all, will have to reason to it or have it revealed in faith. In answer to the question, "Is the existence of God demonstrable by reason?," some have said "No"; some have said "Yes." Grounds for denying the demonstrability of God's existence vary. Some say that it cannot be demonstrated because the beings of experience do, after all, explain themselves. It is therefore not necessary, they say, to come to an efficient cause outside a limited being to account for its being. Or if it is necessary to come to such a cause, this efficient cause is itself simply another limited being, not God. The reason for this position, therefore, is that apparently God is unnecessary. Human knowledge of the universe and of man does not produce any necessity for positing God's existence. Science can explain more and more without God. Natural processes account for existence and the modes of existence, whether these processes be material, psychological, historical, economic, or what have you.

Perhaps the most common reason among contemporary philosophers for rejecting the proofs of the existence of God is the conviction of empiricists that it is impossible for the human mind to break through the bonds of the finite, material world. For these empiricists (and most philosophers in the West today tend toward empiricism), the only acceptable evidence is that which describes discoverable features of the world. They will accept a causal discussion in par-

---

[1] St. Thomas makes the distinction between something that is self-evident in itself and something that is self-evident to us. Accordingly, the existence of God is self-evident in itself but it is not self-evident to us. See *Summa Theologiae,* I, 2, 1.

ticular cases, such as, "How did my breakfast egg get on my plate?" in which "a series of agents from the cook back to the hen on her nest can be distinguished as the cause of the presence of the egg on my plate." [2] The reason for this is that God, or the first cause, cannot exist *in the world as a material being* and the empiricists will admit the existence only of such material beings in the world. Or, to put it the other way around, all matter-of-fact statements (which assert existence) must be empirically verifiable.[3] All meaning is locked inside the visible world. Another way of putting this is given by R. W. Hepburn in *New Essays in Philosophical Theology:* "For if we argue from the existence of a world to a First Cause, we are not in this case recording some observed concomitance of events, or stating a causal law according to which certain sets of events vary reciprocally. We are instead *uprooting* the vocabulary of cause and effect from its habitat in the language, in order to relate the known *to the unknown and unknowable.* It is not the case that every time we have observed a universe, we have noticed a First Cause causing it, and that therefore we feel justified in saying, 'No universes without First Causes.' " [4]

Similarly, within a closed systematic explanation of reality such as given in dialectical materialism, there is no room for God, for anything outside the realm of the beings of experience, since it is man whose existence and activity explains all. "Man can only be his own master when he owes his existence to no one but himself." [5] To one with such a world outlook, the existence of God becomes, not an answer to the question of limited existence, but a threat to the autonomy of man. For such "humanistic" philosophers, to conclude that God exists is a sign of weakness, in the face of which man is cautioned to stand firm. Thus, Nietzsche, after proclaiming that God is dead in the modern world, urges man to break away from any subservience to God: "Ye higher men, this God was your greatest danger. Only since he lay in the grave have ye risen again. Now

---

[2] E. Sprague, *What Is Philosophy?* (New York: Oxford University Press, 1961), p. 62.

[3] *Ibid.*, p. 63.

[4] E. A. Sillem, from R. W. Hepburn, *Christianity and Paradox* (London: A. and C. Watts, Ltd., 1958), p. 160.

[5] Karl Marx, *The German Ideology*, quoted in E. Borne, *Atheism*, trans. S. Tester (New York: Hawthorn Books, Inc., 1961), p. 31.

only cometh the great noontide, now only doth the higher man become—master!"[6] The idea of God is reduced to a dream, not consonant with reality as it is to be lived, not appropriate to man's destiny as it is to be lived out.

For some the rejection of the demonstrability of God's existence is based not merely on the nonnecessity of God as an explanation of the beings of experience, but on something in experience which seems to contradict the existence of God. This aspect of reality which belies God's existence is the very real presence of evil, of suffering, in the world. God, if He exists and is God, must be all-powerful and all-good. If he is all-powerful and yet there is evil, He must not want to eradicate it and therefore is not all-good. If He is all-good, and yet there is evil, He must not have the power to eradicate it. In either case, because there is indeed evil in the world, He would not be God. He must then not exist.

A striking example of the refusal to accept the existence of God because of the evil in the world appears in Camus' *The Plague*. Rieux, the doctor, and Paneloux, the priest, are leaving the room of a young boy who has just died of the plague:

> Rieux was already on his way out, walking so quickly and with such a strange look on his face that Paneloux put out an arm to check him when he was about to pass him in the doorway.
>
> "Come, doctor," he began.
>
> Rieux swung round on him fiercely.
>
> "Ah! That child, anyhow, was innocent, and you know it as well as I do!"
>
> He strode on, brushing past Paneloux, and walked across the school playground. Sitting on a wooden bench . . . he felt like shouting imprecations—anything to loosen the stranglehold lashing his heart with steel. . . .
>
> He heard a voice behind him. "Why was there that anger in your voice just now? What we'd been seeing was as unbearable to me as it was to you."
>
> Rieux turned toward Paneloux.
>
> "I know. I'm sorry. But weariness is a kind of madness. And there are times when the only feeling I have is one of mad revolt."
>
> "I understand," Paneloux said in a low voice. "That sort of thing is

[6] F. Nietzsche, *Thus Spake Zarathustra*, trans. T. Common, in *Complete Works*, 5th ed., ed. O. Levy (New York: The Macmillan Company, 1923), XI, 351.

revolting because it passes our human understanding. But perhaps we should love what we cannot understand."

Rieux straightened up slowly. He gazed at Paneloux, summoning to his gaze all the strength and fervor he could muster against his weariness. Then he shook his head.

"No, Father. I've a very different idea of love. And until my dying day I shall refuse to love a scheme of things in which children are put to torture." [7]

Rieux will not believe in a God who allows this kind of evil in the world.

The above positions are the basis of almost all forms of atheism or agnosticism. There is, however, another kind of rejection of the demonstrability of the existence of God. It is the refusal of those who do not intend to deny God's existence or deny that we know that God exists, but who only want to deny our knowledge of it *by reason.* They say that God exists but that we can know it only *by faith.* Kierkegaard gives us a good example of this in his *Concluding Unscientific Postscript.* There he speaks of the futility of seeking to know God objectively by reason instead of subjectively by faith. In a footnote he explains: "In this manner God certainly becomes a postulate, but not in the otiose manner in which this world is commonly understood. It becomes clear rather that the only way in which an existing individual comes into relation with God is when the dialectical contradiction brings his passion to the point of despair, and helps him to embrace God with the 'category of despair' (faith). The postulate is so far from being arbitrary that it is precisely a life-necessity. It is then not so much that God is a postulate as that the existing individual's postulation of God is a necessity." [8] This is a clear rejection of the way of reason in favor of the way of faith. Today it has become a fairly common position among Protestant theologians.

It would be possible at this point to attempt a somewhat complicated explanation of the possibility of demonstrating the existence of God, but it is perhaps more useful simply to proceed with the

---

[7] *The Plague,* trans. S. Gilbert (New York: Alfred A. Knopf, Inc., 1957), pp. 196–97.

[8] *Concluding Unscientific Postscript,* in *A Kierkegaard Anthology,* ed. R. Bretall (Princeton, N.J.: Princeton University Press, 1936). See Modern Library ed., p. 211.

demonstration, and so show that such a demonstration is possible. In answer to the objection that God is unnecessary to an understanding and explanation of the beings of experience, the only thing to do is to see whether they can be understood and explained without a relationship to Him. And if it becomes necessary to posit the existence of God from the very fact that the beings of experience exist, evil in experience must find an explanation in accord with the existence of God. And if the student unfolds reality and finds it necessary to conclude that God exists, he will thereby know that the existence of God is able to be known by reason as well as by faith.[9]

KINDS OF DEMONSTRATION

The human mind does not always move in the same pattern when it is searching for more knowledge. There is, therefore, more than one pattern which demonstration may take. Most basically, the mind either knows a cause and through this comes to know its effect, or it knows an effect and through this comes to know its cause. These kinds of demonstration are referred to as demonstration from cause to effect (also called *a priori* or *propter quid* reasoning) and demonstration from effect to cause (*a posteriori* or *quia* reasoning). To reason from cause to effect seems impossible when seeking a knowledge of the existence of God. God, of course, has no cause; and He cannot Himself be known as cause without the mediation of His effects, unless by someone who has a direct mystical experience of God causing His effects in the world. The great majority of men, however, do not have this type of mystical experience. Nevertheless, apart from this, there is one form of *a priori* reasoning which attempts to reason from the content of an idea to the existence of the thing represented in the idea. Some have thought that the existence of God can be known in this way: the idea of God which a man has

---

[9] There is a sense in which faith itself affirms reason's demonstrability of God's existence. St. Paul (Romans 1:20) points out that the human mind can know God simply through knowing His effects in Nature. The first Vatican Council explicitly stated that the existence of God can be known from creatures: "*Eadem sancta mater Ecclesia tenet et docet, Deum . . . naturali humanae rationis lumine e rebus creatis certo cognosci potest . . .*" in Denzinger, *Enchiridion Symbolorum,* 30th ed. (St. Louis: B. Herder Book Co., 1955), p. 443.

in his mind is the idea of a being which is most perfect. Now a being most perfect must have the perfection of existence. Necessarily, then, in the idea of God is included the idea of existence. St. Anselm gives a classic statement of this in his *Proslogion*: "Certainly, that than which nothing greater can be thought cannot be only in the mind. For even if it is only in the mind, it can be thought to exist also in reality, which is greater. Therefore, if that than which nothing greater can be thought is only in the mind: that than which nothing greater can be thought is that than which something greater can be thought. But this certainly cannot be. Therefore, without doubt, there exists in mind and in reality something than which it is not possible to think anything greater." [10] Descartes argues in a somewhat similar vein:

"But now, if just because I can draw the idea of something from my thought, it follows that all which I know clearly and distinctly as pertaining to this object does really belong to it, may I not derive from this an argument demonstrating the existence of God? It is certain that I no less find the idea of God, that is to say, the idea of a supremely perfect Being, in me, than that of any figure or number whatever it is; and I do not know any less clearly and distinctly that an [actual and] eternal existence pertains to this nature than I know that all that which I am able to demonstrate of some figure or number truly pertains to the nature of this figure or number, and therefore, although all that I concluded in the preceding Meditations were found to be false, the existence of God would pass with me as at least as certain as I have ever held the truths of mathematics (which concern only numbers and figures) to be.

"This indeed is not at first manifest, since it would seem to present some appearance of being a sophism. For being accustomed in all other things to make a distinction between existence and essence, I easily persuade myself that the existence can be separated from the essence of God, and that we can thus conceive God as not actually existing. But, nevertheless, when I think of it with more attention, I clearly see that existence can no more be separated from the essence of God than can its having its three angles equal to two right

---

[10] *Proslogion*, C. 2. See J. Hick, *Classical and Contemporary Readings in The Philosophy of Religion* (Englewood Cliffs, N.J.: Prentice-Hall, Inc., 1964), p. 29.

angles be separated from the essence of a [rectilinear] triangle, or the idea of a mountain from the idea of a valley; and so there is not any less repugnance to our conceiving a God (that is, a Being supremely perfect) to whom existence is lacking (that is to say, to whom a certain perfection is lacking), than to conceive of a mountain which has no valley.

"But although I cannot really conceive of a God without existence any more than a mountain without a valley, still from the fact that I conceive of a mountain with a valley, it does not follow that there is such a mountain in the world; similarly although I conceive of God as possessing existence, it would seem that it does not follow that there is a God which exists; for my thought does not impose any necessity upon things, and just as I may imagine a winged horse, although no horse with wings exists, so I could perhaps attribute existence to God, although no God existed.

"But a sophism is concealed in this objection; for from the fact that I cannot conceive a mountain without a valley, it does not follow that there is any mountain or any valley in existence, but only that the mountain and the valley, whether they exist or do not exist, cannot in any way be separated one from the other. While from the fact that I cannot conceive God without existence, it follows that existence is inseparable from Him, and hence that He really exists; not that my thought can bring this to pass, or impose any necessity on things, but, on the contrary, because the necessity which lies in the thing itself, that is, the necessity of the existence of God, determines me to think in this way. For it is not within my power to think of God without existence (that is, of a supremely perfect Being devoid of a supreme perfection) though it is in my power to imagine a horse either with wings or without wings." [11]

It is difficult, however, to see any validity in positing the existence of God outside the mind on the basis of the idea of His existence in the mind. From the fact that I have an idea of something, the most that can be concluded is that the thing is somehow possible, not that it exists. Thus, if we follow the laws of logic, Anselm's and Descartes' arguments tell us only that *if God exists* He will exist

---

[11] *Meditations,* V, trans. E. S. Haldane and G. R. T. Ross in *The Philosophical Works of Descartes* (Cambridge: Cambridge University Press, 1911), I, 180–81. (Also in Hick, *Readings in The Philosophy of Religion,* pp. 63–64.)

necessarily and existence will be part of His essence. Our ideas alone, however, give us no guarantee that he does exist.[12]

St. Thomas maintains that the only valid way of demonstrating the existence of God is to reason from His effects to His existence as cause. He claims this because the mind must begin with what is given in experience, with what it knows of reality existing outside itself. If it begins only with its own ideas, it seems impossible to bridge the gap from the world of concepts to the world of concrete beings.[13] This approach of St. Thomas, of course, is intimately connected with the view of knowledge indicated briefly in our introduction, which is that the only valid starting point of human knowledge is knowledge of existing things. The only existing things directly attainable by the human mind are the beings of experience, effects of which God is discovered to be the cause.

DEMONSTRATION OF THE EXISTENCE OF A FIRST, UNLIMITED, UNCAUSED CAUSE OF BEING

Most textbooks since the beginning of the Thomistic revival have studied the proofs for the existence of God by examining the five "ways" which St. Thomas gives in the first part of his *Summa Theologiae.* In the consideration of these ways, however, certain cautions are in order. It is quite possible for a student to assume the completeness and adequacy of any or all of them simply on the authority of St. Thomas, progressing apparently without effort from motion to a first mover, from causes to a first cause, and so forth. Later, however, certain difficulties may arise in relation to these five ways which tend to place in jeopardy the whole question of the demonstrability of the existence of God. The fact is that these five ways have not always been accurately presented, and this does not

---

[12] For further discussion of this see J. Owens, *An Elementary Christian Metaphysics* (Milwaukee: Bruce Publishing Co., 1963), pp. 339–40. Kant agrees with this rejection of the argument for the existence of God based on our idea of God. He claims, however, that all the proofs for God's existence are really no more than restatements of this argument. It would take us too far afield to discuss Kant's arguments here. For such discussion see J. Collins, *A History of Modern European Philosophy* (Milwaukee: Bruce Publishing Co., 1954), pp. 500 ff.

[13] See *Summa Theologiae,* I, 2, 2c and I, 2, 1 ad 2.

help the situation. For example, for us to use the first way to reach a prime mover by a somewhat imprecise demonstration, does not insure our conclusion to the existence of God. Concluding the existence of a prime mover, isolated from the significance of a cause of being, has questionable value. And it is at least not explicit in the argument for a prime mover that the prime mover is the cause of being in the way in which we discussed it in our last chapter. Indeed, it is questionable whether any of the five ways really arrives at the existence of God unless it is seen as ultimately based on a demonstration of an existing first cause of finite being *as* being—not simply as cause of moving, cause of causing, or cause of acting for an end. We cannot here give a full discussion of the five ways; therefore we will attempt to work out one complete demonstration of the existence of God based on the need for a cause of existence in the beings of experience. Only after this will we consider the five ways in relation to this one demonstration. The formulation of an *a posteriori* proof for the existence of a first, unlimited, and uncaused cause of being will come from an integration of two basic insights already acquired: (1) the need for a cause of existence for all beings whose essence and act of existence are distinct; and (2) the impossibility of an infinite regress in a *per se* series of causes. The steps of the demonstration are as follows:

1. *The very existence of the beings of experience is caused by an efficient cause. All finite beings, therefore, as beings, are effects.*

This was the conclusion of our discussion concerning the principle of causality. As we looked at the structure of finite beings, we saw that they are many; and if many, necessarily different; and if different, therefore limited; and finally, if limited, therefore composed at least of essence and existence. We reason from this to the conclusion that since they are not their own existence (they do not exist by their nature), something outside of them is needed to account for their existence. This we identified as their efficient cause or causes.[14] As beings, therefore, they are effects of this cause or these causes.

2. *If this efficient cause is in turn caused, there cannot be an infinite series of caused causes, without arriving at a first uncaused cause.*

---

[14] See pages 108–14.

If the cause in question is itself caused to be, it is here and now dependent for its being on the cause which precedes it. The cause must be acting "here and now" because we are talking about causes of *being*, not causes of becoming. At every moment the beings of our experience depend on a cause of their existing here and now. This holds at every link in the causal series: every cause in the series —if there is a series—must be causing, and so existing simultaneously. This makes it a *per se* series. But in a *per se* series there cannot be an infinite number of members,[15] since all are actual; and if there cannot be an infinite number in this series, the effect—the existence of a limited being in experience—cannot be accounted for simply by an infinite number of caused causes. Only a first uncaused cause can explain the existence and causality of the whole series and the final effect.[16]

The placing of the problem in the present—by the recognition of a present effect which can only exist through the present causality of a presently acting and existing cause—isolates the demonstration of the existence of God from the problem of the eternity of the world. There cannot be a question here of going back in time, coming thus to a first cause at the temporal beginning of the world.[17]

---

[15] See pages 101–3.

[16] As seen above, even if the possibility of an actually infinite number be admitted, there must still be an uncaused first cause outside the series of caused causes. See page 102.

[17] Indeed, if this were the only way to reach a first cause, St. Thomas thinks it impossible to reach it. A series of causes accounting only for the beginning-to-be of the beings in experience, stretching back therefore in time, would be but an accidental series. Such a series could be potentially infinite, so that there would be no need to arrive at a first uncaused cause. Even if one could come in this way to a first cause, there would be no necessity for that cause to be existing now—since it could have long since gone out of existence, having finished its task of putting some beings into existence or into motion.

St. Thomas himself did not think it possible to determine by reason alone whether or not the world had a beginning in time. It was his position that the noneternity of the world can be known by revelation alone. This would indicate that his demonstrations of the existence of God did not depend on finding a starting point for the world in time. Such a view has important implications for all those who fear that a discovery by science that the world has always existed will destroy the proof by reason that God exists and is the sole total cause of all limited being. If the world had existed from eternity, this would simply mean that it and everything in it was utterly dependent upon God from eternity. See *Summa Theologiae,* I, 46, 1.

Whether or not the world had a beginning in time, each existing being in it here and now, at this moment, requires a cause also existing here and now. Whether or not each of us has an infinite number of ancestors, our existing here and now—not just our coming to be at one time—is caused.

3. *Therefore, there must be an existing, first, uncaused cause of the existence of the beings of experience.*

The very existence of each of these beings in experience bears witness to the existence of a being beyond experience. Since the beings of experience are here and now effects, accountable for here and now only by an uncaused, unlimited being which is their cause, such a being must exist.

In order for this cause to be first and to be uncaused, it must be uncaused in its very existence. This means that it must be unlike the composite beings which all require a cause for their existence. It cannot be composed of an essence and of an act of existing which are principles distinct from one another, since such a composition is precisely what requires that a being be caused. If this cause is not, therefore, composed, it is also not limited—for wherever there is limitation there is composition. It must, then, be a pure act of existing, pure act not received in any potency. We will have to investigate the full meaning of this when we attempt to understand not only *that* God is, but *what* He is.

The proof which has just been given is substantially the same as St. Thomas' argument in *De Ente et Essentia,* Chapter 5: "Now, whatever belongs to a being is either caused by the principles of its nature, as the capability of laughter in man, or it comes to it from some extrinsic principle, as light in the air from the sun's influence. But it is impossible that the act of existing be caused by a thing's form or its quiddity (I say *caused* as by an efficient cause); for then something would be the cause of itself and would bring itself into existence—which is impossible. Everything, then, which is such that its act of existing is other than its nature must needs have its act of existing from something else. And since every being which exists through another is reduced, as to its first cause, to one existing in virtue of itself, there must be some being which is the cause of the existing of all things because it itself is the act of existing alone.

If that were not so, we would proceed to infinity among causes, since, as we have said, every being which is not the act of existing alone has a cause of its existence. Evidently, then, an intelligence [that is, separated intelligence] is form and act of existing, and it has its act of existing from the First Being which is simply the act of existing. This is the First Cause, God." [18]

Both of these proofs, ours and that of St. Thomas, are based on the nature of the beings of our experience. They tell us that the finite beings which we know present a limited intelligibility or meaning, which shows its incompleteness and its dependence on Pure Existence. Finite being strikes our mind in somewhat the way an incomplete chord strikes our ear. In both cases they demand completion—the chord by striking the final note, finite being by the affirmation of Pure Existence. The incompleteness, moreover, is not in our mind or in our ear but in the music and in reality. We are not arguing, as Kant would have it, for some mental necessity to think of being as requiring a first cause.[19] Rather, the real beings of our experience present themselves to us as a part of the picture, as effects. It is from this that we argue and not from any internal compulsion. The intelligibility of being, real existing being which we meet in the real world, is our starting point and our guideline throughout this whole argumentation.

Pure Existence is presented to us, therefore, as pre-eminently real being. We must now analyze in greater detail what is involved in this Pure Existence.

---

[18] *De Ente et Essentia*, ed. A. Maurer (Toronto: Pontifical Institute of Mediaeval Studies, 1949), Chapter 4, p. 47. While it may be maintained that St. Thomas did not mean this argument to be a proof for the existence of God—this is Gilson's opinion (*The Christian Philosophy of St. Thomas Aquinas* [New York: Random House, 1956], p. 82)—it nevertheless provides the final insight needed to validate the demonstrations which Thomas does give, and it is therefore at least implied at the heart of them all. Gilson agrees to this (*ibid.*, p. 81).

[19] We are not, of course, denying that our aptitude to know being enters into the picture. Since we are taking a common-sense rather than a transcendental approach, however, we are emphasizing the objective side of the proof. For an approach which puts greater emphasis on the subjective, see Lonergan, *Insight*, pp. 657 ff.

APPENDIX TO CHAPTER 5:

THE FIVE WAYS

The five ways to a reasoned knowledge of the existence of God which St. Thomas points out at the beginning of the *Summa Theologiae* have been revered by some philosophers as sacredly incontrovertible, and have been denounced by other philosophers as falling blasphemously short of the truth of God's existence. It is likely that for St. Thomas himself these five demonstrations were neither intended as the last word in the knowledge of God nor were they considered useless as "ways" in which the human mind might, through philosophical reflection, find the existence of God manifested in the world of experience. They provided five starting points from any of which one might reason to the knowledge that God exists.

St. Thomas wrote as one who believed in the existence of God, guided thus by faith but not, in this instance, founding his conclusions on faith. One who believes in God may well acknowledge that God is manifest in His creation and is discoverable therein by pure philosophical analysis. He may then reflect on the universe of experience precisely to discover by reason what he knows is present. This does not render his philosophy foolish, presumptuous, or superfluous; it is rather an expression of the human mind's natural tendency to establish rationally what is already believed but what can be understood by reason.

It is possible that anyone seeking to lay hold of some aspect of reality given in experience and therein to find an affirmation of the existence of God might light on the aspects of change, of causality, of contingency, of graded perfections, of order. These provide the starting points for the "ways" in which St. Thomas proceeds. If we reflect on our own experience of reality, these aspects seem as significant as any from which to begin. If there are traces of God to be found in the world, they may well be sought in things so forcefully given in experience as the changeableness of all things around us, the apparent influence of one being upon another as cause upon effect, the visible evidences of birth and death, the countless nuances of perfections, and even the isolated instances of the beauty of order.

Although it seemed best to reason to knowledge of the existence of God first in a way that does not exactly parallel any of the five ways, it can now be of benefit to examine the demonstration already made in the light of the five ways and to see the five ways in the light of that demonstration. This can be done simply by looking at the passages in the *Summa Theologiae* in which St. Thomas presents five ways of proving the existence of God and by commenting briefly on those passages in the light of what has already been seen.[20]

THE FIRST WAY: FROM MOTION

"The first and more manifest way is taken from motion. It is certain, and evident to our senses, that in the world some things are in motion. Now, whatever is being moved is being moved by another, for nothing is moved except insofar as it is in potency to that toward which it is moved; whereas a thing moves insofar as it is in act. For 'to move' is nothing else than to reduce something from potency to act. But nothing can be reduced from potency to act except by something existing in act. Thus that which is actually hot —such as fire—makes wood, which is potentially hot, to be actually hot, and thereby 'moves' and alters it. Now it is not possible that the same thing should be at once in act and in potency in the same respect, but only in different respects: what is actually hot cannot simultaneously be potentially hot; rather, it is simultaneously potentially cold. So it is im-

---

[20] While we are treating explicitly the five ways as given in the *Summa Theologiae*, it must be noted that these and other ways are given in other of St. Thomas' works. Four ways are given in the *Summa Contra Gentiles* (I, 13); one is given in the *Compendium of Theology*, and so forth.

possible that in the same respect and in the same way a thing should be both moving and moved; in other words, that it should move itself. Therefore, whatever is being moved must be moved by another. If that by which it is being moved be itself moved, then this also must be moved by another, and that by another again. But this cannot go on to infinity, because then there would be no first mover and consequently, no other mover. For secondary movers move only because they are themselves moved by the primary one; even as the staff moves only because it is moved by the hand. That is why it is necessary to conclude to a First Mover—which is moved by nothing else whatever. And this all understand as being 'God.'"[21]

Outline and Explanation of Argument

1. *Data: things in motion, as given in experience.*

The starting point of the first way is the empirically given evidence that things are moving. By "motion" St. Thomas indicates all forms of change—from mere movement in space to evolutive change. Spatial change, locomotion, is perhaps most evident to the senses, and thus might be considered the primary datum, but Thomas's definition of motion as "to reduce something from potency to act" forbids the interpretation of locomotion as the only starting point for this way. We begin, rather, with any and every experience of change—internal or external, in space or time, quantitative or qualitative, necessary or free.

2. *Whatever is moved is moved by another.*

This step in arriving at the existence of God from things in motion can be understood only if it is seen as expressive of the principle of efficient causality which we have already considered.[22] What St. Thomas is saying is that whatever is changing cannot be the sole source of its own change or its own being. Whatever is changing is in some way an effect and therefore being caused; as long as it is changing, there-

---

[21] *Summa Theologiae,* I, 2, 3, in *Treatise on God,* trans. J. Anderson (Englewood Cliffs, N.J.: Prentice-Hall, Inc., 1963), p. 10.

[22] See page 102.

fore, there is an existing cause of its change, and this cause is outside of itself.

But how do we know that whatever is changing requires a cause for its change? St. Thomas reasons that since change is the passage of something from potentiality to actuality, and since potentiality is a state of not yet having a perfection but only being capable of having it, and since a thing cannot give itself what it does not yet have, whatever is in potency cannot actualize itself.

Certain difficulties arise in regard to this principle. For one thing, it is possible for a being that is actualized in one respect to actualize in itself what is potential in another respect. Thus, living beings are said to move themselves when one part moves another part.[23] In addition, the Aristotelian view of the universe which St. Thomas shared[24] is no longer considered valid. Thus, in a universe where, according to the law of inertia, a thing apparently needs no cause for it to stay in motion, it is more difficult to assert that whatever is in motion is moved by another. A further difficulty will appear when we understand the dynamic orientation of potency to act.[25]

All these difficulties make it imperative that we see beyond the motion or change of a being to the being which moves or changes; that is, that a being changes will still provide a starting point from which to reason to the existence of an outside cause only if we see that a being capable of changing must be a being that cannot ultimately explain its own being, let alone its own change. This can be seen if we recall that change here implies a being somehow composed of act and potency, and any being composed of act and potency is ultimately dependent upon a cause outside itself to account for its being and hence its change.[26] Even if the causes of change, of becoming, were seen to be within the being of the thing that changes, because it is changing, becoming, we know that its very being is itself caused. This ultimately places the way of motion within the demonstration of the existence of God which we have already seen.

---

[23] See Chapter 4, note 17.

[24] *Summa Contra Gentiles,* I, 13; *Compendium Theologiae,* I, 3.

[25] See Chapter 7.

[26] See pages 108–14.

3. *There cannot be an infinite number of moved movers.*

This is essentially the same step which we took in our previous demonstration.[27] If the cause of being in a changing being is itself changing, it must itself be caused in being. This is again, therefore, not a question of a cause merely of something's beginning to move, beginning to change, or even beginning to be. Each changing being, no matter how many there may be in a series, is here and now dependent on its preceding cause for its being and its change. This is, therefore, a *per se* series of causes and cannot proceed to infinity.[28] Only a first uncaused cause can explain the being and the change within the whole series. And a first uncaused cause must be a being that is not changing, for if it, too, were changing, it, too, would have to be caused—for the same reason that any changing being must be caused.

4. *Therefore, it is necessary to arrive at a first mover, unmoved by another: this is God.*

The first unmoved mover is one and the same as the first uncaused cause, and hence not only a Prime Mover in Aristotle's sense, but Pure Act, unlimited, infinite, uncomposed, pure perfection. This, St. Thomas says, everyone understands to be God.

THE SECOND WAY: FROM EFFICIENT CAUSES

"The second way is from the nature of the efficient cause. Among sensible things in our world we find an order of efficient causes. There is no case of a thing's being the efficient cause of itself; nor is such a thing possible, for then it would be prior to itself; which is impossible. Now in efficient causes it is not possible to proceed to infinity, because in all efficient causes following in order, the first is the cause of the intermediate, and the intermediate is the cause of the ultimate, whether the intermediate be several or only one. Now to remove the cause is to remove the effect. So, if there be no first in efficient causes, there will be no last, nor any intermediate, term. But if it is possible to proceed to infinity in efficient causes, there will be no first efficient

---

[27] *Ibid.*

[28] See pages 99–100.

cause; and so there will be no terminal effect, nor any intermediate efficient causes. But this is patently false. Therefore it is necessary to admit a first efficient cause, which all call 'God.' "[29]

Outline and Explanation of Argument

1. *Data: empirical evidence of efficient causes—the whole order of efficient causes.*

Although we tend to think of the first way in terms of efficient causality alone, the cause of motion could be other than an efficient cause; and although we tend to think of efficient causes as always causing change or becoming, we do find in experience efficient causes of being—though it may be only of accidental determinations of being.[30] In other words, the starting point of the second way is not exactly the same as the starting point of the first way. In any case, the focus in the first way is on effects that are caused, and in the second way the focus is on causes that are causing.

Thomas's reference to an order of efficient causes implies not only a series of causes, one ordered to the other, but the very order there is between an efficient cause and its effect. Of course, it is possible to deny any experience of causality, to suppose that one thing follows another without any justification for calling one an effect consequent upon the other as cause. If we were to make this denial upon this supposition, we could not take the experience of efficient causality as a starting point. However, if we find it given in experience that one being does influence another, that there is even reciprocal influence experienced in our universe, then this is a starting point for our second way to prove the existence of God. St. Thomas affirms causality as self-evident in experience, and we affirm it with him.

2. *Whatever is caused is caused by another.*

If any cause is caused to be causing, it cannot be the ultimate source of its own causality. So long as it is caused in any way, it must be caused in its being; for, as we have seen, a being that is in any way in potency—a prerequisite for be-

---

[29] *Summa Theologiae,* I, 2, 3 (Anderson, p. 10).
[30] See pages 93–95.

ing caused—will not ultimately be able to explain its own being, nor then, its own causality. If it cannot explain its own being, cannot cause its own being or its own causality, there must be a cause outside of it which accounts for it.

We might say that perhaps none of the efficient causes given in experience are caused; perhaps they are all uncaused as causes, totally the source of their own causality. Experience clearly gives some examples of causes that exert causality only under the influence of another cause. But even if it did not, we could examine what kind of cause could possibly be uncaused in its causing. Only one that is uncaused in its being could be so, and only a being that is without composition and without limitation could be uncaused in its being.[31]

3. *There cannot be an infinite number of efficient caused causes.*

To explain a caused cause by another caused cause is not finally to explain either one. Even an infinite number of caused causes could not explain any one of them. When one cause is caused by another and that one by still another, we have a series of causes. Since each is dependent upon the one preceding it for its causality here and now, this is a *per se* series of causes. We have already seen that a *per se* series cannot be infinite, or even if it were so, would require a cause outside the whole series to account for the causality of the series as a whole. Without a first cause, or a cause outside the series, none of the causes in the series can be causes —since if each is dependent upon the one preceding it, without the one preceding it it cannot cause.

4. *There must, therefore, be a first uncaused cause, and this is God.*

As we have seen, the first cause is cause in a wholly unique way; it is not merely the first in a series of causes all of which cause in essentially the same way. It is cause as Pure Act, unlimited, infinite, uncomposed, pure perfection.

THE THIRD WAY: FROM "POSSIBLE" BEINGS

"The third way is taken from the possible and the necessary; and it is this. We find in things some which are pos-

[31] See pages 98–99.

sible of being and of not-being, since they are found to be generated, and to be corrupted and, consequently, to be possible of being and of not-being. But it is impossible for all such things always to exist, for that which can not-be at some time is not. So if everything can not-be, then at one time there was nothing. But if this were true, even now there would be nothing, because that which is not does not begin to be except by something which is. So, if at one time nothing existed, it would have been impossible for anything to have begun to exist; and thus even now nothing would be in existence—which is patently false. Therefore, not all beings are possibles, but there must be something whose existence is necessary. But every necessary entity either has its necessity caused by another, or not. Now it is impossible to proceed to infinity in necessary things whose necessity is caused, as has been already proved in regard to efficient causes. It is therefore necessary to admit the existence of a being having its necessity through itself, and not receiving it from another, but rather causing in others their necessity. This all men call 'God.' "[32]

Outline and Explanation of Argument

1. *Data: experience of "possible" beings—that is, beings that are able to be generated and corrupted and therefore able not-to-be.*

Birth and death are realities which easily invite the kind of reflection which might provide another way to knowledge of the existence of God. That beings are seen to begin to be and to cease to be shows them to be somehow contingent—able not to be—and raises the question, not so much of whence comes the possibility of their beginning-to-be, but of how they can be while they are.

If they are as contingent as they appear to be, perhaps they are not only able not to be at one time—that is, before they are generated and after they corrupt—but are, even while they exist, able here and now not to be.

2. *The existence of these contingent—or "possible"—beings must be caused by a necessary being.*

[32] *Summa Theologiae,* I, 2, 3 (Anderson, pp. 10–11).

St. Thomas argues that if everything were in all respects corruptible, at some time there would be nothing. This has been explained as meaning that if a thing did not corrupt in an infinite duration of time, it really would not be corruptible. This would make it a necessary being of sorts. However it is explained, there remain difficulties with this statement of St. Thomas'—not the least of which is that while all things must be generable and corruptible, the corruption of one is the generation of another, and thus there could always be something even though it would always be something new. This, of course, would lead one to investigate the possibility of generation, and in the discovery of a principle like primary matter would come the discovery of something necessary. Nevertheless, it seems best in the understanding of this way to focus less on a factor of time and more on the factor of the present contingency or necessity of generable and corruptible being.

Any being that is generable or corruptible is by its very nature a limited being. It is therefore a composed being, having act and potency. If we make a thorough analysis of corruptible being we should discover that it is corruptible precisely because in the order of essence its potential principle—primary matter—is able to receive a different formal principle—substantial form—than it has. All this, for our purposes, would indicate that although it has being it has no necessary claim on being, not even for the time that it is. Indeed, nothing can account for its being here and now save a cause outside itself that holds it in being.[33]

3. *Every necessary being has its necessity caused by another or not.*

By a necessary being St. Thomas means merely a being that is not corruptible. Thus, a necessary being would be any being or even principle of being that has no passive potency not to be; this means precisely any being not composed in the order of essence, and therefore not susceptible to losing one form and gaining another—thereby corrupting itself and giving rise to a different being. In this sense of the term, the

---

[33] Such a being, composed in the order of essence, would necessarily be composed in the order of existence—for a limited essence limits the existence which it actualizes.

human soul, angelic substance, even primary matter itself, would be necessary beings.

Now the question is, what accounts for the necessity of such beings? Do they have it of themselves, or do they receive it from another? If they have necessity by their very nature, then it is their nature to exist, and they would then be pure act.[34] If it is not their nature to exist, if they are limited beings whose existence is received and limited by essence, then they receive their necessity from a cause outside themselves, for the same reason that all limited beings are caused by an efficient cause other than themselves.

4. *There cannot be an infinite number of caused necessary beings causing.*

To account for what necessity there is in corruptible beings—for even they can be said to have necessity so long as they are caused—it will not be sufficient to point only to incorruptible, necessary beings whose necessity is received from another. For beings whose necessity is a caused necessity depend here and now on their cause, and even supposing a series of such beings causing, this would again be a *per se* series and so could not be infinite. There would then have to be a first cause, a being whose necessity is not received, who is its own necessity and thence the source of the necessity of all beings that are.

5. *There must then exist a being which has of itself its own necessity. This being is God.*

Such a being can have its own absolute necessity only if it is its nature to exist—thus, only if it is Pure Act, unlimited, uncaused, uncomposed. This being we understand to be God.

THE FOURTH WAY: FROM GRADATIONS OF PERFECTIONS

"The fourth way is taken from the grades [of perfection] found in things. Among beings there are some more and some less good, true, and noble; and so in the case of other perfections of this kind. But 'more' and 'less' are predicated of diverse things according as they approach in diverse

---

[34] See pages 108–14.

measures something which is the maximum, as a thing is hotter the more it approaches that which is hottest. There is, then, something which is truest and best and noblest and, consequently, something which is maximally a being. For those things that are greatest in truth are greatest in being, as Aristotle says in Book II of the *Metaphysics*. Now that which is predicated maximally in a genus is the cause of all in the genus; for example, fire, which is maximally hot, is the cause of all hot things, as is said in the same book. Hence there is a reality which is for all things the cause of their being, goodness, and every other perfection; and this we call 'God.'"[35]

Outline and Explanation of Argument

1. *Data: beings given in experience as more and less good, true, noble, and so forth.*

The kinds of perfections referred to here must be what we shall later call "transcendental" perfections—that is, perfections which in themselves denote no imperfection, no limitation, but which can exist in a limited form. They are perfections which transcend any restriction to genus or species and apply to all being insofar as it is. That Thomas is talking about transcendental perfections here and not accidental or essential perfections is clear from the nature of these perfections. He cannot be referring, for example, to accidental perfections because they are not found in all beings and are dependent upon substantial perfections.[36] He cannot be referring to essential perfections (specific and generic) because they are not found in degrees.

2. *If these perfections are "more" and "less" they must be limited, at least in all that is less than the best.*

This step seems a necessary one before proceeding to the conclusion reached by St. Thomas. If we proceed immediately from the fact of graded perfections to a maximum, a best, certain rather serious difficulties arise. Thus, for example, to say that "more" and "less" have no meaning unless

---

[35] *Summa Theologiae,* I, 2, 3 (Anderson, p. 11).
[36] See *Summa Theologiae,* I, 4, 1c.

related to a best, even to an absolute, seems somewhat premature. First of all, an absolute cannot be immediately implied, for "more" and "less" could imply simply a best which may itself be a relative best, the most. Further, even a relative best does not seem immediately deducible, for without any relation to a *per se* causal series there seems no reason why there could not be a series *ad infinitum,* the better being measured by remoteness from the least, or the more and less measured by relation to a mean standard chosen arbitrarily. The matter of graded perfections could thus be handled like numbers, wherein there need be no highest number.

It thus seems impossible to reason to a most perfect without bringing in efficient causality.[37] Rather than try to establish a highest, or an absolute, simply by an appeal to the intelligibility of degrees of being and then go on by another argument to prove that this is the cause of the other—as many have done—we shall appeal first to a *per se* series of causes which must have a first efficient cause which is best.

If we ask how it is possible to have grades of perfection, we can follow the same line of reasoning which we used in first asking how it is possible to have many existing beings. That is, we see first that there can be grades of perfection only if there is plurality, only if the perfections appear in a plurality of beings or principles of being. But if they are plural, that is, many, they must be different—"more" and "less"; and if they are different, they must be limited, at least in all that is not best. This means, of course, that there must be composition, for the perfections must be received in a limiting capacity, must be joined to a principle of potency. It is only thus that they may appear in measures of "more" and "less." By reason of a limiting principle, a being has a certain measure set for its perfection. This measure has a negative and a positive aspect: it is negative inasmuch as it excludes perfection beyond a certain limit, and it is positive inasmuch as it gives a positive order to a cer-

[37] To appeal to exemplary causality, as some do, does not seem satisfactorily to lead to an absolute; for in exemplary causality there is no need for a *per se* series of causes—for an artist may paint a picture, and another artist make a copy, and the original be destroyed, and copies continue to be made, and so forth.

tain degree of perfection, a positive capacity for this much and not for less than this.

3. *Limited being is caused.*

This is clear from all that we have seen in our original demonstration of the existence of God and in our original consideration of the principle of causality.

4. *There cannot be an infinite number of limited causes.*

Once again, precisely because each cause would depend on its preceding cause for its existence and perfection, this would be a *per se* series, which requires a first uncaused cause, and in this context, an absolute—because unlimited—in whatever perfection is considered.

5. *Therefore, we arrive at a first ultimate cause, unlimited, which is "best" and which accounts for all that is "more" and "less." This we call God.*

The fourth way has often been described as the way of "participation." This is because it implies that all transcendental perfections exist in limited form only because they are a limited share in the absolute, even as all limited beings only by reason of their limited share in unlimited, absolute being. This will become clearer when we consider the notion of participation in greater detail.[38]

THE FIFTH WAY: FROM THE DIRECTION OF THINGS TO ENDS

"The fifth way is taken from the governance of things. For we see that certain beings devoid of knowledge, namely natural bodies, act for an end; and this is evident from their acting always, or almost always, in the same way, in order to obtain the best result. Hence it is clear that they achieve their end, not fortuitously, but purposefully. Now whatever lacks knowledge does not tend toward an end unless it be directed by some being endowed with knowledge and intelligence, even as the arrow is directed by the archer. It follows that some intelligent being exists by whom all natural things are directed to their end. This being we call 'God!' "[39]

---

[38] See pages 233–35

[39] *Summa Theologiae,* I, 2, 3 (Anderson, p. 11).

Outline and Explanation of Argument

1. *Data: things without knowledge acting for an end.* What we discover in the activities of all beings in experience is that the activities and the beings are in some way directed toward an end. We learn this by observing the repetition of some actions and by seeing the fulfillment in some way achieved by actions. It would be naïve to say that every activity or even every being achieves the end to which it is directed. The disorder in the world may be as great as the order. But it would also be naïve to conclude that this disorder contradicts the very existence of an order to an end; it may, in fact, negatively confirm that there *is* an order, but one which is oftentimes violated.

A principle emerges which has been called the Principle of Finality: Every agent acts for an end. Whether or not it achieves its end, it is directed toward an end. This may mean simply that all activity is in some way determinate; it is impossible that an agent act in a wholly indeterminate way. But what is implied in the data which is the starting point of the fifth way is that there is some order in the determination of beings in the universe to their proper ends.

Establishing the existence of God from order and design in the universe at one time seemed the most cogent argument available. That is no longer the case. The complete collapse of the Aristotelian universe, a teleological conception of an ordered world, has bequeathed to the fifth way all the ghosts of an outdated scientific theory. This does not necessarily mean that the way is no longer valid, since the core of its argument does not depend upon any scientific theory. However, a more detailed discussion of the meaning of finality in a world of acting beings will be deferred for now,[40] and we shall attempt merely to see the essential lines of the demonstration involved in the fifth way.

However we assess the adaptation of means to ends in the universe, we do find at least some instances of adaptation present. A bodily organ is so structured to perform its proper activity. Water creatures swim to find their food. If

---

[40] See pages 205–8.

we ask for an explanation of these things, one thing is clear: the whole explanation does not seem to lie in the things themselves.

2. *Whatever lacks knowledge and moves toward an end is caused to move toward an end by an intellectual cause.*

The determination of activities to an end, the original ordering of natures to an end, the adaptation of means to ends, all belongs to intelligence. If we find determination and adaptation in beings that do not have intelligence, it would seem that they cannot be themselves the cause of this determination and adaptation. They must then be directed to their proper ends by a being other than themselves, a being which is intelligent.

3. *There cannot be an infinite number of caused intelligent causes.*

If the cause of beings in the universe acting for an end is an intelligent being that is not God but a limited being with limited intelligence, it must in turn be caused—since every being that is in any way limited is dependent for its existence, and hence for its activity, intelligent, or otherwise, on a being that is not limited and not caused. If there is even a series of limited intelligent beings causing, the explanation of their effect is unintelligible without a first uncaused cause, for such a series would once again be a *per se* series.

4. *There must then be an intelligent being that is uncaused and unlimited, whose intelligence is thus identical with its Being, that causes all other beings to be directed to their proper ends. This being is God.*

Although we have chosen to postpone a more thorough treatment of finality, at least brief mention must be made here of some of the specific difficulties which beset the fifth way. The first is raised by the inference that all direction of activity and being to an end must be the effect of an intelligent cause. Such direction might be accounted for merely by a built-in necessity given through efficient causality. In other words, what there is of order in the world may point to a mechanistic meaning for the world rather than to an intelligent first cause.

There is another difficulty which is closely allied to the

first, namely, that the apparent order of things to an end may be the result of chance—either here and now or in the original ordering of things within the universe. Chance, of course, when properly understood, implies two lines of causality, both directed to their proper end, but meeting in a way not included within the causality of either. A chance event is therefore the meeting of two or more causal lines whose convergence is not provided for by the causality of the lines. Chance itself, therefore, presupposes a causal ordering of actions to their ends, even though the causes would not account for the fact that their ordering might converge in a way that would be a further ordering. The difficulty of chance may therefore either be dismissed or be reduced to the original difficulty of necessity or mechanistic determinism in the universe.

This latter difficulty is not resolvable without proceeding once more to the need for a cause of being, this time for a cause of the very being of things which are experienced precisely under the aspect of being directed to an end, and hence to the cause of being and direction. Once again, the cause of the being and the being-of-order can only be a cause outside the limited being and a cause which is in itself in no way limited. This has been seen over and over again. Thus, no mechanistic theory will suffice to explain either the being or the order in the beings given in experience as acting for an end—for it would leave all beings still without an explanation of their being, and thus, without an explanation of their order. Not even the concept of a master architect or clockmaker, so long as he is a limited being in any way, will explain the existence of being ordered to an end, for such a director might indeed direct the order in the universe, but his own being and order would still be utterly received, wholly caused. Only an infinite being, uncaused, whom we call God, can ultimately render this data intelligible. That such a being must be intelligent is indicated in the nature of the causality; and if not there, it is indicated in the fact that an intelligent being must be the cause of the caused intelligent beings that are limited causes; and if not there, it is indicated—as we shall see later—in the very fact that such a cause is all-perfect, and therefore all-knowing, all-wise.

SUGGESTED READINGS

Borne, Etienne, *Atheism,* trans. S. J. Tester. New York: Hawthorn Books, Inc., 1961. Historical analyses of the two main forms of atheism.

Descartes, Rene, "Of God, that He Exists," *Meditations,* V, in *The Philosophical Works of Descartes,* I, trans. E. S. Haldane and G. R. T. Ross. Cambridge: Cambridge University Press, 1911. Also in J. Hick, ed., *Classical and Contemporary Readings in the Philosophy of Religion,* pp. 63–67. Englewood Cliffs, N. J.: Prentice-Hall, Inc., 1964.

de Finance, Joseph, "Being and Subjectivity," *Cross Currents,* VI (1956), 163–78. The personal affirmation of one's own being opens out into the affirmation of God.

Gilson, Etienne, *The Christian Philosophy of Saint Thomas Aquinas,* trans. L. K. Shook, Chapters 2 and 3. New York: Random House, 1956.

———, *Elements of Christian Philosophy,* Chapter 3. Garden City, N. Y.: Doubleday & Company, Inc., 1960.

———, *God and Philosophy,* New Haven, Conn.: Yale University Press, 1941. Historical review of philosophical approaches to God.

———, *The Philosopher and Theology,* trans. C. Gilson, Chapters 4 and 5. New York: Random House, 1962.

Holloway, Maurice R., "Some Invalid Proofs from Science for the Existence of God," *An Introduction to Natural Theology,* Appendix C. New York: Appleton-Century-Crofts, 1957.

Kierkegaard, Søren, *Philosophical Fragments,* trans. D. S. Swenson, pp. 31–36. Princeton, N. J.: Princeton University Press, 1936. Also in J. Hick, pp. 190–94. In opposition to rationalistic proofs of the existence of God.

St. Anselm, "The Ontological Argument for the Existence of God," in *Classical and Contemporary Readings in the Philosophy of Religion,* ed. J. Hick, pp. 28–36. Englewood Cliffs, N. J.: Prentice-Hall, Inc., 1964.

St. Thomas Aquinas, *Concerning Being and Essence,* Chapter 4.

———, *Summa Contra Gentiles,* I, 13.

———, *Summa Theologiae,* I, 2, 3.

Sillem, Edward, *Ways of Thinking About God.* New York: Sheed & Ward, 1961.

Weigel, Gustave, and Arthur G. Madden, *Religion and the Knowledge of God,* Chapter 7. Englewood Cliffs, N. J.: Prentice-Hall, Inc., 1961. Brief history of the problem of the existence of God as it has appeared since the time of Plato.

KNOWLEDGE AND NAMING OF PURE EXISTENCE

INTRODUCTION

Our analysis of existence, as we meet it in the world of our experience, has led us through the way of causality to pure existence which is the first cause and source of all being. Up to this point all that we have shown about this first cause is that it is Pure Existence. Now it will be necessary for us to see what more we can say about it. We have called the First Cause "God," because we identify God with the source of being. Strictly speaking, however, we have said only two things: (1) there is a first efficient cause of being; and (2) this first cause is pure existence. In the present chapter we will have to fill out our notion of First Cause to see whether we can come closer to the general notion of God. With St. Thomas we will take a middle path, affirming that we can know *something* of the nature of God, and yet we will not exaggerate the extent of that knowledge.

As we might expect, many of the contemporary thinkers who reject the proof from causality go a step further and deny that even if we did arrive at a first cause by our argumentation, it would not tell us anything about God. John Hospers, in his introductory text, expresses this conviction with no hesitation. The proof, he says, "If it establishes the existence of a Deity, it establishes nothing whatever about the Deity's characteristics except the characteristic of being the Cause of the universe. It enables us to say nothing about whether God is good or evil, whether God is concerned with the problems of human life or indifferent to them, or whether there is one God or many gods (the divine power could conceivably be a *collective* power). The argument cannot be used to establish any particular kind of Deity."[1] Hospers' reason, of course, is that he sees no way of filling out the notion of cause to include the characteristics of God. However, we have seen that our analysis gives us more than just *First Cause;* it gives us *pure existence.* This will have to be the key to further knowledge about this first cause. Nevertheless, it is true that we have no direct experience of this first cause and so we will have to project from our knowledge of the world about us to fill out the notion of first cause.

We have a personal reason, too, for attempting to learn as much as possible about Pure Existence. For to the degree that a man understands the utter dependency of his own being and of every limited being upon a cause, to that degree is he aware of his need to understand the nature of his relationship to that cause and the nature of the cause itself. If continued finite existence is totally contingent upon the continued activity of the cause of one's being, if one exists so long as he is actualized by an act of existence totally received from another, it is not surprising that questions about that other are perhaps the most crucial questions a man must ask. The questions our human reason addresses to limited being somehow never stop there but reach beyond it to God for their full answer.

THE PROBLEM OF MAN'S KNOWLEDGE OF GOD

To know God becomes a problem in itself. How shall a mind that strains to unveil the beings of experience hope to attain to a knowl-

---

[1] J. Hospers, *An Introduction to Philosophical Analysis* (Englewood Cliffs, N.J.: Prentice-Hall, Inc., 1953), p. 327.

edge of the nature of a first cause, the very existence of which is veiled to experience? When human reason stands before God it is like the eye before the colors beyond infrared and ultraviolet, or like Aristotle's owl in the sunlight, or like mystics in the darkness of the cloud of unknowing. It is easy to shrug one's shoulders at what "sounds too high and too deep" for human reason. And yet, philosophers have been denounced for turning God into a supreme idol reflecting their own spirit.[2] But neither false humility nor supercilious unconcern can satisfy us. For as men we know that we must grasp the meaning of life, and in our search to understand the beings of our experience we find them without meaning apart from God and of necessity we are confronted sooner or later with the problem of the knowledge of God.

This thirst for God must be satisfied in basically the same way as our thirst for knowledge of being in other areas. There is an added difficulty, however, since whatever we know is in us, the knowers, according to our capacity as knowers. This makes knowledge of God more difficult than most of our other forms of knowledge. What we know best, of course, are the forms of material things as abstracted from those things as we meet them in our experience. Everything else we know by some sort of analogy to this fundamental type of human knowing. Our knowledge of the human soul, for instance, beyond our experience of its proper powers, is worked out in terms of an analogy with the material things of experience. How much more, then, must our knowledge of God suffer severe limitations. Our intellect, as finite, has not the capacity to receive unlimited being in any but a very limited way. This is why St. Thomas says that no created intellect by its natural power can see the essence of God.[3] This infinite object of knowledge would overwhelm our intellect, which cannot know perfectly even a limited essence. Nor can we know the whole power of God, since all we can see are the effects of that power, and we have no way of conceiving of the infinity of God's power in itself.

Yet for all this it is possible for man to know something about God. The effects of any cause tell something about their cause. The beings

---

[2] For example, by Karl Barth, as reported in J. Daniélou, *God and the Ways of Knowing* (Cleveland, Ohio: The World Publishing Company, 1957), p. 52.
[3] See *Summa Theologiae,* I, 12, 4, 11 and 12.

of experience, effects of a first cause, say something of their uncaused cause. It is possible to know from God's effects *that* He is and even something of *what* He is. The demonstration of the existence of God has already shown that His existence is revealed by the existence of His effects. And this existence has been shown to be Pure Existence.

We have two principles at work here. First, pure existence as the fullness of being, must contain the full perfection of being. Secondly, every effect tells us something of its cause. Thus it is possible to know, however imperfectly, what God is by His effects because no perfection can be in an effect that is not in its cause.[4] From a knowledge of God as First Cause can come a knowledge of what must necessarily belong to Him as First Cause of all things.[5] Further, as the perfections in His effects speak of the perfection in their cause, so the limitations of the perfections in the effects tell us of what their cause is not.[6] This denial of limitation in the perfections of God at the same time implies that He is immeasurably other than His effects not by defect, but by excellence.[7] This is why historically there have been three ways by which God may be known: the ways of causality, of negation, and of eminence or excellence.[8]

These ways are in a sense inseparable. It is only by the way of causality—knowing God through knowing His effects—that human reason approaches a knowledge of God at all. Yet whatever is known of Him must be conceptually purified by the removal of every notion of imperfection. Thus, whatever is known by the way of causality must be subjected to the way of negation. As Etienne Gilson says, "If we can imagine what something is, then God is beyond it; if we can grasp the definition of a certain thing, then that thing is

---

[4] See pages 104–5.

[5] See *Summa Theologiae,* I, 4, 2.

[6] Whatever perfections are in creatures in a limited way are totally "other" in God, because they are in Him in an unlimited way. To know that God is "other," to know what He is not, is to have positive knowledge of Him. In the words of St. Thomas: "Wisdom consists not only in knowing that God exists, but in attaining to a knowledge of what He is. But in this life we can know this only insofar as we know what He is not. For one who knows something insofar as it differs from all other things approaches the knowledge by which one knows what it is." *De Veritate,* 10, 12 ad 7.

[7] *Summa Theologiae,* I, 4, 3; *De Potentia,* 7, 5 ad 2.

[8] *Summa Theologiae,* I, 12, 12.

not yet God. Nor is it enough to have said this only once; the aim of the doctrine of Thomas Aquinas on this crucial point is to invite us to a sort of intellectual asceticism calculated to rid our intellects of the delusion that we know *what* God is." [9]

This means, for example, that if we find goodness in the effects of God, goodness must be first in God Himself. But goodness as we see it in His effects is always limited, marked by temporality, composed, and so forth. All these limitations to goodness must one by one be removed from our understanding of the goodness of God, so that divine goodness comes to be understood as unlimited, eternal, absolutely simple, and so forth. When we have so purified our notion of goodness, it might be said that we are no longer speaking of what we found in the effects of God. We might just as well say now that he is not-good, for he is not good in the sense in which other things are good. We do not, then, know anymore about what God is than we did before. We only know what He is not.

This conclusion does not follow for even if we hold that a negative knowledge of God is the highest way of knowing Him through reason, all our knowledge of God is not negative. As G. Klubertanz points out, "St. Thomas is not a Dionysian, not an agnostic. He does not limit man's knowledge of God to the negative attributes like eternity, immensity, infinity, immateriality. He serenely asserts that we can know that God exists, that He is good, wise, holy, loving. But in his explanation of our knowledge of God he avoids even a trace of concession to rationalism." [10] For St. Thomas every negative implies something positive, and in denying everything of God, we also affirm in a pre-eminent way everything of Him. So long as the negative element is never left out, we do have positive knowledge of God. Thus, God is good, though He is not good in just the way anything in our experience or in our imagination is good. How we can know His goodness and any other positive perfection will be seen more clearly when we consider the notions of analogy and participation.

---

[9] *Elements of Christian Philosophy* by Etienne Gilson, p. 110. Copyright © 1960 by Doubleday & Company, Inc. Reprinted by permission of the publisher.
[10] G. Klubertanz, *St. Thomas Aquinas on Analogy* (Chicago: Loyola University Press, 1960), p. 151.

NAMING GOD

Taking the philosophical approach, as we have, we are in danger of underemphasizing the personal side of God. Thus far, as we have pointed out, we have not analyzed the meaning of Pure Existence to show that God is personal. Theologian Martin Buber warns us against any depersonalization of God: "Men have addressed their eternal 'Thou' with many names. In singing of Him who was thus named they had always had the 'Thou' in mind: the first myths were hymns of praise. Then the names took refuge in the language of 'It'; men were more and more strongly moved to think of and to address their eternal 'Thou' as an 'It.' But all God's names are hallowed, for in them He is not merely spoken about, but also spoken to." [11]

Buber's admonition is salutary but we must not let it paralyze us from analyzing further our knowledge of God. We must be strong-minded enough to see that although the knowledge which reason gains of the First Cause, of God, is sealed into certain concepts and spoken in certain words—the traditional *attributes* of God—and although metaphysicians and nonmetaphysicians alike have frequently rebelled at the notion of categorizing these attributes, this procedure of analyzing our knowledge of God is valid. It is true, of course, that individual thinkers have claimed too much or too little for this knowledge. Since Descartes, for instance, scholastic thinkers in general have placed too much confidence in this knowledge, not realizing that when all that reason can do is done, little is really known of God. Perhaps this is due in part to the use of "attribute" to designate what we know about God. It gives the impression that we know God from the inside, as it were. Hence to use language like this, which seems to express more than we can know from our conclusion that God is first cause, is perhaps a disservice to reason and certainly a disservice to man.

Consequently, although maintaining the validity of the discussion of the divine attributes, for the reasons just given, we will discuss

[11] M. Buber, *I and Thou*, 2nd ed., trans. R. G. Smith (New York: Charles Scribner's Sons, 1958), p. 75.

the *names* of God, rather than His *attributes.* This may seem an over-technical distinction, but it will be worthwhile if it serves to prevent a kind of rationalism in metaphysics which is a recurrent danger. "Name" may simply be a logical synonym for a term or word—the expression of a concept. It may also carry the connotations here of proper name.

Names, or words, are signs of ideas. Ideas are signs of things—of realities. Accordingly, men name things as they know them. If this theory of naming is followed in naming God, it yields the following: Men name as they know. They know God from His effects—that is, concepts of God are drawn from creatures. Hence, they name God through their concepts of creatures. These names carry an experientially derived meaning, yet, through causal reasoning, they transcend the limitations of the beings of experience. The concepts and judgments they signify do apply to God, and a recognition of their limitation allows them to point beyond to the mystery they cannot encompass.[12]

A further advantage of treating of names rather than of attributes is that the personal character of God shows through the names more clearly than through the attributes. As we shall see, almost every name makes sense only if it refers to someone who has the perfection of what we call personality. We will see God as an intelligent, loving agent whom we will want to know and love in a personal way.

Finally, since names correspond to knowledge, the names which may be philosophically formed for God correspond to the ways in which He may be philosophically known. There are names, therefore, which express the relationship of the beings of experience to their cause and names which signify something of what that cause is in itself apart from its relationship to its effects. The former may be referred to as the "relative" names of God, and they include such names as First Cause, Creator, Power, Presence, Providence, Justice, Mercy.[13] Names which signify what God is apart from any

---

[12] J. Collins, *God in Modern Philosophy* (Chicago: Henry Regnery Co., 1959), pp. 308–403.

[13] See *Summa Theologiae,* I, 13, 7. St. Thomas indicates that these names signify the relation which is in creatures in regard to God, not a relation which is in God in regard to creatures. The reason for this distinction is that Thomas implies dependence whenever he speaks of real relation in this context.

relationship to creatures may be referred to as "absolute" names, and they are of two kinds: those which signify what He is not and those which signify what He is. The first of these, the negative absolute names, correspond to the knowledge of God by way of negation.[14] They signify His total "otherness," negating any limitation in God—whether it be limitation to time, space, or any particular mode of existence whatever. Such names, therefore, as Uncaused, Immense, Immutable, Eternal, One, Simple, Infinite, are negative names.

The affirmative absolute names which affirm what God is, for example, Being, Truth, Beauty, Goodness, present the greatest problem for human understanding. Yet it is possible to name God in this way, however inadequately, because of what has already been seen: the effects of any cause have a likeness to their cause. God's effects are infinitely removed from Him in similarity, yet their perfections do reflect the perfection of their cause. Thus, goodness, as our example has shown, cannot be in creatures if it is not first in their cause. Still it is limited in creatures and unlimited in their cause. This is why the meaning of any affirmative name of God must be purified by negation, the removal of any notion of limitation or imperfection, so that it may apply to God by way of excellence.[15] These names, therefore, need not be mere metaphors, however far short of God they fall. They apply to Him properly and substantially. Nor are they mere synonyms, but each carries a portion of the fullness of meaning in the perfection of God.[16] Finally, since these names derive from creatures and signify a meaning that is somewhat

---

[14] See page 151.

[15] See *Summa Theologiae,* I, 13, 2 and 3.

[16] In examining the question of whether or not these affirmative absolute names are to be only metaphorically applied to God, St. Thomas distinguishes between names signifying "pure" and "mixed" perfections. "Pure" perfections are perfections found in creatures in a limited form, but perfections which are not in themselves necessarily to be understood as including limitation in their very notion. "Mixed" perfections, on the contrary, are those perfections such as materiality, and so forth, which include imperfection in their very meaning. Pure perfections may be predicated of God substantially and properly; mixed perfections may be predicated of God only metaphorically. See *Summa Theologiae,* I, 13, 3.

the same and somewhat different when applied to creatures and to God, they are all analogous when predicated of God.[17]

It is not possible in an introductory study of metaphysics such as this to consider all the philosophical names of God. Some few which are perhaps central, which will make possible a continuing effort to hold in perspective the vast polarities of being, and which will be of greatest help in deepening insight into the beings of experience, will be looked at separately. Of the relative names, some consideration will be given first of all to the two names which fill out the meaning of First Cause: *Creator* and *Presence.* Later we will examine the name *Providence* to some extent in the context of activity. From an understanding of these names we can reach an incipient understanding of all the relative names, and so attain at least a glimpse-through to the relatedness of man and the world to God.

Of the negative names, *Immutable* and *Eternal* have been selected for discussion to give perspective to our understanding of becoming and time. We will not treat the other negative names separately but our general discussion of the names of God should clarify them so that in the end we attain at least some idea of the pure transcendence of the divine being.

Finally, we will consider in this chapter just one of the affirmative absolute names, *Being,* the first from which the rest unfold. The names *Truth, Goodness,* and *Beauty* will be studied in our consideration of the "transcendentals," which indicate the universal breadth of the participation in them by the limited beings of our experience.

Since our purpose in discussing the names of God is to help us to reach a fuller understanding of the meaning of God, we will not be rigid in restricting these names to the categories in which we have originally placed them. There is a certain arbitrariness in the choice of categories for the names of God since there are numerous ways of categorizing the names which philosophy can give to God.

---

[17] St. Thomas discusses the synonymity of these names in *Summa Theologiae,* I, 13, 4. See also *In I Sententiarum,* d.2, q.1, art. 3. He makes here the point that not only the limitation of the human intellect but the fullness of the divine perfection allows for many concepts signifying the one reality which is God. On the question of the analogous predication of these names, see *Summa Theologiae,* I, 13, 5. For a further discussion of analogy, see pages 227–35.

Although all are perhaps helpful, we have chosen the categories of relative and absolute, affirmative and negative, simply because they seem to represent as satisfactorily as any the different ways in which we can know and name God's being in Himself and His being for us. But the full meaning of each name comes only in the context of them all—so that the First Cause is an all-powerful creative cause, present in the created world, provident with the justice of mercy. Furthermore, the creative activity of the First Cause comes forth from and effects existence, truth, goodness, and beauty—and this wisely, in love and joy. Finally what is created is a limited and temporal, multiple and sometimes spatial, participation in the uncaused, unchanging, eternal, one, simple, absolute, infinite, Being, Truth, Goodness, and Beauty.

We can group the names as follows. The names with an asterisk are those which we will discuss in succeeding pages.

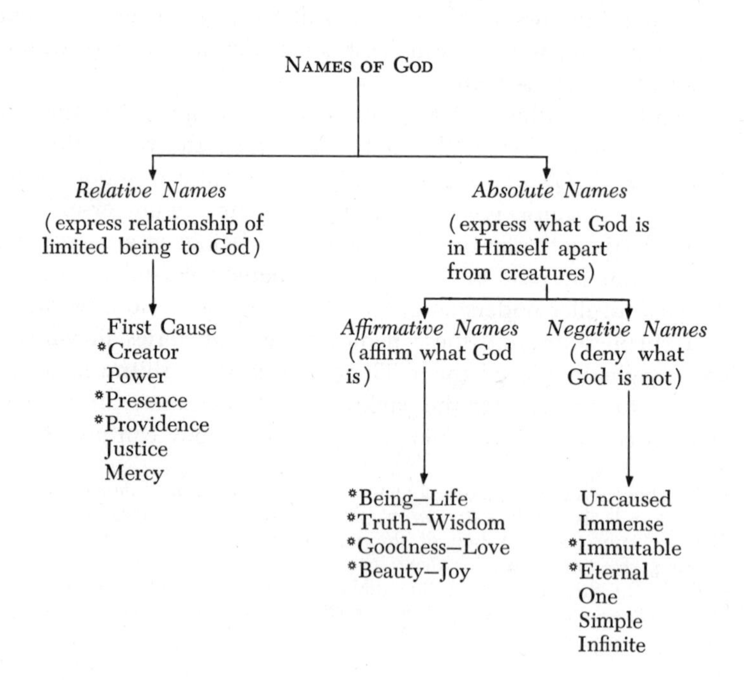

LIMITED BEINGS IN RELATION TO GOD: THE NAME "CREATOR"

We have seen that we can know more than the bare fact that God is, and so we must look into the nature of the bond which relates ourselves and all the world to God. For it is in this relationship between us and God that we will have to learn more about God. We know that God is the First Cause of all limited being. We know, too, that all limited beings are wholly dependent upon their First Cause for what they have of existence. We could express this by saying that the ground of all finite being is in the First Cause, Pure Existence. The relationship of the grounded to the ground, between the caused finite being and the uncaused First Cause of being has long been called the relationship of creature to Creator.

What is implied in our understanding of First Cause is perhaps not self-evident, and what is rendered explicit by the name "Creator" does not perhaps always remain explicit. Contemporary concern for the "loosening of the ontological bond which unites each particular being to Being in its fullness" and consequently for "a humanity which has broken, or thinks it has broken, its ontological moorings,"[18] reflects the fact that the ground of being is not found by all in a First Cause and that the meaning of finite existence is not then always characterized as being-created. One of the philosophical positions which "breaks" these moorings, however, serves to throw light on the meaning of the moorings themselves. The atheistic existentialism which recognizes the absurdity of man's existence apart from any ground for his being points to the ultimate source and end of existence in nothingness. "The Encounter initiating crisis is not an encounter with God who discovers our Nothingness but with Nothingness as the vacuum left by the nonexistent God as in Sartre, or the absent God as in Heidegger."[19] It is this very concern with nothingness that provides a context within which to understand by contrast the philosophical meaning of creation.

---

[18] G. Marcel, *Homo Viator*, trans. E. Craufurd (Chicago: Henry Regnery Co., 1951). See Gateway Paperback edition, pp. 210–11.

[19] H. Kuhn, *Encounter with Nothingness* (Chicago: Henry Regnery Co., 1949), p. xix.

It is consistent to say that beings grounded in nothingness are absurd, but it is not consistent to accept absurdity in reality as well as in understanding as a ground for anything but nothingness. If a being is ultimately grounded in nothingness, it is not only absurd, it does not exist. But if it is, all that it is must ultimately be grounded in whatever grounds its very existence. And our examination of causality has indicated that the existence of the world of our experience does have a ground, namely, Pure Existence.

Traditionally the meaning of "to create" has been defined in terms of calling forth and fashioning "out of nothing" *ex nihilo*. This abyss of nothingness is perhaps even more radical than the abyss postulated by those who ground human existence in a nothingness beyond which there is no Creator. At least for those who originally coined the terms, "to create" and "out of nothing" meant just what they say, not-out-of-something. For those who inherit these terms, there is, of course, the danger that the "nothing" can be imagined as a vague something out of which comes something else; but the "nothing" means still precisely that: "no thing at all." [20]

However meaningful or absurd may be the existence of men or of any other beings in our experience, they do exist. And we have seen, so long as they exist they exist only as caused. If, as we have come to understand, they are caused in their act of existing, then, as we shall see more explicitly now, they are totally caused, that is, their whole being, with nothing at all presupposed except the causal power of the First Cause, is caused to be. This is what it means to say that they are created "out of nothing."

What is rendered explicit in now naming the First Cause "Creator" is the causing "out of nothing." Perhaps this is better when put positively as a causing which is total. If God, the First Cause, is the cause of the act of existing in a being, then He is the cause of that being totally, completely, wholly. Everything in a being is real by reason of its act of existing. Thus, whoever or whatever causes the act of existing in the being causes the being integrally, absolutely. There can be no part nor aspect of the being which is not caused to be by the cause of its existence, and which is not being held in

---

[20] See *Summa Theologiae,* I, 45, 1.

being so long as the existence of that being is radically dependent upon its cause.[21]

It may not be immediately apparent why the cause of the act of existing in a being is necessarily the cause of the total being. Our difficulties in understanding why whoever gives existence gives the whole being sometimes stem from a mistaken view of the act of existence as something spatial, a point, a *locus,* in the being. But just as the soul is not spatially located in one part of the body but informs the whole body, contains the whole body, makes the whole body to be alive and to be a human body, so the act of existing makes the whole being be. Wherever there is reality, there it is, and where it is not there is no reality of that being. Thus it is said that the cause which causes the act of existing causes everything in the being, its constituent principles, even its activity. Creation, therefore, is an all-encompassing causality, a causality which reaches to the depths of each being caused, and from the depths to the breadth and height, causing it absolutely, "out of nothing."

A distinction is sometimes made between creation and "conservation," the former signifying the beginning of a being's existence, the latter its continuance in existence. In fact, the causality referred to is the same. Whether two terms are used or only one, the causality indicated is the complete causality which gives being to a limited being, holding it from the abyss of nothingness so that it is in a sense newly caused at every moment of its existence. Such a conception of creation is not necessarily at odds with the maturing insight into the beings of experience which is offered by the natural sciences or any other branch of knowledge. There is no reason why it cannot apply whether creation is seen as evolutive or static—indeed, whether it is one or the other raises a different question which demands different evidence. But in either case, the creative causality of God is total, accounting for whatever there is in created being, evolving or otherwise. What there is of evolution in the world is no less the effect of God's creative activity than is anything else in the world.

The name, therefore, which signifies God as He causes totally every other being and every aspect of being is the name "Creator."

---

[21] *Ibid.,* I, 44, 2.

LIMITED BEINGS IN RELATION TO GOD: THE NAME "ALL PRESENCE"

An effect here and now present means causality here and now present. Present causality means here and now a present cause. Creation permeated with causality is creation permeated with a presence. Contemporary man concerned with man, concerned with the meaning of human life and personality, has looked long and hard at the meaning of presence in human existence and destiny. Philosophers speak of the presence of one person to another, the presence of things to persons, presence with and presence for, presence ultimately to an Absolute Presence, to the Eternal Thou, to God. We can see what it means for God to be called "Presence" if we look more closely at the relationship which obtains between creatures and their First Cause.

Once again, however, a name which has been passed down from generation to generation may not hold the explicit fullness of meaning which it once signified. To make sure that we appreciate the full meaning of "presence" we shall take advantage of the insights gained through contemporary considerations of this idea and work out the meaning of "presence" before we turn to questions of the presence and manner of presence of the First Cause.

The meaning of "presence" may be caught partially, at least, by comparing the many ways in which it appears in our everyday language, all of which basically mean "someone or something being somewhere." Ordinary notions of presence are drawn from material things, where one thing is present to another when it is spatially close to or in contact with it or when it is in view of or exercising some influence on the other. Thus, for example, two peas are present in the same pod, and all the students in the classroom are said to be present there with one another even though the substance of each one is in a different part of space.

Presence is understood, too, in terms of power, as for example, when a ruler is said to be present in his whole kingdom by his power. Similarly, immaterial things are said to be present somewhere when their power is brought to bear in that place, as the soul is in the body wherever it activates the body.[22] A being is said to be "essentially" present, present according to its essence or substance, when

[22] See *Summa Contra Gentiles,* III, 68, n. 3.

its whole being is in some particular place, as for example, a student is in that particular part of the room which is occupied by his body.

Presence is used to apply to conscious experience. We are said to be present to ourselves when we are aware of ourselves in some way. We are present to another, or the other is present to us, when we have this awareness in knowledge and in love. We speak of things or persons as being present to our thoughts or present in our hearts. Things feared and dreaded, or things eagerly anticipated and fondly remembered, are said to be "with" us, present to us. Contemporary thinkers such as Gabriel Marcel and Martin Buber have an intense interest in personal presence in community and communion, the openness of one being to another, the availability and responsibility of one for another.[23] There is, finally, a kind of preconscious presence, an ontological union in being, which underlies every other meaning of presence. But since it is not found in our experience in the way the other presences are, we will postpone our discussion of it until we consider the notion of "participation" in being,[24] and until we discuss love in Chapter 11.

Having these meanings of presence, however, is not enough. We must decide whether any or all of them apply in the relationship between the beings of experience and their cause. Beginning only with the knowledge that this relationship is causal, a certain kind of presence can be discovered. It has already been seen [25] that causal activity takes place in the patient, in the effect. To this we may add the observation that an agent, a cause, is always joined to its immediate effect.[26] The immediate effect of the First Cause is the

---

[23] For the notion of presence as it applies to divine presence, see, for example, G. Marcel, *The Mystery of Being, I, Reflection and Mystery,* trans. G. Fraser (Chicago: Henry Regnery Co., 1960), pp. 187–209; and *Creative Fidelity,* trans. R. Rosthal (New York: The Noonday Press, 1964), p. 36. See also M. Buber, *I and Thou,* pp. 110–11.

[24] See pages 233–35.

[25] See page 97.

[26] That an agent is joined to its immediate effect can be clarified in experience. When a picture is painted the artist does not perhaps touch the canvas with his hand, but he does touch the brush; and the movement of the brush is his immediate effect. There is even a sense in which it is the movement of his hand, or something even prior to that, which is his immediate effect. When causes are spoken of as acting "at a distance," this does not belie the fact that every cause is joined to its immediate effect; what it does is require a clarification of what is meant by immediate effect and what is meant by "at a distance." See, for example, James Tallarico, "Action at a Distance," *The Thomist,* XXV (April 1962), 252–92.

existence of the beings of experience, and thereby their total reality. It follows, therefore, that the First Cause, God, is present to every being, joined directly to each as cause is joined to effect. As long as the being has being, God is present to it. In St. Thomas' words, "Now, since God is being itself by His own essence, created being must be His proper effect; as to ignite is the proper effect of fire. But God causes this effect in things not only when they first begin to be, but as long as they are preserved in being; as light is caused in the air by the sun as long as the air remains illuminated. Therefore, as long as a thing has being, so long must God be present to it, according to its mode of being. But being is innermost in each thing and most fundamentally present within all things, since it is formal in respect of everything found in a thing. Hence it must be that God is in all things and innermostly." [27]

It is for this reason that St. Thomas has maintained that God is present in all things by His power and by His essence.[28] Since all things are subject to His power, His presence to them extends as far as His causality. Since there is no composition in God,[29] wherever He is present He is present wholly, present essentially.[30] For God there can be no such thing as acting at any distance, even "at arm's length." He is wholly, substantially, wherever He is. And wherever He is He is acting. He is, therefore, wholly present in every being.

The presence of God in and to His effects which we see, the beings of experience, is not to be understood as a material presence, since God is not a material being.[31] On the other hand, this presence is not to be considered in a way that is inferior to the closest possible material presence. For in the last analysis, being materially joined to another being demands that one still be outside the other. The union or presence is still external. But the presence of God to His effects is not subject to the limitations of material presence. It

---

[27] *Summa Theologiae,* I, 8, 1.
[28] See *ibid.,* 3 and 4.
[29] See page 127.
[30] Presence by essence, as seen above, means substantial presence of one's own whole being; where one's whole being is.
[31] Although the immateriality of God has not been explicitly considered yet, it follows from the fact that in God there is no composition, no limitation, no potency. Material beings are constituted, as has been seen, by a composition in the order of essence.

is not the presence of material contact, but it is for that reason a more, not a less, intimate presence.

There is a third kind of presence attributed to God, that presence whereby things are present to Him in His knowledge and love. Since this is the presence of a personal God, we cannot discuss it in terms of what we have seen about God the First Cause, for we have not shown that He is a person, capable of knowledge and love, capable of having all things present to Himself and of rendering Himself present to the persons He constitutes in being. This is why we must return to the name "Presence" later when the presence of God as a personal being can be seen, and when perhaps all metaphysics can be summed up in the understanding that for limited being to be is to be known and loved by God.[32]

There is, however, one more insight which we can gain even at this point: God's presence to all things is an intimate, innermost presence, and this precisely because it is the act of existing which He causes. The act of existing is what is innermost in each thing. God is therefore at the heart of every being. He is, in a most metaphysical sense, "more intimate to each thing than its own self." Yet, because He causes the other's existence as other, He is fully present without being part of the being He causes, nor His effect being part of Him. St. Thomas has said, "God is essentially present in all things, not however, in such a way that He is mixed with them as a part of anything . . . the act of being of each thing, and each of its parts, comes immediately from God, since . . . only God creates. Now to create is to give the act of being . . . the cause of the act of being cannot cease from the operation by which that act is given without the consequence that the thing itself ceases to be. . . . Suppress any given efficient cause and its effect is suppressed. . . . From all these ideas we may gather that God is intimately present to each thing, in the same way as the act of being proper to each thing is immediately present to it; for the thing cannot begin to be or endure without the activity of God, through which God is joined to what He does so as to be present in it." [33]

Etienne Gilson, in commenting on this aspect of the relationship

---

[32] See pages 260–61, 267–69, 284–86.

[33] *In I Sententiarum,* d.38, q.1, a.1. See also *Summa Theologiae,* I, 8, 1; I, 4, 1 ad 3; and I, 7, 1.

between creature and Creator, points to the statement, "God is present in all things," as a true metaphysical proposition, and says of it, "There is no more important and central notion than this one in the doctrine of Thomas Aquinas."[34] Although it is a metaphysical proposition in a proper sense, Gilson notes also its theological and religious significance: ". . . a truth that places man, along with the whole world, in the constant presence of God, or rather . . . a truth that turns man into a God-inhabited being living in a God-inhabited world."[35] It is this truth that is contained in the name, "Presence."

GOD IN HIMSELF: ABSOLUTE BEING

Knowledge of God in relation to His effects not only leads inevitably to a need for knowledge of Him as He is in Himself, apart from any relation to creatures, but also prepares the way for knowing Him in Himself, and so we turn from a consideration of the relative names of God to consider an absolute name. When we look at our world constituted by beings, each of which has a limited fullness and limiting emptiness, there blazes forth the testimony acceptable to reason of a being whose activity and presence constantly and gloriously hold them away from nothingness, a being who is totally other because He is an unlimited fullness with no part of emptiness. The perfection of all perfections in every limited being is totally accounted for by a being whose perfection is not received, needs no accounting for, is boundless in its transcendence. To be, for limited beings, is to receive existence from Pure Existence. To be, for God, is just to be, simply and absolutely.

The first affirmative absolute name, then, which expresses what the First Cause is in Himself, not just in relation to creatures, is the name "Being." But if the question "What, after all, does it mean to be?" does not give a completely illuminating answer when asked of finite being, how shall there be any illumination when the answer is sought in the inaccessible heights and depths of infinite being?

In one sense, we have already discussed the name "Being," for

---

[34] *Elements of Christian Philosophy,* p. 180.
[35] *Ibid.,* p. 181.

we have seen that God is Pure Existence. It is doubtful that anything more can be said to fill out its meaning than has already been said in Chapter 5. In arriving at the discovery of Pure Existence through our probing of finite existence, it has already become clear that the First Cause must be uncaused. And the only kind of being that could be uncaused is a being with no composition, with no potency conjoined to its act, with no distinction between existence and essence, and hence a being that is Pure Act, Pure Existence. This is what is signified in the name "Being," the name which St. Thomas, at least, thinks to be the proper name of God.[36]

He refers us to Exodus 3:14, where Moses asks God what He should be called and receives the answer that His name is: *I am who am.* St. Augustine had used the same text in a similar way.[37] Contemporary Scripture scholars do not generally agree that the text is meant to give us God's nature or essence, as St. Thomas interprets it. However, the name, I AM WHO AM, the Hebrew YHWH, was a symbol accorded great reverence among the Jews. It was never pronounced YAHWEH as it is written, but either JEHOVAH (Lord) or simply NAME. The Tetragrammaton (four-lettered: YHWH) was a name known only to the high priests, transmitted from one to another. It has been interpreted as meaning that no one has the right to know God's name, as Pure Existence, with St. Thomas, and as signifying God's presence to man.[38]

Whether St. Thomas' interpretation is the literal meaning of I AM WHO AM, or not, is not the important issue. The text dramatizes the identity between Absolute Being or Existence and the God of the Judaeo-Christian revelation, and so it is certainly a valid application of the text. "Absolute Being," however, is so compact that we will have to unfold it as best we can in terms of Life, Truth, Goodness, and Beauty. The first of these we shall treat in Chapter 8, the others in Chapters 10 and 11, when we discuss the transcendentals.

---

[36] See *Summa Theologiae,* I, 13, 11; and I, 4, 1 and 2.
[37] *De Civitate Dei,* V, c.2, n. 3.
[38] See *A Gilson Reader,* ed. A. Pegis (Garden City, N.Y.: Image Books, 1957), pp. 192–93; see also M. Bourke, "Yahweh, the Divine Name," in *The Bridge,* III, ed. J. Oesterreicher (New York: Pantheon Books, Inc., 1958), 271–87.

SUGGESTED READINGS

Bourke, Myles M., "Yahweh, the Divine Name," *The Bridge,* ed. J. M. Oesterreicher, III, 271–87. New York: Pantheon Books, Inc., 1958.

Buber, Martin, *Eclipse of God,* Chapters 3 and 4. New York: Harper & Row, Publishers, Inc., 1957. On the disparity of philosophy and religion, and of the God of philosophy and the God of faith.

———, *I and Thou,* Part 3. New York: Charles Scribner's Sons, 1958. I-Thou understood in relation to the Eternal Thou.

Collins, James, *God in Modern Philosophy,* pp. 398–409. Chicago: Henry Regnery Co., 1959. On the nature of a true philosophy of God.

Daniélou, Jean, *God and the Ways of Knowing,* trans. Walter Roberts, Chapter 2. Cleveland, Ohio: The World Publishing Company (Meridian Books), 1957. Concerning philosophical knowledge of God.

Gilson, Etienne, *Elements of Christian Philosophy,* pp. 104–11 (on knowledge of God); Chapter 7 (on creation); pp. 137–45 (on the problem of naming God); pp. 178–83 (on the divine presence). New York: Doubleday & Company, Inc., 1960.

de Lubac, Henri, *The Discovery of God,* trans. A. Dru, Chapter 4. New York: P. J. Kenedy & Sons, 1960. On man's knowledge of God.

Marcel, Gabriel, *The Mystery of Being, I. Reflection and Mystery,* trans. G. Fraser, pp. 187–209. Chicago: Henry Regnery Co., 1960. On the divine presence.

Pieper, Josef, *The Silence of St. Thomas,* trans. John Murray, and Daniel O'Connor, Part II. New York: Pantheon Books, Inc., 1957. Treats of knowledge of God by way of negation; the meaning of creation.

St. Thomas Aquinas, *Summa Contra Gentiles,* I, 32–34 (on naming God).

———, *Summa Theologiae,* I, 4, 2 and 3; I, 12, 4 and 11–12 (on the names of God); I, 13, 11 (on Being); I, 8, 1 and 3 (on presence); I, 44; I, 45, 1–5 (on creation).

Tillich, Paul, "Two Types of Philosophy of Religion," in *Classi-*

cal and Contemporary Readings in the Philosophy of Religion, ed. J. Hick, pp. 387–98. Englewood Cliffs, N.J.: Prentice-Hall, Inc., 1964. Tillich contrasts the "ontological" and "cosmological" methods in a philosophical approach to God, pointing to the ontological as the key to uniting philosophy and religion.

7 BEING AND BECOMING

INTRODUCTION

There is something about the view of finite beings in the concrete which suggests that the explanation of their being which has been given in the previous chapters does not yet give an adequate picture of their existential reality. At least there is something else given in the experience of being which has not yet been accounted for except briefly and in passing at the end of Chapter 3. The structure of finite beings, even seen as throbbing with the causality of God, may appear to be a static manifestation of a static reality. But even a brief glance at the beings of experience shows that they are anything but static. Being reveals itself as dynamic, as changing and being changed, acting and reacting, vibrant, and even fruitful.

The phenomenon of change alone requires us to take another look at the explanation of being. Everything in experience seems constantly to be in flux, coming into and going out of being, gaining and losing, always becoming something other than it was. How can there be an explanation of what it means "to be" in a world where everything becomes and nothing ever fully is? How can a thing be and yet not be; be what it is and become what it is not? A changing universe may call for a changing understanding of being. One thing is certain, an explanation of being which ignores its dynamic aspect, its "dynamism" [1] can be nothing but an artificially constructed theory which will serve ultimately to falsify our knowledge of being.

Beings which become while they continue to exist, a universe that continues to exist while beings come and go, beings that come and never go—all these place the problem of being in a world of time. And if time is somehow bound up with the fabric of the beings of experience, it, too, must shed some light on a true understanding of reality. This description of the world involves two things: activity and becoming. Activity does not present itself as necessarily identical with change, nor change as necessarily identical with activity. Consequently, if we attempt to understand change or activity only as it effects change, we will not discover the full meaning of activity in its relation to being.

Any study of the significance of activity raises so many questions about the beings which are acting that no discussion of being can be in any way complete without a discussion of activity. Existing beings are acting beings, and the mystery of action lies at the heart of the mystery of being. Activity may reveal being, but it does so by revealing something of itself within being, giving its light within the light of being, and showing itself forth in an epiphany of being.

If activity reveals itself as a pure perfection, rooted in the existential aspect of being, we must investigate it with relation to the pure existence of absolute being. The poles of reality—finite and infinite—infinitely different, but intimately related, must somehow fit into our understanding of being. If a being which becomes cannot fully be, absolute being cannot become, cannot change, cannot be in a world of time because its fullness of being precludes the modifica-

---

[1] The use of the word "dynamism" in our discussion is not to be confused with eighteenth- and nineteenth-century theories of materialistic dynamism, nor to be identified with twentieth-century doctrines. It refers simply to the tendential aspect of limited beings. For some general background see J. de Finance, *Etre et Agir, passim* and J. M. Henri-Rousseau, "L'être et l'agir," *Revue Thomiste,* LIII (1953), 488–531; LIV (1954), 85–118.

tions which these imply. But even though absolute being cannot change, if the cause and effect relationship between God and creatures is as total as it has been seen to be, then God's causality will permeate activity as it permeates being. Once we say this, we raise the centuries-old questions once more for ourselves in today's world, for each of us needs to know whose activity he performs, whose life he lives, whose freedom he exercises, or to what necessity he bows. If God is First Cause, is there any second cause? If all being and activity come from God, can man have any true activity or any true freedom? We can answer these questions only when we understand the nature of becoming and activity in created beings.

Change, time, dynamism, activity, and freedom on the one hand, and infinite Life, Eternity, and Providence on the other, will help us to understand the total reality of being. What we have elaborated in our previous chapters has truly opened being for us; the questions we are now raising and the answers we are now trying to give must confirm and deepen the sense of direction already achieved.

THE PROBLEM OF CHANGE

That things change is a fundamental fact of experience. A child grows into a man, a leaf changes from green to scarlet, man is happy and then sad, a student learns and forgets, an animal lives and then dies. How is such instability in being to be explained? How, and indeed why, do existing beings, which have the actuality of their individual and specific natures and all that is necessary for them to exist, add a further actualization, add a new kind of being to what they already are?

Since reality presents itself as changing, it makes sense to raise the question of change and its meaning. It is not at all surprising that the men who began to probe the darkness and mystery into which being stretches should wonder first about the fleeting nature of reality, the fragmented existence of the beings around them and of their own being. The constantly changing reality around us is like a rushing torrent and our attempts to understand it are sometimes like trying to hold a torrent in the cup of one's hand. Almost immediately, of course, it overflows our hands and splashes around us.

Since change is so fundamental in our experience, it is not surprising that some have thought that it was the most ultimate of all things in reality. Heraclitus, as we have seen,[2] conceived of our world in this way. In fact he and similar thinkers were convinced that change is real and that being, in its static permanence, is unreal. Reality, therefore, is the flux, becoming, and conflict, and many accept it as the explanation of all things, the point beyond which explanations cannot go. This view of reality is by no means merely naïve; since the time of the ancient Greeks many thinkers have accepted it as the true picture of our world. Today, for example, dialectical materialism, in which the universe is understood to be a complex of processes in which things have only the appearance of stability, continues the Heraclitean tradition. Thus Friedrich Engels says: "The world is not to be comprehended as a complex of ready-made things, but as a complex of processes, in which things apparently stable . . . go through an uninterrupted change of coming into being and passing away." [3]

It is important to realize that change poses some real problems. Having already seen that the ultimate reality in a being is the act of existing and that Pure Existence is the source of all limited beings, we may be tempted to ask the questions of change in an unauthentic way. Our questions may seem already answered by what we have seen and we might seem only to pretend to find a serious difficulty where there is none in an artificial attempt to stimulate academic curiosity. We must not assume too quickly that all the answers are ready and waiting in a prefabricated explanation of being. We must ask indeed how beings with so stable a structure as discovered in Chapter 3 can change, change constantly, and change so radically. We must inquire, too, how in our own personal lives we remain who and what we are and yet continue to change, to become, in so essential a way that our very consent to our own lives depends on our continued changing and becoming.

Although the experience of change cannot of itself deny the discoveries already made in regard to the constituent principles of

---

[2] See pages 40–41.

[3] From his *Ludwig Feuerbach,* Chapter 4; quoted in M. Cornforth, *Dialectical Materialism,* 2nd ed. (London: Lawrence & Wishart, Ltd., 1955), I, 48.

finite being, it can make us take a new metaphysical look at our procedure of discovery. If the original conclusions appear still valid, change must somehow be intelligible, not in spite of, but perhaps because of, what we know about being. We must, therefore, render change intelligible, and if its explanation is already contained within our understanding of being, we must show explicitly that this is so and not rest content with only an implicit explanation.

We must first ask what is given in the experience of change. What happens when something becomes other than it was? Obviously, there is some kind of "transition from one mode of being to another." Something remains and something passes. A man's hair turns grey with age. If he is lucky, there is only a change in color—the hair remains, but the color changes. A man dies; his body changes from a human body to a corpse. Something in the body remains, but something very radically changes. A seed grows into a beautiful flower. In this there is no mere substitution of a full-grown plant for a seed. Rather something in the seed remains but something also changes. All the beauty now in the flower was not first in the seed.

We can summarize these facts of experience by giving the three basic situations in change: (1) something may be added; (2) something may be taken away; or (3) something may be added and something taken away. We may diagram this:

$x \longrightarrow xy$ (something added)
$xy \longrightarrow x$ (something taken away)
$xy \longrightarrow xz$ (something taken away, something added)

In each instance of change there must be something in the result which was in the beginning—otherwise there would not be change but substitution. In substitution, of course, we remove one thing, for example, billiard ball *A* from a table, and replace it with something else, for example, with billiard ball *B*. This is quite different from changing the color of billiard ball *A* to a new color. To have change there must be something which persists before, during, and after the change. Properly speaking, without such a beginning, middle, and end there is no change. Where there is no starting point, as in creation, what happens can be called change only improperly. The same is true in cases in which there is no true ending point, as would happen if something were annihilated, that is, simply dropped out of existence. In such cases, nothing carries through as the "subject" of the change. If in every change, therefore, something remains and something is added or taken away, two "principles of being" must be involved. The principle of being, as we have seen, is a special kind of "part" of being.[4]

One of these principles will be the "subject" of the change which can be determined in different ways (for example, a man's hair can change from black to grey, and a woman's can change from almost any color to any other color). The other "principle" must be the particular determination or determinations which are added or taken away (for example, the black, grey, and other colors of one's hair). We can describe these two "principles" in terms of potency and act. The principle which we call the subject (which can receive the determinations) is a potential principle. It has the capacity to exist in one way before the change and in another way after the change, as the hair mentioned above exists as black before the change and as grey after the change. With respect to the various colors the hair is considered potency. The instances of the other principle, here the colors, are actual determinations and actual principles, which make the hair actually be this or that color. In this context, therefore, color is act with reference to the hair, which we have just said is potency. We can conclude from this description that changing being reveals itself as composed of potency and act. We can summarize this discussion with the following chart.

EVERY CHANGE REQUIRES TWO PRINCIPLES:
ONE POTENTIAL, ONE ACTUAL

Something remains throughout the change.	Something is added and/or taken away.
What remains is a continuing subject which is *capable* of different determinations.	What comes or goes is an actual determination, an *actualization* of the potency.
A principle which is a "capacity" for determination is a *potential* principle.	A principle which is an "actualization" of a determination is an *actual* principle.
Hence, change demands a principle which is *Potency.*	Hence, change demands a principle which is *Act.*

[4] See Chapter 3, note 14.

In change, therefore, either a potential in a being becomes actualized, an actualized possibility returns to a state of potency, or both, that is, a subject loses one actuality and gains another. In other words, the subject of change receives an act which it did not have, loses an act which it did have, or exchanges one act for another. We must be careful to avoid confusion here. The facts which we are discussing are fairly simple, so that if we are careful in our use of terminology, especially in our use of the term "subject of change," we should have little trouble. Part of the difficulty arises because we use subjective change in connection with two sets of terms: act and potency, and "being in act" and "being in potency." Strictly speaking, when we refer to the subject of change we are referring to that which continues through the change, and which loses and/or receives the actual determinations. Some of the difficulty arises because we are talking of two kinds of subjects. Some subjects can exist without a given determination and then receive the determination, as a bush may exist in the winter without leaves and then in the spring develop leaves. Other subjects must have some determination to exist at all and so must exchange one determination for another in change, as in the case of a leaf, which must have some color but which changes from green to red in the fall. We must keep our discussion general enough to include cases similar to both of these.

When in the context of change we speak of act and potency, the act we are considering is the actual determination (the leaves on the branch or the color in the leaves, in our examples) which a given subject receives. The branch without leaves or the leaf considered apart from its color is the subject, or potency, which receives the actualization. Thus, when we speak of act and potency, we sharply distinguish between the subject and the determination or actualization which it receives. In speaking of being-in-act and being-in-potency the situation is a little different. When in the context of change we speak of something "being in act," we are referring to the subject *with* its determination: the branch with the leaves, the leaf with the particular color. When we speak of something as "being in potency," we are referring to something which can receive a determination which it does not now have. This includes subjects which will not lose a determination in order to gain a new determination (the branch which will receive the leaves), and subjects with determinations which they must exchange for the new determination (the green leaf which will become red). The branch and the green leaf can both be described as "being in potency." We must be careful, however, to realize to what they are in potency. The branch is in potency to having new leaves, the green leaf is in potency to becoming a red leaf. From a different point of view, both the branch and the green leaf can be considered as being in act, since the branch has the actual determination of being a branch and the green leaf has the actual determination of being a green leaf.

Furthermore, since there can be a series of changes following upon one another, the terminal point of one change can be the beginning point of another, so that in looking at any stage in these series of changes we must ask ourselves whether we are looking at it as the result of a previous change or as the beginning point for a new change. Like the midpoint in a journey which is terminus for the first half of the trip and starting point for the second half of the trip, a given stage in a series of changes must be considered as "being in act" with reference to the actual determination as received from a previous change and as "being in potency" to the determinations it will receive from the next change. These distinctions will become clearer as we apply them to the two kinds of changes, accidental change and substantial change.

Accidental Change

When a child becomes a man, or a green leaf becomes red, or a dog barks and then is silent, a change occurs within a given being which does not bring about a new being with a new essence. The man is the same person the child was, the red leaf is the same leaf that was green, the silent dog is the same dog which barked. What changes is not the essential nature of the being (man, leaf, dog) but an accidental characteristic which modifies the being and its nature. Abraham Lincoln was Abraham Lincoln when he was three months old and when he was thirty years old; yet the change over thirty years was so great that if we had no experience of seeing the child grow to manhood, we would hardly accept the fact that this was indeed the same being—the same permanent self, the same permanent existing human nature, the same permanent substance, which endures but which also undergoes a true and profound modification over the minutes and years of constant change.

When in the fall a green leaf becomes red, a change is certainly evident, as we have seen, though not so profound a change as the maturing of a person. The leaf is still a leaf, modified now by a different color. It has a new accidental form, to which before it was only in potency. The difference here is truly a difference, but only in a more superficial and external way. Clearly, however, there is question of a change in the accidental characteristics of the leaf.

When a dog barks and then stops barking, a change occurs—not in the essence of his being, but merely in an accidental way. The "accident" here is different from that in the leaf. Color is a static characteristic; barking is an activity. However, when we are speaking of change, the change from barking to nonbarking is similar to the change in which one loses a characteristic. We are speaking of the same being before and after the change, but this being exists now in an accidentally different way from which it existed before. The dog passes from "being in act," that is, barking, to "being in potency," that is, silent. Something has been taken away ($xy \longrightarrow x$) without changing the essential nature of the being, here the dog.

When we study this kind of change, therefore, it becomes apparent that beings can change in a way in which their substance remains the same substance, but accidental forms or activities change—are lost, gained, or both. We have already seen in Chapter 3 that substance is related to accident, and power to activity, as potency is to act. We can see this relationship more clearly now as we understand that substances can be modified by different accidental forms and that beings can undertake certain activities and so be actualized in different ways. The consequences of this act-potency relationship appear in our everyday experience.

We see that a substance potency sets limits to the kinds of accidents (acts) it may receive. As a potency for accidental form, it is a limiting factor in that it has only a certain capacity for rather definite actualizations. An oak tree is limited to the accidental color and size of an oak tree. It cannot receive the accidental forms which a sunflower is capable of receiving. A human person is limited by his capacities. He cannot receive either the intellectual perfections of an angel nor the power of hearing or smelling that belongs to the essence of a dog. But a human being—or any other being—is limited not only by his essential capacity, inasmuch as he is a particular kind of being, but also in his individual capacity, insomuch as he is this particular individual with his particular history. Thus, as an individual, Peter has not the same individual capacities as does Paul, and *vice versa.* Neither Peter nor Paul, therefore, may be actualized with exactly the same accidental forms as the other; nor may either have exactly the same activities as the other.

We must make one final point concerning accidental change. Since some accidental changes are so obvious, we may be tempted to think of accidental change as we would think of pinning a tail on a donkey or spreading paint on a wall. Accidental forms and activities are not appendages which can be tacked on to a substance or coatings that can be spread over a substance. Rather they truly actualize and so modify the whole substance. One cannot scrape the color off the leaf in the way one can scrape paint off a wall, nor can one extract the changes between the boy and the man and put them in a box like so many coins, nor separate the bark from the dog. These characteristics and activities exist in the substance and cannot exist outside of it. They modify the substance without changing it into a totally new substance. In one sense, they are that which makes substance dynamic and which keeps our world from becoming dead and static. Accidental forms and activities are the key to the process of becoming, which is what makes our world go around.

Substantial Change

When a living being dies, absorbs food, or is divided into two living beings, we are faced with deeper and more radical changes than those accidental modifications which we have just discussed. These changes are so radical that an individual goes out of existence and/or a new individual comes into existence. Yet even in such a change something endures, something carries through the change, something participates in both the old and the new being.

When a man dies, his body ceases to be a human body, and a corpse, or an aggregate of chemicals, results.[5] Somehow there is a

[5] What some philosophers have called an "I know not what."

different being here; it is no longer a man, but something else. Obviously, what made this body a human body is no longer present and something else, that which makes it a corpse or an aggregate of chemicals or whatever being or beings actually is here, has taken its place. In our discussion of the limitation of being, we pointed out that material beings are composed of matter and form. If this is so, and if change means the substitution of one act for another, it should follow that matter is what carries through the change and that substantial form is the act which is lost or gained. As the leaf which was green becomes red, so the matter which was man becomes corpse. And just as the leaf cannot exist without having some color, so matter cannot exist except as man or corpse or something else. In substantial change, therefore, matter as capable of being determined by different substantial forms remains through the change; but after the change it has a new substantial form to which it was only in potency while it was in act by reason of the previous substantial form.[6] This kind of matter, matter as pure determinability, mere substrate for form, has already been named "primary matter."[7]

When a horse eats an apple, the apple ceases to be. It loses its essence and its identity as an apple. Only the horse remains, having absorbed the apple into its being by the process of digestion. Yet the primary matter which was the constituent principle of the apple endures under a new and different substantial form, the form of the horse. There are no longer two beings—apple and horse—but only one, because now there is only one substantial form actualized by one act of existence. The apple is gone, the horse remains. When a

---

[6] There is some reason for thinking that in every instance of substantial change in a material being, a new being results. In other words, there is reason for thinking that no being is simply annihilated; something always remains. Material beings go out of existence because they corrupt; that is, their primary matter loses its substantial form. However, since primary matter itself cannot corrupt—for it has no parts—it is not threatened with decomposition and could go out of being only if, once given existence, this act of existence were totally withdrawn by the First Cause. Since primary matter cannot exist without being informed by some substantial form, on the losing of one form it is informed by another. No being returns totally to nonbeing. Of course, there is always the possibility that God may annihilate, but St. Thomas thinks it unlikely that He would. See *De Potentia,* 5, 3; *Summa Theologiae,* I, 104, 4; and E. Gilson, *Elements of Christian Philosophy* (New York: Doubleday & Company, Inc., 1960), pp. 198 ff.

[7] See pages 71–72.

living being divides into two living beings, as for example, when a worm is cut in half, the original being and a new being exist. The primary matter which originally was determined by only one form is now determined by two.

In these instances of change, therefore, what remains is not the original *substance* itself, but a principle within the substance—primary matter. The three examples given can be diagrammed to illustrate this:

$$\frac{\text{man}}{x} \dashrightarrow \frac{\text{corpse}}{x} \quad \text{or} \quad \frac{\text{man}}{x} \dashrightarrow \frac{\text{element 1}}{x_1} \; \frac{\text{element 2}}{x_2} \; \frac{\text{element 3}}{x_3}$$

$$\frac{\text{horse}}{x_1} + \frac{\text{apple}}{x_2} \dashrightarrow \frac{\text{horse}}{x_1 + x_2}$$

$$\frac{\text{worm 1}}{x_1} \dashrightarrow \frac{\text{worm 1}}{x_1 - x_2} + \frac{\text{worm 2}}{x_2}$$

In each of these changes x represents the principle which has remained throughout the change. This is the primary matter, the determinable principle which can exist as man, corpse, horse, apple, worm, or what have you, once it is actuated by the substantial form of one of these.

It is often extremely difficult to decide whether or not a real substantial change has taken place. However, if in any case a real change in essence occurs, it can be understood as possible only if we say that something still remains and something passes: primary matter remains and substantial form changes. If this is not so we do not have change but only substitution. Since it is substantial form which determines the essence of a being, and since essence is what limits the act of existence to be this kind of act of existence constituting this being, once the substantial form changes,[8] what continues to exist cannot be the same being which existed before. Let us re-

[8] That is, once the substantial form and the essence change, not according to an accidental modification, but so that there is an entirely new substantial form and so an entirely new kind of being, the previous being cannot continue to exist.

peat, we are saying that where one being ceases to be and another being comes into existence there must be substantial change.

We are not saying that we can identify this in every case or even in a majority of the cases. Examples of substantial change are fairly clear in living beings since we are able to identify them as individual beings. The question becomes exceedingly difficult once we begin talking about nonliving beings, precisely because it is extremely difficult, if not impossible, to identify the unit of being in nonliving things. For instance, a stone which one chips off a block of marble is fairly obviously not one being. But in the stone is it the molecules, or the atoms, or the electrons which are the individual beings? Only a foolhardy philosopher would attempt to decide.

Our consideration, therefore, of accidental and substantial change has not proved incompatible with our discoveries about the structure of finite beings. It is, rather, in terms of these principles which constitute being that we have been able to explain change. For when a thing changes, its potency must be actualized in a new way. From this it becomes clear that change can only occur where there is potency. Thus every being subject to change must be a limited, composite being, one which can become other than it is. This is true of all the beings of experience, since all are finite material things.

THE TEMPORALITY OF FINITE BEING

Beings which never fully "are," which are constantly becoming, changing, are beings whose existence is given to them piecemeal, as it were, and in a constant succession. A being which changes has not one static mode of being, but a flowing succession of modes of being, a continuing sequence of befores and afters. Such beings are said to be in time. Time is thus bound up with the fabric of the beings of experience, and has its place in a metaphysical consideration of reality.

What do men mean when they speak of time? Many would answer with St. Augustine, "What is time? I know what it is if no one asks me what it is; but if I want to explain it to someone who has asked me, I find that I do not know." [9] Nevertheless, just as Augus-

---

[9] *Confessions,* XI, 14.

tine became preoccupied with time and temporal becoming, so others have felt the need to seek an understanding of the meaning of a reality which is subject to the limitations and the opportunities of time. The concern of contemporary philosophy and literature bears ample witness to this fascination which the questions of time hold for man.

Whatever else is understood by time, it always involves a before and an after—a past, present, and future. This context implies successive duration, a successive plurality of moments in a being's existence. There is a sense in which only the present is bound up with reality, since the *now* alone is actual. The past was but it is no more; it has no reality save in the mind that remembers. The future does not exist now but it will be at some time; it too has no reality save in the mind which anticipates. But there is another sense in which the past and the future partake in the reality of the present and are taken up within and fulfilled or anticipated in the present. For the meaning of the past can be determined from the present and in a way the meaning of the present carries over into the future. But neither past nor future exists in the way the present does.

The now of the present is actual, but even its actuality is only a flow, a transition from the past to the future, never stationary for an instant, a *nunc fluens*, or "flowing now." Thus, time is associated with change because it is possible to be temporal, in time, only if a being is changeable. Indeed, only where there is change or the possibility of change can there be past, present, and future,[10] and so time—whether it be an abstract concept of time or time concretely existing within being itself. The essential mode of existence of changing beings is a temporal mode.

Philosophers have disagreed about the nature of time itself. It has been considered as if it were only a mental measure with no foundation in reality, an abstract and arbitrary measure of change which divides the duration of changing being into minutes or hours or years. It has been considered, on the other hand, as part and parcel of the very being of changing things, and so not only a reality independent of the mind which measures it, but a reality which

---

[10] For a being capable of change, temporality will appear also as measure of not changing.

can only be distorted by the numbering of minutes, seconds, or centuries which the mind imposes upon it. There are difficulties with either position. On the one hand, time does seem to be stamped into the being of changing things, into the evolving being which carries within itself its own history. It seems more than a mental construct which can merely point to the successive duration in the being which time measures. Yet, on the other hand, there is an arbitrariness about the abstract measures of time, an irrelevance which seems to divorce it from the real world outside of our minds. Thus, for example, to measure two beings by an hour is not to truly indicate the temporality of their existence. One may have changed twice as much as the other in that time. To place the succession of all beings in a framework which measures them all in the same way tends also to distort our understanding of their existence. There are two things to be considered. There is something in being which demands that there be a measuring of change, and at the same time there is something in our measuring of time (to a greater or lesser extent, depending on how one looks at it) which as such is not given in reality. Perhaps, then, time is best understood as having a foundation in reality, and also as being a mental measurement. In a metaphysical study our emphasis is not on the arbitrary aspect of the mental measurement, but with the changing aspect of the temporal being. Temporality as a mode of being confronts us when we attempt to penetrate reality metaphysically.

Each being continues to exist so long as it has being, but it undergoes accidental changes which modify it (accidentally). As long as it is changing accidentally, it has a succession of perfections and activities and is in potency to ever-different actualizations. Thus it is never given all at once. Its duration is successive. Even when beings cease to be, drop out of existence through substantial change, the reality of the universe endures. Scientific hypotheses about the indestructibility of matter in the world indicate that the coming into existence and dropping out of existence which we see in substantial change does not mark a setback in the progressive duration of the total universe.

If substantial beings in the world are continually being actualized, continually becoming, continually stretching out their existence in time because they cannot exist all at once; and if the universe exists as a whole, continuing in being not as a thing in itself separate from the beings which compose it, but nevertheless more than the individual beings that come and go within it; if all this is so, then there is a sense in which time is more than simply a counting of changes, a mere succession, a "marking time" like a clock. It is not simply time for enduring or time running out, not a fatal framework whose ravages are to be feared. In a way time is all these, but it is also time for growth, the measure of maturation, a mode of existence whereby beings which are largely potential when they begin to be are gradually transformed and made full in act by the changes they undertake and undergo. Just as a tree bears in its rings the stamp of its time, so every being has the evolutionary aspect of its changing as a constitutive characteristic of its very way of being. Contemporary philosophers speak of evolutionary time as opposed to cyclic time,[11] a kind of cosmogenesis in finite being leading to a fullness of being. Time, thus, would mark limited being as limited, and indeed would be a limitation—in that limited beings do not and cannot fully exist at any one moment. But time is also the opportunity for limited being to transcend its limitations, to fill out in many moments the existence which it cannot achieve in one moment.

There is, therefore, a sense in which past, present, and future have meaning within temporal being itself—not only within the memory and anticipation of man's mind.[12] If every change modifies a being, and if every being bears the mark of its time and its changes, it has the past taken up into it, fulfilled in the present. The present, too, will find its meaning and fulfillment in the future. The point of this discussion of time for an understanding of the beings of experience is that it helps us to see the beings of our experience as beings in time, constantly becoming as they exist, filling out the potencies of their nature, while remaining limited by those same potencies.

---

[11] See Bruno de Solages, "The Concepts of Cyclic and Evolutionary Time," in *The Human Person and the World of Values*, ed. B. Schwarz (New York: Fordham University Press, 1960), pp. 49–56; C. Tresmontant, *Study in Hebrew Thought*, trans. M. Gibson (New York: Desclee Company, 1960); and H. Bergson, *Creative Evolution*, trans. A. Mitchell (New York: Modern Library, Inc., 1944).

[12] The grasping of past, present, and future in the mind of man is perhaps the highest form of time impressed in being.

ORIENTATION OF BEING TO ACTIVITY

Our discussion of time has indicated that beings have a tendency to push ahead. However, some may consider this conclusion as based only on speculation about the temporality of the beings of our experience. We must ask now whether there is anything in beings which will account for the dynamic characteristics which we have found in change. To put it another way, we have seen how change is possible, but there remains the question of why change should take place and take place so universally and so continuously. We must ask whether changes are completely patternless, indicating no orientation in the beings in which they take place. We must ask finally, what the relationship is which exists between change and activity.

In our experience of finite material beings we find in them a certain "tendential" aspect. Certain inclinations, certain tendencies seem to pervade the whole gamut of the orders of finite beings. Beings appear ordered to their own fullness, so that at least some changes within them are part of their progressive coming-to-be. They have within their own beings an inclination to expand, so that all their changes are not merely a totally passive reception of forms either completely without order or with an order simply imposed from without. Further, the orientation of beings to their own completion manifests itself as an ordering to activity.

There is plenty of evidence for the tendential nature of limited being. Discoveries in the natural sciences indicate forces at work, energies within and between every kind of material being, organic and inorganic. The "natural processes" observed in biology and even chemistry are examples of this. Studies in the behavioral sciences such as psychology and sociology indicate similar forces at the psychological level in man. Ordinary everyday observation provides common knowledge of the tendencies in living beings to get what they need in order to preserve their being and to grow in being. The tree sends its roots through countless obstacles to reach the water it needs for life and nourishment. Every animal has its built-in instinctual patterns for the attainment of food, for self-defense, and for reproduction. Personal experience reveals to man the drives within him for self-fulfillment at every level of his being, and the frustration he suffers at anything which hinders the satisfaction of his needs, whether it be felt as hunger, sickness, ignorance, loneliness, or despair. It reveals to him, too, his own spontaneous tendencies for self-preservation and security in being, for self-affirmation and union with others. Finally, he may find in himself and in others an inclination not only to receive but to give, as the artist is moved to communicate his intuition, the scientist to share his discoveries, and the saint to express his holiness in action.

Countless philosophers have pointed to an energy, a dynamism, in being and have sought to explain it in various ways. The Greek expression of this dynamism ranged all the way from the conflicting opposites of Anaximander to the fruitfulness of human love in Plato.[13] Down through the ages it appears from time to time in such thinkers as Plotinus, Origen, Avicenna, Leibniz and Spinoza, Hegel, and Marx.[14] In more recent philosophical history it has been the concern of such men as Henri Bergson, Maurice Blondel, and Teilhard de Chardin. No two of these thinkers speak of the dynamic orientation in being in just the same way, but all indicate in some way that it is there and that it is important to an understanding of being. Many of the explanations imply a theory of being which is incompatible with the discoveries made in the preceding chapters. Some explanations have led to what has been called a "cult of action," [15] not at all in accord with the insight into existence which we have gained. On the other hand, many of these philosophers can give us a helpful insight into the reality of this dynamism in existing beings.

For St. Thomas, too, the dynamic nature of being is presented as a kind of existential dynamism, rooted in the act of existence it-

---

[13] See *Symposium,* 205A–210D, *The Dialogues of Plato,* I, 330–34; *Republic,* VI, 508C; 509B, *ibid.,* I, pp. 770–71; *Timaeus,* 41B, 46D, *ibid.,* II, pp. 22–23, 26.

[14] See Plotinus, *Enneads,* IV, 8; Origen, *De Principiis,* III, 5, 3; Avicenna, *Metaphysica,* VII, 7, f100; 4, f104; 6, f106; Spinoza, *Ethics,* I, 17 Scholium; Leibniz, *The Exigency to Exist in Essences: The Principle of Plenitude,* in *Leibniz Selections,* trans. P. Wiener (New York: Charles Scribner's Sons, 1951), pp. 91–93.

[15] H. Rauschning, "Russian and German Nihilism," *Dublin Review,* CCVIII (April 1941), 187–208.

self. It manifests itself in three ways: (1) as a tendency of being to preserve perfection possessed; (2) as a tendency to attain perfection not yet possessed; and (3) as a tendency to communicate perfection consequent upon possession.[16] We can express these three in another way: (1) a being in act tends to be acting; (2) a being in potency tends to act; (3) a being in act acts to communicate itself. All these tendencies are expressed concretely in terms of a translation of the energy of existence into activity. Imperfect being strives for the preservation of its own perfection and for the full actualization of that perfection. Activity is necessary for imperfect being in order that it may become perfect and necessary for perfect being because it is perfect. And being insofar as it is perfect tends to act to pour forth from its fullness.

None of this must be taken for granted. It will be helpful in understanding what experience tells us of existential dynamism if we recall what we have already considered in regard to nature, being, and activity. We have seen that activity in a being is not simply another accidental form such as quality or quantity. It is not an *essential,* but an *existential* act. Its correlative potency is what we have called a "power" and a power is not a mere capacity for actualization—not merely a "passive potency"—but is itself an act in relation to essence or nature. Since a power is related to nature as act is to potency, it is limited by the nature in which it inheres. This is, as we saw in the introductory chapter, why "action follows being." A being has certain powers for acting in keeping with its nature as a being: as a being is so can it act. It follows from this that if a being changes in such a way that it becomes fuller in being, its activity then can be that much more perfect.[17] Indeed, any change in the nature of a being will be reflected in the activity of that being. Thus activity can be the indirect result of a change. Activity may also be a cause of change—in the obvious way that

---

[16] St. Thomas does not use the term "existential dynamism," nor does he put together the tendencies spoken of herein into an *ex professo* theory of dynamism. Each of the tendencies appears under separate considerations in his work, but each points to a unified energy in being. See, for example, *Summa Theologiae,* I, 4, 2; I, 59, 1c; I–II, 1, 4 ad 1; I–II, 27, 1 and 3; *Summa Contra Gentiles,* II, 82, n. 4; III, 24, n. 6; III, 69; IV, 11.

[17] We do not imply here that a being gains new and proper powers, but only that both nature and powers may undergo changes. In common parlance we speak of powers (and being) developing.

one being's activity produces an effect in another being, and in a less obvious way when the activity of one power in a being brings about a change in the activity of another power or reflexively affects other activities of the power from which it flows.

But the relationship between activity and change is more intimate than these cause-effect statements may indicate. The dynamic orientation of a being to self-expansion and completion is precisely, as we have said, the translation of existential dynamism into activity. The complete actuality of a being comes in activity. But beings in our experience are not always immediately capable of their most perfect activity. However, their orientation to that activity directs the changes which make them ultimately capable of it and orients those changes in terms of the tendency of the particular being to full being. This will become clearer if we look more closely at the threefold manifestation of this tendency.

Being in Act Tends to Be Acting

Here, once again, we can turn to experience, for it shows us that as soon as a being exists it is performing some activity. This is clear in the case of living beings, and modern science is making it ever more clear in the case of nonliving beings. St. Thomas was aware of this fact: "A natural thing, through the form by which it is perfected in its species, has an inclination to its proper operations." [18] Insofar as a thing is actual, and is not hindered in acting, its actuality flows into activity.[19] These refer to the instinctive activities of living beings and the natural reactions of nonliving beings. In passing, we may note that the powers we referred to above are needed as the proximate source of activity, for unless the activity were mediated through them it would flow directly from the nature and so, since the nature is always fully there, the being would be exercising its full activity at every instant. Obviously, this is not what happens. And so there must be powers to mediate the activity from the nature.

The tendency of a being to preserve its being is manifest in the tendency to preserve itself as acting. St. Thomas again says: "Every

---

[18] *Summa Contra Gentiles,* IV, 19, n.2. See also *Summa Theologiae,* I, 77, 1; I, 87, 4c.
[19] See *Summa Theologiae,* I, 77, 1.

creature endeavors by its activity, first of all to keep itself in perfect being, so far as this is possible." [20] Again, we must not let the terminology get between us and the facts. Everything we experience is throbbing with activity, whether we can see it with the naked eye or under the microscope or in the test tube. In every one of these cases we see being in act tending to be acting.

Being in Potency Tends to Act

The second form which the existential dynamism of being takes is the tendency of being to attain its full perfection, the orientation of what is in potency to its actualization. ". . . Every being in potency tends to become actual, insofar as that is possible." [21] A flower thirsts for water and sunlight. A normal newborn animal immediately begins to grow into an adult of its species. Every power, for example sight or hearing, seeks its object. Even nonliving things tend to a kind of perfection in relation to other things.

To say that being insofar as it is in potency has a tendency to act is not to affirm that every potency does indeed become actualized. Wherever there is interaction between conflicting tendencies—between one being and another or within a single being—one or more tendencies may never be fulfilled. The cow and the grass both tend to grow but when the cow eats the grass, the grass, as grass, drops out of existence, whereas the cow continues to grow. However, this does not contradict the reality of the tendency to a fuller perfection of being anymore than despair contradicts the fact that a man has desires.[22]

---

[20] *Compendium Theologiae,* I, 103.

[21] *Summa Contra Gentiles,* III, 39, n.7. See also *ibid.,* II, 82, n.4; III, 22, n.6; *Summa Theologiae,* I, 4, 2; I, 59, 1; *Compendium Theologiae,* I, 103; *De Veritate,* 21, 2c; 22, 1 ad 4. This point is made by St. Thomas in all his texts concerning natural appetite.

[22] A difficulty arises if we think in terms of potencies which allow substantial, rather than accidental change. There may seem to be a sense in which beings are in potency for nonbeing. The difficulty, however, is more apparent than real. Strictly speaking, there can be no such thing as a potency for nonbeing, since potency is potency precisely insofar as it is ordered to act. We are, of course, concerned primarily with dynamism, change, and activity within a given being—not a dynamism for one being to become another. In substantial changes we have instances of one tendency superseding another.

The tendency of being in potency toward being in act belongs, of course, only to limited beings. For only such beings are in potency to further act. Pure act, infinite being, has no potency. Only beings in time, which are capable of changing and are constituted with possibilities for the future, can stretch toward greater and greater actualization. Only beings not yet fulfilled can have a tendency for fulfillment. Only beings which do not fully exist all at once can be said to continue to become.[23]

The dynamic tendency of a being toward fuller being is realized in and through its activity. Not only does a being in act tend to be acting, but it tends to be acting in the fullest way possible. This statement may seem to be a bit puzzling in view of the fact that most things do not act to their full capacity. If they did, teachers would have fewer problems with failing students, doctors and veterinarians would have much less business in dealing with human and animal ills, and automobile mechanics would soon lose much of their business. In view of this, how can we say that a being tends to be acting in the fullest way possible?

The answer is perhaps a bit subtle. For we have to distinguish between the tendency of the being itself toward perfect activity and the concrete conditions which sometimes frustrate this tendency to a large extent. The child's desire to learn, for instance, can be dampened in a dozen ways. Parental attitudes, competition from other members of the family, frustrations in early attempts to learn, physical sickness, and psychological problems—all these and many others can keep the young child from realizing his learning potential. Similarly, our physical powers do not operate at their highest level because of the various germs and viruses and diseases that attack them. We must bear in mind, too, that not every being of a given species has the same fullness of activity. Each of us is limited by the gene structure which he has inherited. Congenital weakness of the heart or lungs puts very definite limitations on our activity. Someone with short, stubby fingers and poor coordination will hardly be a concert pianist. And so for the thousands of limitations

---

[23] We are not considering purely spiritual finite beings here. Since it is only from revelation that we can know that such beings exist, we need not discuss their activity or the peculiar type of succession (*aevum*) which belongs to them.

we find among us. Consequently, the fact that we do not attain to the fullness of activity of which we are capable, and especially of which "man" is capable, does not in any way refute the statement that a being tends to be acting in the fullest way possible. This tendency is there but it is subject to intrinsic and extrinsic limitations.

We can understand this a little better perhaps if we try to distinguish between change and activity. We speak of a being as changing so long as it is coming to be, so long as it is *passing* from potency to act (and so still is in potency). This gives change a double aspect. For insofar as change produces a new perfection or at least is a stage on the way to a new perfection, we can say that change partakes of perfection. However, when change leads to a lower level of perfection, we should say that it partakes of imperfection. Furthermore, there is an imperfection in *every* change insofar as change implies a passage on the way to a perfection and not the actual possession of a perfection. As long as I am on the way to learning how to play the piano and do not actually know how to play, there is necessarily imperfection in this passage from not being able to play to being able to play the piano. The case is not the same with activity. For if we take activity in itself and disregard the limitations that are put on it by the fact that it is the activity of limited beings like ourselves, we can say that of itself it need not be limited, need not be the act of a potency. Such an activity would have to be the activity of an infinite being, whose activity is identified with his being. We spoke of this when we discussed the names of God and His activity. It is fairly simple to say "God is His activity," but we must admit that we have only the vaguest concept of what this really means. The principle is clear. Infinite activity is identified with infinite being and so need not imply limitation. Activity in limited beings, therefore, is limited not because it is activity but because it is the activity of limited beings.

However, even in finite beings activity must not be regarded as merely a means to a perfection, to fullness or expansion. Activities (especially spiritual activities), when fully actualized, can continue in their perfection. An art lover who comprehends the structure of a masterpiece may stand enthralled for minutes savoring this new insight. The scientist who for the first time sees an orderly relationship in a conglomeration of elements, can hold this in his mind for hours while he seeks new relationships. And on a lower level, a child who grasps the meaning of multiplication has acquired an activity which he can use for life. In material things the same phenomenon could occur, for instance, if in keeping with Newton's laws of motion, we were to put a body in motion at a certain speed and protect it from the gravitational influence of other bodies. But, even if as happens in our actual world, other influences are at work, the moving body does tend to keep its original motion and this tendency is a factor in plotting the course it will take when influenced by other bodies. In all these cases we should note that "activity follows being." Activity is the expression of the existential perfection in a being.

Being in Act Acts to Communicate Itself

From what we have said, it should be clear that the tendency in being for self-expansion does not disappear with the attainment of a given perfection, but may transform itself, using in a new way all the dynamism previously manifested in a tendency to fullness. This new way is manifested by self-communication or self-giving, in which every being engages. For it follows not only from the highest level of perfection, but rather from every level of perfection. And every being has a certain level of perfection, and so on its own level will communicate itself in some way.

If we take this generally, we see that active communication will mean causal activity whereby the acting being produces an effect in another or it may mean an internal activity by which the acting being relates and unites itself with another. The first of these has been called "transient" activity because it "goes out beyond," the being acting; and the second has been called "immanent" because the activity "remains within" the acting being. The communicative aspect of activity appears more clearly in transient activity, since in some way it produces a perfection outside of itself in another. Somehow it shares the fullness of being which it has with another being. And, of course, it does this to the extent that it has some perfection in itself. Thus when an apple tree matures sufficiently it produces fruit. It reproduces itself, gives rise to new beings.[24] Or when a student has reached a certain degree of proficiency in his studies, he may communicate his knowledge to others through some form of teaching. Or again, a billiard ball in motion may transmit some of its motion to another billiard ball when it strikes it.

In these cases, "When a form exists perfectly and naturally in something it can be the principle of action on something else, . . . But if a form exists in something imperfectly and not naturally, it cannot be the principle whereby it is communicated to something else." [25] The distinction between having the form perfectly and naturally and having it imperfectly and not naturally can best be understood in an example. The billiard ball actually in motion has the motion perfectly and naturally and so can produce motion in the billiard ball which it strikes. However, when I have the idea of motion in my mind, I have the form imperfectly and not naturally, and so my idea of the motion of the billiard ball cannot physically bring about the effect of moving another billiard ball.[26] This is the kind of perfection of being St. Thomas is talking about when he says: "To pour out acquired perfection upon others is of the nature of what is perfect, considered as perfect." [27] Since being is existentially self-expansive, it is dynamically oriented to seek and preserve the actuality which it possesses and to give from its fullness by causing being in another.

Immanent activity, which remains essentially within the being, differs from transient activity precisely in that it does remain within the being, and its effect, so to speak, is not something distinct from the actual activity itself. But it, too, can be considered as communication in an extended sense, for by immanent activity an agent can participate in the perfection of other beings, entering into immanent union with them. Thus, when I know the billiard ball, in the example above, my activity of knowing remains within me but somehow

---

[24] This, of course, in no way implies that it does so as First Cause. The whole question of secondary causality will be taken up in the following chapter.

[25] *Summa Theologiae,* I–II, 5, 6 ad 2. See also *ibid.,* I, 19, 2; *Summa Contra Gentiles,* II, 6, nn. 4 and 7; II, 45; III, 21, nn. 6 and 8; III, 24 n. 8.

[26] This distinction between having a form perfectly and imperfectly is connected with St. Thomas' Aristotelian physics. Compare "media" in sensation, in which forms exist imperfectly.

[27] *Summa Theologiae,* I, 62, 9 ad 2.

unites me to the billiard ball in letting me know it. So too, when an automobile designer has the completed picture of his new model in his mind, the activity of conceiving it remains within his mind and so is an immanent activity, but it points outward to the car which is to be made. Similarly, when I love another person, my act of love remains within me, but it is an act of union whereby I am in the one I love and he in me. In all these cases we are talking of an activity which is a perfection of the agent, since my acts of knowing and loving perfect me as a human being. This is the internal reference; the external reference, which we have seen in our examples, can be expressed technically as intentional and affective union with an object. In knowledge, a being is intentionally united to what it knows, knowing by an intentional affirmation of the being which is its object. In love, a being is affectively united to what it loves, loving by an affective affirmation of the being which is its object.

Existential Source of Dynamism

Since a being is a being because it exists, and since everything in a being is real by reason of its act of existing, the dynamism which being exhibits must have its source in the act of existing and its reality from the act of existing. Given this primacy of the perfection of existence, the tendencies striving for fuller existence and flowing from fuller existence must in the first instance rise from existence itself. Existence, limited by essence, actualizes essence and along with it constitutes a being which is tendential at its very heart. This existential tendency or dynamism is mediated by powers, active potencies, which tend toward their proper activity, for example, the mind toward knowing and the will toward loving. As growth and development make more and more perfect activity possible, and as the essence of a being grows in perfection, the being manifests more and more the fullness which was virtually contained in the perfection of its existence from the beginning of its being. If this is so, it becomes more and more clear how a finite being holds its own history within it, bears witness to its own time, comes to be and so to act.

In this and in previous chapters we have made some reference to the identity of being and activity in the infinite being of God. In our next chapter we will consider Pure Existence with reference to its activity.

SUGGESTED READINGS

Aristotle, *Physics,* Book I, Chapters 7–9, 190a32–192b2. Regarding change.

Bergson, Henri, *Creative Evolution,* pp. 330–85. New York: Random House [The Modern Library], 1944. Bergson here treats of evolutive continuity in time.

de Chardin, Pierre Teilhard, *The Phenomenon of Man,* trans. B. Wall, pp. 62–66, 264–72. New York: Harper & Row, Publishers, Inc. [Harper Torchbooks], 1961. Interpretation of the universe in terms of cosmic dynamism.

de Finance, Joseph, *Etre et Agir.* Rome: Librarie Editrice de l'Université Gregorienne, 1960.

Gilson, Etienne, *Elements of Christian Philosophy,* Chapter 11. Garden City, N.Y.: Doubleday & Company, Inc., 1960. In explaining the human will, Gilson treats of St. Thomas' understanding of the dynamism in being for activity.

Henri-Rousseau, J. M., "L'etre et l'agir," *Revue Thomiste,* LIII (1953), 488–531; LIV (1954), 85–118.

Koren, Henry J., *An Introduction to the Philosophy of Nature,* Chapter 10. Pittsburgh: Duquesne University Press, 1960. Deals with time, its concept, measurement, and relativity, in the light of modern scientific theories.

Lonergan, Bernard J. F., "The Concept of the *Verbum* in the Writings of St. Thomas Aquinas," Part III, "Procession and Related Notions," *Theological Studies,* VIII (1947), 408–13. On meaning of activity.

St. Thomas Aquinas, *Summa Contra Gentiles,* III, 21 and 24. Treats of the relationship between being and activity.

de Solages, Bruno, "The Concepts of Cyclic and Evolutionary Time," *The Human Person and the World of Values,* ed. B. Schwartz, pp. 49–56. New York: Fordham University Press, 1960.

Somerville, James M., "Maurice Blondel and the Philosophy of Action," *Spiritual Life,* VII (June 1961), 111–23.

Tresmontant, Claude, *A Study in Hebrew Thought,* trans.

Michael F. Gibson, pp. 17–29. New York: Desclee Company, 1960. Regarding the concept of time.

Van Melsen, Andrew G., *The Philosophy of Nature* (2nd ed.), Chapter 4, pp. 107–14, 126–29. Pittsburgh: Duquesne University Press, 1954. On substantial change.

Wild, John, "Tendency: The Ontological Ground of Ethics," *Journal of Philosophy,* XLIX (1952), 468–72. Gives metaphysical view of tendency in being.

THE DIVINE LIFE AND ACTIVITY

GOD'S ACTIVITY IN HIMSELF

We have seen what it means to call God Creator, All Presence, and Absolute Being. The first two tell us that God is not some vast, inert, static being. Rather, He creates and He is actively present in all that He creates. In other words, God is a living God, an active God. But what does it mean for us to say that Absolute Being is living and active? Obviously we are not talking about De Lawd, as portrayed in *Green Pastures,* a sort of grandfatherly old head of the household. But what do we mean? The only life and activity we know is that of creatures, so that the only way we can talk about life and activity in God is to work out something in terms of the highest life and activity of the creatures which we know. For the more closely a creature approaches God, the more perfection of existence it possesses. Hence we must look to whatever fullness of being we can find in experience and purify it by negating all limitation of it. When we have finished, we may begin to have some understanding of the divine life and activity.

The Meaning of Divine Life

When we say that God is living, we say this because life is the highest dynamic force in finite being. In creatures it is a way of existing marked by an activity which at its highest, in man, is bound up with knowing and loving. Since we are interested in life at the highest level, and in stretching beyond that to get some ideas about God, we are not concerned with the difficulties faced by philosophers and scientists who attempt to define life in a way that will allow a clear-cut distinction between living and nonliving beings. They are working at the other end of the spectrum in the "grey area" where the highest forms of nonliving beings and the lowest forms of living beings seem almost to overlap. We can take life from, for example, the middle range to the highest range in creatures, and there we find that whatever else it is, life is a mode of existence whose full actuality is expressed in self-activity of a certain degree of perfection. Thus, in one sense, perfect self-activity is perfect life. Consequently a Being who is His own activity has the perfect self-activity and can be said very properly to have life. This is to say that if finite being is dynamic, if its activity is bound up with perfection, and if its full existence is not only achieved but constituted by activity and fruitful activity, somehow activity, too, must have its ultimate meaning from God.

Now this means that the perfection of activity must somehow be included in the Pure Existence which is God. But as soon as we say activity is in God, the question arises, "How?" That it must be in God in some way is clear because whatever is in an effect must somehow first be in its cause. In creatures activity is a perfection, and it is a perfection which, as we have seen,[1] does not of itself imply limitation. It appears in a limited form in every being of our experience only because it is limited by the limited capacities of the being in which it inheres. A perfection [2] which of itself implies

[1] See page 186.

[2] See page 154 for the distinction between "pure" and "mixed" perfections. In applying "pure" perfections to God the same pattern may always be followed: the perfection is in the effect and hence must be in the cause. The problem which remains, therefore, is to understand the meaning of the perfection—in the effect, first, and then similarly in the cause.

no limitation can exist in the First Cause really, substantially, in a way similar to that in which it is found in finite being. In the finite being it is limited by the potencies of that being, but wherever it is not joined to potency, as in God, it is unlimited, since it has there no limiting factor whatsoever.

We can say, then, that the perfection of activity is found first of all in God. It is in Him as unlimited, infinite activity. We have already seen that since there is no composition in God's being in the order of existence, and hence no distinction between essence and existence in God, He is Pure Act, Pure Existence. If a being has no potency, no limitation in the order of existence, it is already all act, already all there is of being, Absolute Being. And if there is act on this highest level of being, there can be no potency for more being at any level in the being. Thus, since there is no composition of essence and existence, there can be no composition in any other regard—hence no composition between substance and accident or nature and operation. It follows, therefore, that if there is activity in God, it must be identified with His act of existence. And since we have seen that activity is a perfection which of itself implies no limitation, it must be in the Pure Existence of God, identified with it, Pure Activity.

One may also reason that if in finite beings the dynamism of existence gives rise to the dynamism of activity, if the relationship between existence and activity is so intimate that the one immediately implies, whether abstractly or concretely, the other, if as soon as a being exists it is acting, if activity belongs to—leads to, preserves, and flows from—the fullness of existence, then He who is perfect existence will also be perfect activity. If a being acts insofar as it is perfect, He who is perfect in being will be perfect in activity.

The name for God which carries the meaning of perfect and infinite activity, an affirmative absolute name which indicates what God is in Himself, is "Life." We use this name because when it is applied to the beings of experience, it signifies a kind of existence which is known and marked by activity which in some way is self-activity.[3] Like every other affirmative absolute name, it is used

---

[3] See *Summa Theologiae,* I, 18.

analogously, that is, in such a way that it refers to God and creatures in a way somewhat similar yet somewhat different. There is an infinite distance between finite and infinite life, but there is nevertheless a basis of similarity which offers us the possibility of knowing life in God. Life, like every other affirmative absolute name, must be purified in its meaning so that every form of limitation is removed from it when it refers to God. One of the limitations which cannot belong to the perfect activity of God is the limitation which marks a changing, temporal being.

As we have seen in Chapter 7, activity is not to be completely identified with change. Because of the limited nature of the beings of experience, it is easy to equate change and activity. A finite being is always changing in and through its activity. But even in finite beings, the perfection of activity does not lie in the change involved but in the actualization which takes place through the change. If, for instance, a being were to achieve all the perfection possible to it, and be somehow irrevocably confirmed in that perfection, it would no longer undergo change, no longer pass from a state of potency to a state of act. Yet this would not mean that it would at this point cease its activity. On the contrary, its activity is part and parcel of its perfection. It would therefore be performing its peak activity. Thus, for example, when a child is learning to play the piano, each time he plays he is growing in skill. Each time his potentiality in this regard is being more and more actualized. But suppose that he finally actualizes that potency completely,[4] its actualization would be in the playing, in the activity which would signify the peak of his being in this regard and not his growth or progress.

We have already said that only limited beings, only beings with potency, may change. God's activity may not in any way, therefore, be marked by change. There is in Him neither composition nor potency, and without these change is impossible. He is therefore named "Immutable," unchanging and unchangeable. As such, He is not frozen in being in some static state, but is fully in act, the infinite source of existential dynamism and of all finite act and activity.

At this juncture we must stretch our minds to the breaking point.

---

[4] This is quite impossible in this life.

The words are plain enough: God's activity is the fullness of His being. But what do we have left of activity when we empty out all passage from potency to act? The examples we have given above of human acts which seem to break through the framework of time help us somewhat, but we are still talking about activity which is different from the being of the people engaged in it. In God this activity is identified with His being. This we can argue to and affirm, but cannot understand. This is part of the mystery of God which our finite minds cannot fathom.

Eternity

We have the same problem when we conclude that if there is no change or possibility of change in God, then it is impossible for Him to be subject to limitations of time either in His being or in His activity. Temporality is the mode of existence of a changing being. In no way can it be applied to unchanging being. When we say thus that God in His infinite life is not subject to the limitations of time, we call Him "Eternal." This is another name of God, a name which we use of Him inasmuch as He exists in Himself apart from any relation to creatures. It is therefore an absolute name of God. The knowledge it gives of God, however, tells us what He is not. It says that He is not limited to time or by time; therefore, it is a negative name.

We apprehend eternity, then, only as a negation or transcendence of time. Eternity has many meanings in ordinary speech. Usually it refers to whatever has long duration or whatever is thought to have no beginning or end in time. But if eternity is to be truly a negation of the limitation of time, it cannot be taken to mean merely a long time, or time with no beginning or end. As St. Thomas has pointed out, "It is manifest that time and eternity are not the same. Some have founded this diversity on the fact that eternity has neither beginning nor an end, whereas time has a beginning and an end. This, however, makes a merely accidental, and not essential, difference; because, granted that time always was and always will be . . . there would yet remain a difference between eternity and time, as Boethius says, arising from the fact that eternity is simultaneously whole, which cannot be applied to time; for eternity is the measure of a permanent being, while time is the measure of movement [change]." [5] In the strict sense eternity must negate the mode of being which time signifies. It must indicate existence *without successive duration.* In this sense it is outside of time altogether, for it refers no longer to an existence which is a *nunc fluens,* but to an existence which is a *nunc stans.*[6] St. Thomas, following Boethius, speaks of eternity as the "simultaneous-whole and perfect possession of interminable life." [7] We can expand this somewhat cryptic definition by analyzing its parts. By "simultaneous-whole" St. Thomas and Boethius meant to signify an existence which is all at once, as opposed to an existence which is given part after part or act after act in a succession. For example, if we were given perfect knowledge at birth, we would have it all at once. In our present state of existence, however, our knowledge is attained piecemeal and in succession, so that we never do have it all at once. "Perfect possession of interminable life" refers to the absolute fullness of being, which is held firmly and in the peace of permanence and immutability. There is no past or future for a being which is eternal, only an eternal now, a "now" which is pure and perfect because it has the complete fullness of its activity and being. Unlike the "now" of time it is not fleeting or incomplete. We must insist again, however, that although it is not in a state of becoming, it is nevertheless not static, for "life" signifies Perfect Being which is Perfect Activity. Eternity, therefore, does not deny activity, but the protraction of activity in time. In a being which is all at once, and whose activity is its being, activity, too, is all at once, all now. Eternity is the total presentness of a being which is infinitely active, infinitely dynamic, infinitely fruitful. As St. Thomas has pointed out, eternity excludes the "now" of time and the succession of time: "Two things are to be considered in time: time itself, which is successive, and the 'now' of time, which is imperfect. Hence the expression 'simultaneously-whole' is used to remove the idea of time, and the word 'perfect' is used to exclude the 'now' of time." [8]

Eternity, therefore, is a negation of time. But every negative im-

---

[5] *Summa Theologiae,* I, 10, 4c.
[6] See *ibid.,* I, 10, 1, 2, 3, 4.
[7] *Ibid.,* I, 10, 1, obj. 1.
[8] *Ibid.,* ad 5.

plies something positive. Naturally, when we are talking about something so far above and beyond our ordinary experience, we will have difficulty in analyzing this positive aspect. Since we know that somehow eternity is a mysterious Eternal Now, we will have to find some analogy, however inadequate, in our human experience in terms of which to explain the positive side of eternity. We must, therefore, look for instances in human experience where what is successive at one level is taken up into a totality, a "now," at another level. Perhaps the best examples of this are found at the peak of knowing and loving. For instance, an art lover standing before a masterpiece sees the picture as a whole. He does not have to go over the picture or run through the reasons why he enjoys it. As he stands rapt before the picture, time seems to stop as he contemplates it. He is very definitely in act—seeing, knowing, appreciating the work of art, yet there is no passage from potency to act, no succession of activities. He knows and loves the picture. He is in act in a timeless sort of way. He has, if you will, a taste of eternity. Multiply this to infinity in breadth and depth, and we have some idea of the infinite act which is God, the infinite eternal now of Pure Act. As another example, take two people deeply in love. They sit before the fire, holding hands perhaps, but saying nothing, doing nothing—no, not really doing nothing for there is a communion of love between them which is intense activity. They are loving in *act,* and again an act which slips out of the time category. They might be there for half an hour, a full hour, or more, but they are not aware of any succession or passage of time. Again, take this timeless act, multiply it by infinity in breadth and intensity, and we begin to understand the infinite act of God, the eternal now of Pure Act. There are many similar human acts which concentrate their intensity into a "now" and seem to escape the limits of time. The astronomer gazing at the skies, the mathematician who grasps a complicated formula for the first time, the philosopher who shares an important insight into the nature of being, the scientist who discovers a new correlation of elements, all these people are *in act,* all of them actually contemplate the truth. In a small way each of these finite agents shares in some finite way in *act without succession, act without continued passing from potency to act.* This participation in act helps us to get some idea of what it means for God to be in eternity, to be in the eternal now of Pure Act. In a weak, analogous way we see in these examples a finite participation in eternity, which helps us to understand the Eternal Now, the positive aspect of eternity.

Life: Infinite Knowledge and Love

So far we have said that the activity of Pure Existence is perfect and infinite activity, unchanging but charged with unlimited dynamism, eternally present and whole, however little has been said about the nature of this activity. Our experience acquaints us with all kinds of activities—walking, talking, painting, hoping, giving. What kind of activity is in God? Or rather, since being and activity are one in God, what kind of activity is God?

Perhaps the best way to approach this question is to examine the highest kinds of activity known in human experience, activities which of themselves imply no limitation and which therefore can be considered as pure perfections. These are the noblest activities of personal beings, knowing and loving. These are our most "spiritual" activities and so are the highest perfections in our world. Like all perfections, they are the effects of God, and so they must be in Him as in their First Cause. Since of themselves they imply no imperfection, they may be included in God's activity in some way. Thus the activity of God, in Himself and in relation to creatures, must in some infinite way include knowledge and love.

The names of God which refer to this knowledge and love will be considered separately in Chapters 10 and 11. For now we need only see that this is the kind of activity which God performs, that God is therefore a personal being, and that God knows and loves not only in Himself but in relation to creatures. We shall have to devote more time to this in later chapters, as we have seen. But even this rudimentary insight into God's knowledge and love gives us some idea of the name "Providence" as applied to God.

GOD'S ACTIVITY IN RELATION TO HIS EFFECTS

God: Cause of All Finite Activity

We must now ask ourselves about the relation between the activities of beings in experience and the infinite activity of God. Once more we will have to study the finite activity which we experience and try to see what it implies in relation to the divine activity. In the first place, when we speak of the activity of limited being in all its dimensions, we are speaking of something over and above what we might call its substantial being or existence. This activity, as we have explained, is a kind of extension of the substantial existence of the being and is distinct from it. If limited being does not fully explain its own substantial existence, it cannot fully explain the further extension of this existence in activity. Activity, like the being of the agent, must be related in some way to infinite activity as its source. Furthermore, this infinite source is creative, so that the dependence of finite beings is total. Their existence is wholly received and so they are effects in every respect. There is no other ultimate source for anything in finite reality. Consequently finite activity, change, existential dynamism, even time—all are totally the effect of the creative causality of God. He exerts a continuing causality which holds its effects continuously not only in their being but also in their tending and acting.

Since existence is the key to being, whatever is the cause of existence is thereby the direct cause of everything in a being. And if, as we have just seen, there can be no continued existence without the continuing influence of divine causality, it is impossible that there be finite beings which would be placed in existence and which would then proceed to act on their own. The activity, like the being, of creatures is the direct and immediate effect of the First Cause, a cause who is intimately present wherever He is acting, even in the most insignificant activities of created being. All reality, from the highest to the lowest, is saturated with God's direct and immediate presence.

Now if finite beings are totally caused by Infinite Being, this causality must extend to the ordering of these beings and their activities in keeping with the intentions of the First Cause. Thus, whether we look at them under the aspect of their efficient causality —as seeking perfection and pouring forth perfection—or under the aspect of final causality—as drawn to perfection and led from perfection—all finite beings are ordered to their end totally under the direct causality of God. There are no exceptions. When we think of God as orderer in this way, and look for a name which expresses

His ordering of creatures and bringing them to their end, we find the name "Providence." [9]

Providence

As a kind of introduction to our discussion of Providence, it might be helpful to examine the meaning of the word "providence" before it is used as a name of God. Literally it means "to see beforehand," "to look out for," "to care for," or "to plan for." It comes from the two Latin words *pro,* meaning "before" or "in behalf of," and *videre,* meaning "to see," "to look at," "to observe," or "to attend to." Put together, *providere* has been used to mean providence. In this sense of the word it implies not simply a causing in general, but the causing which comes from knowledge—practical knowledge about an action to be performed in order to reach some end. A father who is *provident* looks out for, plans ahead for, provides for, his family. The kind of practical knowledge which providence involves includes both a plan—an "exemplar"—and the carrying out of the plan—its execution.[10] Thus, when "providence" is applied to God, it indicates His knowing plan for each creature and for the universe as a whole, and His carrying out of this plan, His directing of creatures to their end. As St. Thomas has said, "For the same reason is God the ruler of things as He is their cause, because the same cause gives being that gives perfection; and this belongs to government." [11]

Although it is fairly easy to see what providence means and also to see that if there is order-to-end in creation, it is there as an effect of God, it may be very difficult at first glance to show that there is indeed order-to-end in the world on any large scale. For if we had to prove every relationship of order-to-end experimentally, we could never succeed. We simply do not know enough about the interrelations of the beings of our experience to set up such an order on

---

[9] *Ibid.,* I, 22, 1.

[10] Some further distinctions or clarifications of terminology may be helpful for the student who reads directly in St. Thomas. Thomas uses the term "Government" to refer to the carrying out of the plan. Sometimes by "Providence" he means both the plan and government; at times, however, he reserves the term "Providence" for the plan alone, distinguishing thus between "Providence" and "Government."

[11] *Summa Theologiae,* I, 103, 5c.

a large scale. What we have seen of the tendential nature of finite beings we could perhaps interpret in a way which would establish the existence of this order even though we could not say in any detail what this order is. This, however, is so unclear and inconclusive that we have preferred to consider the dynamic nature of existence from the point of view of its source within the acting beings rather than from its end or goal—arguing more from agent (efficient cause), the source of order, than from the end (final cause), its goal.

In human actions we can speak of goals fairly easily, especially in those actions in which we consciously direct ourselves to certain goals. Especially in living things can we see certain lines of finality,[12] for example, in the development of the acorn into the oak tree and in the complex of vital functions which keeps us alive and healthy. In each case, however, we are dealing with an *instance* of finality. We are not able to fit all these instances into any grand over-all pattern. One indication of our limitation in this regard is the relative sterility of the Aristotelian type of natural science, which attempted to solve its problems in terms of finality, and so failed for centuries to make any substantial progress. When modern science arose, one of its first moves was to proceed completely in terms of efficient causality and to banish final causes from natural science. The success of modern science speaks for itself of the wisdom of this procedure. We would be unwise, therefore, to attempt any explanation of final causes which would take us back to the days of medieval science.

When we speak of order-to-end in the world, therefore, we are not attempting in the twentieth century to redo something which was abandoned in the seventeenth century. If what we are doing is to be valid, it must ask another question and seek a different type of answer. Actually, we will handle finality in a broader context. We cannot, it is true, give a picture of the world into which we fit all the details of a plan for the universe. Only God with His

---

[12] By "finality" is meant simply the order of agents to an end. It partakes of the meaning of final cause, as seen above, pages 90–91. It is sometimes spoken of in terms of a "Principle of Finality," which is stated thus: Every agent acts for an end.

infinite mind can do this. We can, however, show how there must be an order and plan, even though our minds are too small to grasp it. In its most general lines, this is no more than an affirmation of the Principle of Contradiction to the nature of being. Or to put it more concretely, perhaps, we can say that since being is determinate—it is what it is and not something else—action, especially causal action, is also determinate. Every action is what it is and does what it does. Since it does what it does, we can say it is therefore oriented to an end. To this extent at least, the very notion of causality implies finality and every cause acts for an end. Men concretely experience that action occurs for certain purposes, and reflection shows that there is an end for every action—whether consciously intended or not. Even the spontaneous movements, or automatic processes, have their specific objects, purposes, and terminations. We pull our hands away when we think something heavy is going to fall on them. Our eyes blink and our heads jerk back to avoid being struck. When there is need for "fight or flight," adrenalin pours into our bloodstream. The same orientation to ends appears in the natural patterns of activity of other living beings, too. Even nonliving beings give evidence of finality insofar as natural forces tend to uniform results. In any case, it is clear that there is no such thing as a wholly undetermined activity. If one goes to write, but to write no particular word or character, he will never write.

This, however, gives us a very limited picture of finality. It tells us nothing of the further relationships between causes and between more remote effects. There is not much point in trying to go further along this line, however, for we simply do not have the necessary knowledge. In order to get the fullest picture of providence, we must argue the other way around, from God's causality and providence. We see, therefore, that if God is the First Cause, as He is, every finite cause must receive its power to cause from Him. And so every effect is an effect of God and must, therefore, be ordered by His providence. This means that corresponding to the providence in the divine mind there is an objective order in the universe. And in this order everything is directed to its particular end, on the one hand, and fits into God's total plan for the universe, on the other. God makes creatures to exist, dynamically ordering them to a goal, and causes them to move toward this goal by means of their activities. In God's providence a being placed in existence tends to reach the fullness of its being and to diffuse being from its fullness. It is in the light of this double dynamic tendency that every activity of a being and every passivity it undergoes in the duration of its existence will take on meaning. Whether or not a being actually achieves its full being, its whole development must be within the causality of God. Nothing, no reality whatsoever, may exist or take place outside this causality.[13] In the words of St. Thomas, ". . . all things are subject to divine providence, not only in general, but even in their own individual being. This is made evident thus. For since every agent acts for an end, the ordering of effects towards that end extends as far as the causality of the first agent extends. Whence it happens that in the effects of an agent something takes place which has no reference towards the end, because the effect comes from some other cause outside the intention of the agent. But the causality of God, Who is the first agent, extends to all beings not only as to the constituent principles of species, but also as to the individualizing principles; not only of things incorruptible, but also of things corruptible. Hence all things that exist in whatsoever manner are necessarily directed by God towards the end. . . . Since, therefore, the providence of God is nothing other than the notion of the order of things toward an end, as we have said, it necessarily follows that all things, inasmuch as they participate in being, must to that extent be subject to divine providence." [14] But since the being of creatures is totally "participated being," they are totally subject to divine providence.

---

[13] Even what is ordinarily thought of in terms of chance cannot be outside the range of divine causality. Every chance event presupposes causality, for what happens in such a situation is that two lines of causality meet in a way that was not intended in the single effect of each cause. For example, if two automobiles collide, their collision presupposes that each automobile was being caused to go in a certain direction; what was not given in their causality is the meeting of the two directions. Although the individual secondary causes did not intend the crossing of paths, nothing is outside the range of the universal First Cause; thus, both lines of causality have their ultimate source in the First Cause, and even their meeting is given in the causality of the First Cause. See *Summa Theologiae,* I, 103, 1; I, 22, 2 ad 1.

[14] *Summa Theologiae,* I, 22, 2c.

Secondary Causality and Freedom

There is a question which almost asks itself at this point: "What about freedom?" It is a question which touches the springs of human activity, and one which almost no thoughtful person can avoid grappling with from time to time. We, too, must therefore face it.[15]

If the activity of God reaches, as it does, to the height and depth and breadth of created reality, is there any place for a finite activity which belongs to the being from which it comes? Can I as a creature in any way initiate activity and have its effects be truly mine? Is there really any such thing as finite activity, or is it God rather than man who acts at the center of man's being?

The answer depends largely on one's idea of God. The eighteenth-century deists, for instance, whose God created the world, set its laws in motion, and then left it largely to its own devices, could allow man to act independently of God. Thus Voltaire, who professes to believe in God and accepts Him as the "cause of order," wants to leave ample room for human free will to operate.[16] This kind of God should stay in His heaven and leave the world to men and to natural forces, which is about what Voltaire wanted. David Hume, too, although rejecting the deists' proofs for the existence of God and denying a free will in man,[17] still espouses a deistic

---

[15] There are many questions which freedom raises. It will not be our task here to answer any of them save that which is concerned with the relationship of freedom to divine causality. A deeper understanding of the meaning of freedom, its nature, conditions, role in human life, and so forth, will come from the study of the questions concerning it which arise in the philosophy of man and ethics.

[16] See E. Gilson and T. Langan, *Modern Philosophy: Descartes to Kant* (New York: Random House, 1963), p. 335.

[17] By freedom is meant here not the mere possibility of selection between two alternatives. Such an experience might show nothing more than the following of the strongest impulse. Even dogs must sometimes select between two bones. What is referred to here, rather, is the experience of freedom in an act which requires a reaching to the more profound levels of one's being in order to determine one's life. It implies a self-determination which transcends external determinations and even the spontaneous inclinations which arise from within. Only in such an experience does one know that he is free.

sort of God. The most we can say about Hume's God is "that the cause or causes of order in the universe probably bear some remote analogy to human intelligence." [18] Not entirely consistently, Hume refers to God as "an omnipotent mind," whose existence is proved by "the order of the universe." [19] This omnipotence, however, is not entirely effective because "reason," which is founded on the nature of things, has a standard "eternal and inflexible even by the will of the Supreme Being." [20] This viewpoint involves a conception of an inflexible nature which leaves no room for free will,[21] for freedom is merely chance, and chance is "but a secret and conceal'd cause." [22]

The whole trend of modern scientific thought has been to banish God and freedom from the world. Alexandre Koyré tells us that Newton had a God who " 'ran' the universe according to His free will and decision," but "the Divine Artifex had . . . less and less to do in the world. He did not even need to conserve it, as the world, more and more, became able to dispense with this service. Thus the mighty energetic God of Newton . . . became in quick succession, a conservative power, an *intelligentia supra-mundana*, a '*Dieu faineánt*.' . . . The infinite Universe of the New Cosmology, infinite in duration as well as in extension, in which eternal matter in accordance with eternal and necessary laws moves endlessly and aimlessly in eternal space, inherited all the ontological attributes of divinity. Yet only those—all the others the departed God took away with Him." [23] Koyré's conclusion shows how the causality of God was suppressed by the successors of Newton. Without getting involved in a full-scale discussion of this kind of determinism, we can point out that it is completely unaware of the meaning of God as Pure Act. The infinity of Newton's God is a pseudoinfinity; and here lies the basic error.

---

[18] D. Hume, *Dialogues Concerning Natural Religion*, ed. N. K. Smith, 2nd ed. (New York: Thomas Nelson & Sons, 1947), p. 227.
[19] *A Treatise of Human Nature*, ed. L. A. Selby-Bigge (Oxford: Clarendon Press, Ltd., 1896), p. 633n.
[20] D. Hume, *An Enquiry Concerning Human Understanding*, ed. L. A. Selby-Bigge (Oxford: Clarendon Press, Ltd., 1902), p. 40.
[21] Hume, *Treatise*, p. 40.
[22] *Ibid.*, p. 130.
[23] A. Koyré, *From the Closed World to the Infinite Universe* (Baltimore: The Johns Hopkins Press [Harper Torchbook ed.], 1957), p. 276.

Others in the eighteenth century were more zealous for the primacy of God and conceived His infinite causality in such a way that they emptied finite being of all causal effectiveness. For them God does everything. When I seem to move my arm, it is really God who moves it *on the occasion* of my willing to move it. When one billiard ball strikes another, God takes this *occasion* to move the second ball. As might be expected, this theory is called "occasionalism." Its father was Malebranche (1620–1675) and it was espoused by his Cartesian followers.[24] As a philosophical doctrine, it did not enjoy any widespread popularity.

We have been discussing two extreme positions, one of which practically excludes God from the world, the other which deprives man of all causal influence. These thinkers take various stands on the question of human freedom. Some in both schools espouse it, others reject it. Neither can give any satisfactory explanation of freedom because both accept a basic determinism either by God or by natural physical laws. As modern science has expanded, it has been more and more difficult for philosophers to find any place for human freedom. Man has become a pawn in the evolution of the universe, bound by its laws just as the solar system is bound by the laws of motion. Martin Buber sums up this attitude in a strong passage in *I and Thou:* "The quasi-biological and quasi-historical thought of today, however different the aims of each, have worked together to establish a more tenacious and oppressive belief in fate than has ever before existed. The might of *karma* or of the stars no longer controls inevitably the lot of man; many powers claim the mastery, but rightly considered most of our contemporaries believe in a mixture of them, just as the late Romans believed in a mixture of gods. This is made easier by the nature of the claim. Whether it is the 'law of life' of a universal struggle in which all must take part or renounce life, or the 'law of the soul' which completely builds up the psychical person from innate habitual instincts, or the 'social law' of an irresistible social process to which will and consciousness may only be accompaniments, or the 'cultural law' of an unchangeably uniform coming and going of historical structures—whatever form it takes, it always means that man is set in the frame of an

---

[24] Gilson and Langan, *Modern Philosophy,* pp. 93–107.

inescapable happening that he cannot, or can only in his frenzy, resist." [25]

Recently, however, a more sophisticated approach is being taken. Many contemporary philosophers are moving toward a more consistent empiricism, which simply refuses to engage in metaphysical discussion. Consequently, they can now admit a common-sense sort of freedom without having to justify it metaphysically. Thus Gilbert Ryle can point out: "The fears expressed by some moral philosophers that the advance of the natural sciences diminishes the field within which the moral virtues can be exercised rests on the assumption that there is some contradiction in saying that one and the same occurrence is governed both by mechanical laws and by moral principles, an assumption as baseless as the assumption that a golfer cannot at once conform to the laws of ballistics *and* obey the rules of golf *and* play with elegance and skill. Not only is there plenty of room for purpose where everything is governed by mechanical laws, but there would be no place for purpose if things were not so governed." [26] The same approach appears in Morris Ginsberg's *On the Diversity of Morals,* in which, writing in an ethical context, he says: "I cannot attempt here to settle the ancient controversy between the determinists and the indeterminists. But I will ask you to consider whether anyone seriously doubts that a man can be influenced in his action by the judgment he forms of the consequences of his acts and of the relative value or worth of the alternatives open to him. We make such judgments every day, and we do so more or less impartially, that is, with greater or lesser freedom from bias. The freedom that is required as a minimum condition of moral accountability is the ability to make an impartial estimate of the relative worth of the alternatives open to me and of acting accordingly. If I am not capable of any measure of impartiality, if I am unable to know what I am doing, or whether what I am doing is right or wrong; or again if having such knowledge I have not the emotional or cognitive energy to act in accordance with it, then I am neither free nor responsible.

---

[25] *I and Thou* (New York: Charles Scribner's Sons, 1958), p. 56.
[26] G. Ryle, *The Concept of Mind* (New York: Barnes & Noble, Inc., 1960), pp. 80–81.

"If it be maintained that a man's judgments are themselves completely determined, that he cannot help making the judgments he makes, the answer is that this would make nonsense of all knowledge." [27]

It is up to us to consult our own experience for the evidence of freedom. If we reject its reality, we must join the determinists and say that there is no paradox of divine and human causality. If not, we must attempt to solve the paradox. The extent to which we can solve it may be very limited. Perhaps the most we can do is to show that the affirmation of both divine and human causality is not a contradiction. Let us make the attempt.

Our starting point is clear. If God is Pure Act, as we have shown Him to be, He is the source of all being and so is the cause of all things. If there is anything in finite reality to be explained, its explanation cannot come outside of, or in spite of, the creative and providential causality of Absolute Being. This is to say that true secondary principal causality of any kind, and free activity in particular, can only be understood because of divine causality and never in spite of it.[28]

The relationship between divine causality and human freedom is therefore one of cause and effect. There are ways in which such a relationship is not so surprising as it might appear at first glance. For finite beings really exist, and it makes very great sense indeed that such beings, which receive existence as their own and exist in themselves, should receive activity as their own and act in themselves. In the words of St. Thomas, "If He has communicated His likeness, as far as actual being is concerned, to other things, by virtue of the fact that He has brought things into being, it follows that He has communicated to them His likeness, as far as acting is concerned, so that created things may also have their own actions." [29] This is to say that it makes sense that Absolute Being, Who is in-

---

[27] *On the Diversity of Morals* (New York: The Macmillan Company, 1957), pp. 81–82.

[28] ". . . Whatsoever causes He assigns to certain effects, He gives them the power to produce those effects . . . He governs things inferior by superior, not because of any defect in His power, but by reason of the abundance of His goodness; so that the dignity of causality is imparted even to creatures." *Summa Theologiae,* I, 22, 3.

[29] *Summa Contra Gentiles,* III, 69, n. 14.

finitely fruitful, should in the power of His effective activity bring forth beings which are in turn productive.[30] It would be strange to find beings with proper powers permanently and intrinsically possessed by virtue of their natures, but whose activities did not truly rise from those powers.

It is reasonable to conclude that a being with infinite power could not only cause the existence of the effects which He wishes, but cause them to exist in the way He wishes. St. Thomas puts it this way, "When a cause is efficacious to act, the effect follows upon the cause, not only as to the thing done, but also as to its manner of being done or being. . . . Since then the divine will is perfectly efficacious, it follows not only that things are done, which God wills to be done, but also that they are done in the way that He wills. Now God wills some things to be done necessarily, some contingently, so that there be a right order in things for the perfection of the universe." [31] If, therefore, God wishes some creatures to act freely, and if His power is indeed unlimited, it is reasonable to conclude that He cannot only cause activities but also cause free activities, however paradoxical that may seem. There is freedom in human acts precisely because God causes them and causes them to be done freely. This is a paradox, but a paradox is not a contradiction. It might be a contradiction indeed were God, who is Providence, to cause beings with a certain nature and then not provide for the activities which belong to that nature. Again, St. Thomas considers this, "Free choice is the cause of its own movement, because by his free choice man moves himself to act. But it does not of necessity belong to liberty that what is free should be the first cause of itself, as neither for one thing to be cause of another need it be the first cause. God, therefore, is the first cause, who moves causes both natural and voluntary. And just as by moving natural causes He does not prevent their actions from being natural, so by moving voluntary causes He does not deprive their actions from being volun-

---

[30] "Now it is a greater perfection for a thing to be good in itself and also the cause of goodness in others, than only to be good in itself. Therefore God so governs things that He makes some of them to be causes of others in government; as in the case of a teacher, who not only imparts knowledge to his pupils, but also makes some of them to be the teachers of others." *Summa Theologiae,* I, 103, 6c.

[31] *Ibid.,* I, 19, 8c. See also I, 22, 4.

tary; but rather is He the cause of this very thing in them, for He operates in each thing according to its own nature."[32]

The reason, perhaps, why the human intellect stumbles so in an effort to harmonize primary and secondary causality, and causality and freedom, is that it tends to see causality in terms of physical causality. If we see a man pull a trigger of a gun, see the hammer of the gun strike the shell, hear the report of the powder exploding, and see the bullet strike the target, we parcel out the various causal elements and assign them to each of the causes involved. What we cannot do is to ascribe the total effect of a series of causes totally to each of the causes. Where the causality of one begins, the causality of the others leaves off.

In human experience, however, there is one instance of causality which is not physical, and wherein freedom is not destroyed but perfected. This is in the causality of love. It is possible for a human person to love another and by love cause being and activity—by a second cause—so that the activity is at once the result of the lover and of the beloved, an activity which could not have been performed without the love of the lover nor without the answering love and freedom of the beloved. An example of this might be the following: If a person stands at the window of a tall building, threatening to jump and so destroy his life, it is possible for another who loves him and loves him intensely, and is in some way able to communicate that love, to save his life. The decision not to jump may depend on the love of another and, at the same time, on the freedom of the one threatening to jump. The freedom of the latter may indeed be released through the love of the former. And so in a real way his love is the cause of the other's not jumping.

Again, if a person approaching one of those points of crucial decision wherein a personality is made or broken, can be made to develop in being, insight, and courage through the trust and love of another, he may grow enough in the power of self-determination, which is freedom, to take hold of his life at the depths of his being and move forward in the achievement of his destiny. Perhaps he is dissuaded from a life of crime, or encouraged to marriage rather

---

[32] *Ibid.*, I, 83, 1 ad 3. See also I–II, 109, 1; *Summa Contra Gentiles,* III, 94; III, 73.

than an illicit affair, or to loyalty to his family when he was thinking of desertion. In each of these cases there is personal growth and development caused by love.

If human love can have such an effect without destroying the freedom of the beloved, how much more the infinite love of God, which is infinitely more present, more intimate, more powerful, more effective, more freeing. This is not the whole answer but it begins to give us some insight into what it means to say that divine causality and human freedom are not contradictory to one another, but meet in a paradox of cause and effect. Buber states the paradox: "Destiny and freedom are solemnly promised to one another. Only the man who makes freedom real to himself meets destiny . . . destiny confronts him as the counterpart of his freedom. It is not his boundary, but his fulfillment; freedom and destiny are linked together in meaning." [33]

Kierkegaard, the great inspiration of contemporary existentialism, expresses the same idea in his stark, striking way. He sharpens the problem even more by introducing the question of evil in the world: "The whole question of God's omnipotence and goodness and its relation to evil (instead of the distinction that God works good and only permits evil) can perhaps be explained quite simply in this manner. The greatest act that can be performed by any being, greater even than any end to which it can be created, is to make it free. In order to be able to do that omnipotence is necessary. . . . God's omnipotence is therefore His goodness. For goodness means to give absolutely, yet in such a way that by taking oneself back one makes the recipient independent. From finite power comes only dependence, and omnipotence alone can make something independent, can create something out of nothing which endures of itself, because omnipotence is always taking itself back. Omnipotence cannot be involved in any relation to the other, since there is nothing to which it has any relation; it can give without giving away the least part of its power: it can make the other independent. This is what is inconceivable; omnipotence can not only bring forth the most imposing of all things, the world in its visible totality, but it can create the most delicate of all things, a creature independent

---

[33] *I and Thou,* p. 53.

of it. Omnipotence can lay its hands so heavily upon the world and yet can make its touch so light that the creature receives independence. It is only a miserable and worldly picture of the dialectic of power to say that it becomes greater in proportion as it can compel and make things dependent. Socrates knew better: the art of using power is to make free. . . . Creation out of nothing is once again the expression of omnipotence for being able to make things independent. It is to him who made me independent, while he nevertheless retained everything, that I owe all things. If in order to create man God had lost any of His power, then He could not have made man independent."[34] Kierkegaard puts the mystery of freedom in God's omnipotence. There it belongs. Perhaps we can do no more than locate the mystery properly.

From all this there begins to unfold a picture of Providence—intimately causing, intimately present—directing the beings which it places and holds in existence to the fullness of their being through activity. Created beings become creatively, some (free beings) even in such a way that the achievement of their being is at once their own and God's. Primary causality is the source and provider for secondary causality. There is a paradox in principal causality, for the greater the independence of the second cause the greater its dependence on the first cause. Where we find a higher perfection—of freedom or anything else—there we find a greater dependence on the source of that perfection. The intimacy between Pure Existence and finite existents is greatest of all when they meet in a joint activity.[35]

---

[34] From *The Journals of Søren Kierkegaard: A Selection,* ed. and trans. A. Dru (Oxford: University Press, 1938), pp. 180–81; quoted in H. Roos, *Søren Kierkegaard and Catholicism,* trans. R. Brackett (Westminster: The Newman Press, 1954), pp. 17–18.

[35] We have chosen in this chapter to meet the problem of human freedom in relation to divine causality precisely under the aspect of an effect in relation to its cause. In so doing, we might be said to have addressed ourselves to the problem of human freedom in relation to the divine will without, however, raising the question of the relationship of free human acts to divine knowledge.

The problem which divine knowledge presents in relation to free human activities may be formulated thus: if God knows, foresees, the activity of every being, must not every activity take place of necessity according as it was foreknown? The resolution of this problem comes in applying what we have seen of the Eternity of God (see pp. 200–3) to His knowledge. Since God

What we have given is perhaps a partial answer to a partial question, but it inevitably leads to yet another question, and this second question becomes more and more pressing as we unfold the meaning of Providence. We say that beings are created and tend to full being and to the diffusion of being. We say, too, that they are cared for in this tendency toward full being so that nothing touches their existence at any time save what is provided for in divine causality. If this is true, how can we explain why some beings are cut short before the fullness of their time, that forces of disintegration are at work which are no less real in experience than the forces of integration, that the world is plagued by the ravages and perversions of beings and tendencies which might have been whole, but actually are crippled in their being. How, in other words, can we explain the problem of evil?

---

is not limited to time, there is in His knowledge no before and after. All is now. Strictly speaking, it is therefore not correct to say that God "foreknows" anything. He sees all as present.

Because God's knowledge is eternal, He can know free human actions without making those actions unfree. St. Thomas explains this (see *Summa Theologiae,* I, 14, 13) by pointing out that a contingent event—which a free act would be—can be known in two ways: in its cause and in itself. To know it in its cause would be to know the agent capable of making a free choice between alternatives. To know it in itself would be to know the actual choice once it is made. Our knowledge of a free act before it takes place can only be knowledge of it in its cause. Only when it is actually made, and thus determined—freely—can we know it in itself. But God, in whose knowledge there is no before and after, can know it always both in its cause and in itself. Just as our knowledge, after-the-fact, does not impose necessity on the event, so God's knowledge holding all in the present, does not impose necessity on the event. This can be clarified with an example: Before John comes to class in the morning, we can only know that as a free agent he may or may not choose to come to class. If he actually walks in the door, we then know that he has determined his choice to attend class. The only way we can know his choice in itself is to wait and see what he chooses. The difference between our knowledge and God's is that God does not have to "wait and see." Every event is known as present. But neither our knowledge nor God's imposes necessity on the event.

If, however, God's knowledge is considered as a creative cause, our problem becomes more difficult. St. Thomas treats the causal aspect of God's knowledge in terms of His will (*Summa Theologiae,* I, 14, 8). Our treatment of divine causality and human freedom in this chapter has been an attempt to meet this aspect of the problem.

CONCLUSION

Here we have another problem, another question. Once more we must sift the truths which we have already discovered and see how we can square them with the facts which force this problem upon us. We are faced with another pair of apparent opposites—the goodness of God and the reality of evil in the world of our experience. We will face this problem, but before we do so we must advance further in our understanding of being. We will postpone our consideration of this problem, then, until we discuss goodness.[36]

Our study of the divine life and activity has told us not only about God but has helped us explain the becoming, changing, acting, stretching out of the being of creatures in time, their dynamic tendencies toward fuller being, because we have seen that the infinite activity and all-embracing Providence of God causes them to be and to become. Finite existence participates in Pure Existence, finite becoming in Absolute Being, limited activity in Infinite Life, time in Eternity, secondary causality in Primary Causality. Beings exist from their First Cause and tend toward their First Cause, for an existence received is an existence from being and from God, and every tendency is a tendency toward being and toward God.

SUGGESTED READINGS

Buber, Martin, *I and Thou,* trans. Ronald Gregor Smith (2nd ed.), pp. 51–61. New York: Charles Scribner's Sons, 1958. Buber here treats of human freedom in relation to destiny.

Gilson, Etienne, *Elements of Christian Philosophy,* pp. 193–95. Garden City, N.Y.: Doubleday & Company, Inc., 1960. Regarding secondary causality.

———, *The Spirit of Medieval Philosophy,* trans. A. H. C. Downes, Chapters 8 and 15. New York: Charles Scribner's Sons, 1936. On providence and on human freedom.

James, William, "The Dilemma of Determinism," *The Will to Believe.* New York: Dover Publications, 1956. Reprinted

---

[36] See Chapter 11.

in *A Modern Introduction to Metaphysics*, ed. D. A. Drennen, pp. 634–43. New York: The Free Press of Glencoe, Inc., 1962.

Jaspers, Karl, "Freedom and Transcendence," *The Perennial Scope of Philosophy*. New York: Philosophical Library, Inc., 1949. Also in Drennen, pp. 643–51.

Luijpen, William, *Existential Phenomenology*, Chapter 4. Pittsburgh: Duquesne University Press, 1960. Phenomenology of freedom and its destiny.

Marcel, Gabriel, "Sketch of A Phenomenology and a Metaphysic of Hope," *Homo Viator*, pp. 29–67. New York: Harper & Row, Publishers, Inc., 1962. Hope as man's response within and to his destiny.

Potter, Karl H., "Freedom and Causation," *Presuppositions of India's Philosophies*, Chapter 6, pp. 93–116. Englewood Cliffs, N.J.: Prentice-Hall, Inc., 1963. Gives overview of one aspect of Eastern thought in regard to destiny and human freedom.

St. Thomas Aquinas, *Summa Contra Gentiles*, III, 69. Concerning secondary causality.

———, *Summa Theologiae*, I, 18, 3 (regarding life in God); I, 9, 1 (on God's immutability); I, 10, 1 and 4 (on the name "Eternal"); I, 22; I, 103, 5 and 6 (on divine Providence); I, 19, 8; I, 45, 5 (on divine causality and its relation to secondary causality).

A NOTION OF BEING

INTRODUCTION

In the preceding chapters we have covered the range of being. Beginning with the material, changing beings of our experience, we analyzed them to discover their structures and argued from their insufficiency to the need to posit the existence of Pure Act, God. We studied, too, the activity of God and creatures. This has given us some idea of the richness of being, a richness which we must now investigate to see what unity we can find in it, to discover what sort of notion of being we may now be able to elaborate. We have waited until now to raise this question of a notion of being because we are convinced that it is better first to accumulate the materials, so to speak, out of which we can form a notion of being before we attempt to elaborate such a notion. It is true, of course, that we have been using an implicit notion of being throughout our whole discussion. Certainly, as soon as we discovered the primacy of existence, we discovered a way to use the name "being" to cover everything which is real. We could have stopped at this point to work out a notion of being.[1] Our decision to delay the discussion until now was based primarily on pedagogical motives. We hope that at this point "being" will be more than an empty generalization, the meaning of which is supposed to be grasped as the discussion proceeds. Having seen the range of being, we hope to be able to understand it more fully.

FORMING A NOTION OF BEING

Not by Abstraction

There is a sense in which "being" is the first concept anyone forms. St. Thomas affirms this, adding that it is the most evident concept and that every other concept is reducible to it.[2] This first conceptualization of being, however, is almost wholly implicit, and any attempt at this level to formulate explicitly the content of this idea invariably produces tautology or vague scatterings of fuzzy traces of common-sense recognition. Although we can say that being is what is, is what is real, and that reality is being, we have no grasp of the meaning of "to be" and "to be real." At such an early stage there is no way to define it or get any clear idea of it. The most we could do would be to oversimplify being into an empty concept. Heidegger warns us against this: ". . . It has been maintained that 'being' is the 'most universal' concept. . . . But the 'universality' of 'being' is not that of a *class* or *genus*. The term 'being' does not define that realm of entities which is uppermost when these are articulated conceptually according to genus and species. . . . The 'universality' of being 'transcends' any universality of genus. . . . Aristotle himself knew the unity of the transcendental universal as a *unity of analogy* in contrast to the multiplicity of the highest generic concepts applicable to things. . . . So if it is said that 'being' is the most universal concept, this cannot mean that it is the one which is clearest or that it needs no further discussion. It is rather the

---

[1] It is essentially at this point that authors such as Klubertanz explain their notion of being.
[2] *De Veritate,* 1, 1c.

darkest of all."[3] Heidegger's thought takes a different turn from ours at this point but what he says shows clearly his insight into the nature of being. He sees that it is not an essence and cannot be defined as an essence is defined, by genus and specific difference.

This understanding of the complexity of being is brought out perhaps even more clearly by Bernard Lonergan in *Insight:* "Just as other concepts, the notion of being is represented by instrumental acts that are the name, being, and the verb, to be. By mistaken analogy it is inferred that the notion of being resembles concepts in their other aspects. But, in fact, the notion of being is unique; for it is the core of all acts of meaning; and it underpins, penetrates, and goes beyond all other cognitional contents. Hence, it is idle to characterize the notion of being by appealing to the ordinary rules or laws of conception. . . . Other concepts result from some insight either into the use of their name, or into things-for-us, or into things-themselves. The notion of being penetrates all other contents, and so it is present in the formulation of every concept. It cannot result from an insight into being, for such an insight would be an understanding of everything about everything, and such understanding we have not attained."[4]

These remarks of Heidegger and Lonergan justify our reluctance to define being in the way essences are defined. Being is not essence and so we cannot, strictly speaking, form any idea or concept of being because ideas are formed by abstraction, leaving out of consideration whatever is not relevant to the idea we are elaborating. But being encompasses the whole of reality, and so we cannot leave anything out of consideration. Being therefore is not a universal concept, for such concepts are limited to the area of essence, and being must include existence. Or to put this in yet another way, our notion of being must provide for what is common in all being without reducing it to a mere common denominator (which would make it the concept with the least meaning).[5] For if we did this, the dif-

---

[3] M. Heidegger, *Being and Time,* trans. John Macquarrie and Edward Robinson (New York: Harper & Row, Publishers, Inc., 1962), pp. 22–23.
[4] B. Lonergan, *Insight* (New York: Philosophical Library, 1956), pp. 359–60.
[5] See St. Thomas, *De Potentia,* 7, 3; and *Summa Contra Gentiles,* I, 25, n. 10. On the other hand, for Thomas' consideration of *ens commune* (an abstract notion of being, the most general of all concepts), see *Super Dionysii de Divinis Nominibus,* V, lect. 2, n. 660.

ferences between beings would have to be outside of being, and so "nonbeing," which is absurd. We are trying to form a notion of being which includes all reality; but a notion of being reached by abstraction excludes all reality, and so does just the opposite of what we intend.

Negative Judgment of Separation

Clearly, therefore, we cannot proceed by way of abstraction, but must find a different route. We can do this by reviewing some of our previous discussions and studying them for clues. We have discovered in our examination of the beings of our experience that no being is merely an essence. Conversely, we have seen that none of these beings is its own "being," or in other words it is not the nature of any of these beings to be, simply and absolutely, but only to be this or that kind of being. *That they are* is due to their existence; *what they are* is due to their essence. And essence and existence are not the same. Furthermore, we attain our knowledge of existence in judgment, not in the formation of ideas. As Lonergan points out, horses and centaurs, electrons and phlogiston are equally *conceivable,* but it is in *judgment* that we decide which is real [existing] and which is not.[6] The fact that judgment puts us in contact with existence may serve as a hint that we will need judgment to elaborate our notion of being. Taking this hint, we can examine our judgments about being.

The first of these judgments deals with particular things: John is; this tree is; Fido is; this stone is; and so forth. As we study these judgments, we see that each has a particular: John, this tree, Fido, this stone, and so forth, as subject and the verb "is" as predicate. If we substitute the general pronoun for these subjects we can state our judgment generally: Something is. The important thing about this generalized statement of the judgment is that it does not leave out the particularity of the individual judgment. "Something is" can stand for each one without excluding the others. We can diagram this generalization in this way:

---

[6] *Insight,* p. 353.

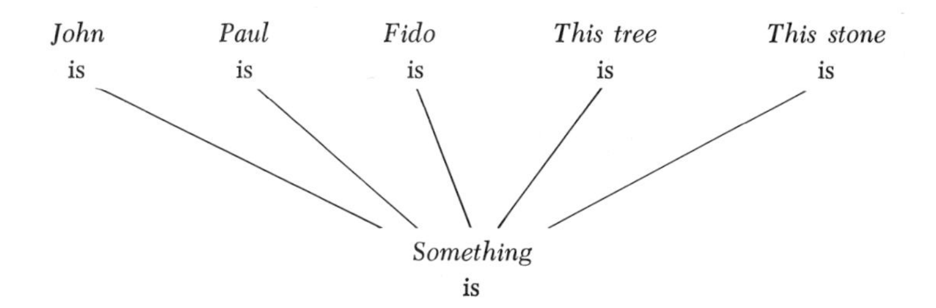

Here *Something* is expresses the being of each individual and of the whole community of being. It is a general way of expressing the common intelligibility of all beings without abstraction. In this judgment the "something" refers to the essence of the particular objects and expresses their individuality in an indeterminate, unspecified way, without, however, abstracting from any of the individuality of the essence. The "is" refers to the unique act of existing of the individual objects. It also points to the fact that the "isness," the existence of a being, is what makes it a being. A being is being not because it is material or living or intelligent, but simply because it is. Being is, therefore, *that which is.*[7]

This is an important conclusion, for it explains the meaning of what is referred to as the "negative judgment of separation." Most simply put, this judgment says that being is not limited to any genus—being is not any essence or even essence itself. It is not limited to material being or any kind of being. Thus it is a *negative* judgment. Similarly, it is a judgment of *separation,* for it separates "something is" from any class of being—material being, substance, essence. Or to put it as we did earlier: something is being not because it has this or that kind of nature but because it *is.* To be, therefore, does not mean to be material or sensible or any particular kind of thing, but to *be.*

This negative judgment of separation gives us an insight into being. It tells us that being is not limited to any genus or category

[7] *"Ens est id cujus actus est esse." Super Boethii de Hebdomadibus,* lect. 2; *Quaestiones Quodlibetales,* 2, art. 3. Literally, the quotation says: "Being is that the act of which is existence." This does not mean, "that which *has* existence," for if Thomas meant it in this way, he could not apply it to God, who, as Pure Act, does not *have* being, but *is* Being.

of reality. It gives us the synthetic notion, "something is," which respects the diversity of being while giving us some unity. We must look now to this unity in order to see whether we can understand it more fully. To do this we must see how "something is" applies to the various areas of being. This is not merely a logical consideration, but a metaphysical one, since it seeks to find the *real* unity of being which is the basis of the *logical* unity.

THE ANALOGY OF BEING

Univocal and Equivocal Predication

When we look for the unity of being in the multiplicity of being, we raise the question of the nature of our notion of being. How, we ask, can we conceptualize our insight that being is that which is? Obviously when we say "conceptualize," we are not talking about forming an essentialistic type of concept. Being, to repeat once again, is not an essence. The concept we have of an essence is a univocal concept,[8] one which has the same meaning each time it is applied. Thus, for example, a concept such as "man" means the same thing when applied to James, John, Peter, and Paul. And "flower" applied to rose, daffodil, gardenia, and hibiscus means the same thing. Such univocal concepts are elaborated by way of "abstraction," that is, we pick out the meaning common among a group of things and conceptualize it in one idea, for example, man or flower. This gives another reason why "being" cannot be conceptualized by a univocal concept. For if it were, it would have to abstract from some of reality and leave it out of consideration. And this is precisely what we cannot do with our notion of being. It must include the whole of reality.

A second type of predication is possible, namely, *equivocal* predication, in which there are different meanings for different uses of a term, for example, "bark" as applied to a dog and to a tree. We must examine this type of predication to see whether our use of "being" is an equivocal use of the word. We have to say "equivocal predication," rather than "equivocal concept," because in equivocal usage there is no single concept, but only the same word and differ-

[8] For the types of predication see *In Metaphysicam,* IV, lect. 1, n. 534.

ent concepts. An example will clarify this. When "bark" is predicated equivocally of a dog and of a tree, there is not one concept or meaning, "bark," but two. In one case it refers to the noise a dog makes and in the other to the outer surface of a tree. The two meanings are simply different. What about "being"? Is the meaning simply different in each case? When I say, John is a being; this rose is a being; this horse is a being, am I saying something simply different in each case? Clearly not. For although each thing is what it is, and so is unique, yet each being does share in existence. Consequently, being cannot mean something totally different each time it is applied.

The Meaning of Analogy

There is a third alternative. Although being is not a univocal concept nor an equivocal term, it may be used "analogously," that is, in a way at once alike and different. We speak this way, for instance, when we say a person is healthy and food is healthy, or when we say that someone has a fiery temper and that autumn leaves are fiery. We call a person healthy because he has health, and food healthy because it is health-giving. We call someone's temper fiery because it is hot and flashes like fire, and autumn leaves fiery because they have the red color of fire. There is a relationship to health in the first two examples and to fire in the second two, but the relationship is not the same in each case. Hence the terms are used in a way which is partly the same and partly different.

From these examples we see that analogy is not used uniquely by the metaphysician, but has become part and parcel, whether consciously or not, of our thought and vocabulary long before we encounter it in the analogy of being. But although we use it every day it is still in itself difficult to understand, for when we try to analyze it we find many usages which defy classification, and there are centuries of theories of analogy which tend to confuse the issue, at least for the beginner. If we stay with the fundamentals, however, we can say that two things are said to be analogous when, though they are unlike one another, they do share some basis of resemblance. The analogy between them points to some relationship of similarity which they have to one another, and some proportion [9] or ratio

---

[9] The word "analogy" derives from the Greek word for "proportion" or "ratio."

which makes possible the comparison between the two. Thus, for instance, all the uses of the word "healthy" relate in some way to the favorable condition of a living body. The body possesses health, food causes health, a climate conduces to health, a complexion manifests health. Scientists use analogy in a similar way when they try to explain the subatomic world to laymen in terms of the macroscopic world of direct experience. The poet, too, uses analogy in his metaphors when he compares one thing to another on the basis of some likeness—the angry wind, the lonely beach, the sighing trees, and so on. We, too, continually use analogy in the ordinary conversation of our workaday world: strong as an ox, a brogue so thick one could cut it, as neat as a pin, and as sly as a serpent. It is no wonder that we find this at all levels, for reality at every level is pervaded with likeness and yet unlikeness, with unity and diversity.

Kinds of Analogy

If reality is analogous and has this unity and diversity, it follows that our knowledge of reality will be formulated and expressed analogously. To see how this analogous formulation and expression of being and our knowledge of being is to be worked out, we will have to look at the unity and diversity of being. We have already seen that there is some unity in the diversity of being: each being shares in existence. We know from this that there must be some analogy of being. To be able to make this general statement, however, is only the beginning, for to understand the analogy of being we must understand what analogy or what analogies are involved in the analogy of being. There are various types of analogy, not all of which are easily categorized. Some analogies involve a comparison of one thing to others on the basis of an attribute which only one of the analogates [10] possesses intrinsically. In this kind of analogy the other things referred to do not actually possess the attribute but have some resemblance or relationship to it. Thus, in the example of health, which we used before, health as an attribute exists

---

[10] "Analogates," or "analogues," are the objects of comparison to which an analogous concept applies. For example, steak and leather are two analogates to which the term "good" can apply analogously; both steak and leather are good, but in an analogous way.

intrinsically only in living bodies. It is attributed to food, complexion, climate, and so forth, because they are a cause, an effect, or an indication of health, or bear some relation to health. Similarly, the comparison involved in any purely metaphorical analogy is based on the same sort of intrinsic possession by one analogate and "attribution" in some way to the other analogates. So, when we say that a man has a fiery temper or the autumn leaves are fiery, they do not possess fire intrinsically, but are somehow compared to the flames of the fire.

On the other hand, sometimes two things are analogous because of some perfection or attribute which both possess intrinsically, but not in the same way. For instance, the perfection may belong primarily and perfectly to one and only secondarily and imperfectly to the other. Every cause and effect relationship is analogous to some extent in this way. We can see this best in a few examples. Parents, for instance, possess the human nature which they cause in their children, and the artist possesses the beauty which he puts into the picture, and the inventor possesses the idea which he embodies in the new mousetrap which brings the world to his door.

We can discover a third type of analogy by looking at the first type in a different way. If in our examples of "healthy" and "fiery" we take the analogates which do not possess health and fire intrinsically, we can say that they are analogous not because of a direct relation to each other, but because of a shared relationship to something else, to that which possesses the attribute intrinsically. In this way, complexion and climate and food would be analogously called healthy because of their relationship to a living being who can, properly speaking, possess the perfection of health.

Although these and other forms of analogy have received various names, they can perhaps all be classified generically as analogies of attribution, because in each of them something which belongs primarily to one of the terms, for example, health to living beings, fiery to fire, and so forth, is *attributed* to something else, which, properly speaking, does not possess it. There is also another type of analogy which is not between individual terms but between sets of these terms, or rather between the relationships or proportions between the two terms in each set. For instance, we find this sort of analogy between the relationship between sense knowledge and the sensible world and the relationship between intellectual knowledge and intelligible objects. This type of analogy is called analogy of proportionality. The proportionality is "proper" when we are referring to an intrinsic perfection, and "improper" when we are speaking metaphorically. Thus when we say, "A mighty fortress is our God," we do not literally mean that the relationship between God and us is like that between a fortress and the people within the fortress. The fortress is obviously not a personal protector of those within it.[11] Our interest is in the analogy of *proper* proportionality, in which there is a similarity of proportions, a proportion between proportions.

Being and the Analogy of Proper Proportionality

We are interested in this type of analogy because it has meaning for our study of the analogy of being. Since in considering the limited beings of experience we have come to an understanding of essence and existence as the ultimate constituent principles of each being, we can see that it is common to each being to have essence and existence, but not common to each to have a common essence and existence—since each has a unique individual essence and a unique individual existence proportioned to that essence. There is therefore no common nature of essence or existence; there is no one essence or one existence which all possess, but in each being there is a relationship between its individual essence and its individual existence which is similar to the relationship between individual essence and individual existence in other beings. This is, of course, a similarity of proportions, of the relationships between each essence and each existence. Each essence is related to its existence in a way similar to that in which every other essence is related to its existence. John's essence is to John's existence as Peter's essence is to Peter's existence as this tree's essence is to this tree's existence, and so forth. This is to say that although no two beings exist in the same way, each nevertheless exists in a way which is according to its nature, its essence. Since there is this relationship in finite beings, they are

[11] For a discussion of metaphor see R. Boyle, "The Nature of Metaphor," *Modern Schoolman,* XXXI, No. 4 (May 1954), 267–80.

thus analogous by an analogy of proper proportionality, and every finite being can thus be called and be understood to be "being" by this analogy.[12]

Not only is there an analogy of proportionality between being and being, but there is the same sort of analogous relationship within each being. For example, existence, substantial form, and accidental forms are all actual principles, but the term "act" applies to them not univocally but analogously. Act does not have the same meaning with regard to existence as it has in regard to substantial form. Act in regard to accidental form means something the same yet somehow different from act as applied to existence and substantial form.[13] This is so because each "act" *actuates* its correlate in its own way. Existence makes a thing to be simply (that is, to exist), all forms whether accidental or substantial make the thing to be this or that type of being, rather than to be simply. The relationship, however, of existence to essence and of substantial form to primary matter and of accidental form to substance is similar in that it is in each case an act-potency relationship. Thus, by an analogy of proper proportionality, existence : essence : : substanial form : primary mat-

---

[12] A great deal of controversy in recent years has surrounded the analogy of proper proportionality in regard to the analogy of being. Some Thomists have held that it is the only analogy possible in the analogous understanding of being, since it is the only form of analogy which preserves the infinite distance between God and creatures. Others have argued that it cannot be used at all in regard to the relation between God and creatures because it implies a distinction between essence and existence in God. This latter, of course, is avoided by pointing out that all that is meant is that each being exercises its act of existence in accord with its nature, and it is the nature of God to be His own act of existence. However, the sole use of analogy of proper proportionality was for years based on the supposed position of St. Thomas; recent studies have indicated St. Thomas held this position only briefly, later rejecting it in favor of an analogy of causality between God and His effects. Certainly his texts on the names of God seem to favor this latter conclusion. This question is discussed more fully in succeeding chapters. See G. Klubertanz, *Saint Thomas Aquinas on Analogy* (Chicago: Loyola University Press, 1960); Gerald Phelan, *St. Thomas and Analogy* (Milwaukee: Marquette University Press, 1941). By limiting this analogy to finite beings we can bypass this controversy.

[13] An example of the difference in the meaning of act when applied to existence from its meaning when applied to substantial form is that in the former it is determined, and in the latter, it is the determining principle.

ter : : accidental form : substance : : activity : nature : : act : potency. This reads: existence is to essence as substantial form is to primary matter as accidental form is to substance as activity is to nature as act is to potency.

We can see from this that the analogy of proper proportionality unifies our notion of finite being. Without entering into the debate about how it can be applied to God, we can say that we may use it at least for *our knowledge* of God. For when we think of God as infinite being, we have to think of essence and existence in God, even though we must immediately add that although we think of God in this way, we know that essence and existence are one in God. This, of course, is to stretch our notion of essence to mean only what God is and to exclude the necessary notes of essence in creatures, namely *potency* and subject of existence. As long as we are careful to understand what we are saying, we may say that God's "essence" is to exist. Similarly, we may have to think of God's knowing, willing, and loving as "acts" of God which have a proportion to His being. Again, as soon as we say this, we have to add that in God His "act of knowing" is identified with His being. God is Pure Act and absolutely simple Pure Existence, but we have to *think* of His being in terms of proper proportionality. In this sense proper proportionality enters into our total notion of being.

Being and the Analogy of Causality

Perhaps, however, the analogy of causality may give us a less confusing notion of the unity of being in its diversity. This, as we have intimated, is an analogy of attribution. To see its meaning we must review some of the conclusions which we reached in our discovery of Pure Existence. In this and in the ensuing discussion we saw that all finite beings are composed of essence and existence, potency and act in the order of being, and so do not explain their existence. We saw, too, that only Pure Act, God, explains His own existence and the existence of all finite being. He explains finite reality as the Creator of its total being.

If we examine the range of being, therefore, from God down through spiritual beings to the lowest material being we see existence at all of its various levels.[14] God, the highest and greatest being, is the source of all existence and so of all being (since existence is the act of being). Under God all creatures share in being as effects of God's being. They therefore have existence, and so being, by *attribution;* being is *attributed* to them by God their cause, hence they have their being by *causal* attribution. Since they possess being intrinsically, this is an intrinsic attribution. Since the being in each is shared a different way, the unity of this causal attribution is not univocal but *analogous.* Each finite being intrinsically and in its own way possesses being as an effect, and so shares in being by an analogy of intrinsic causal attribution.

This analogy can be extended to God because God is being by His essence and is the source and cause of all being. Consequently, He is the primary analogate. What finite beings possess as effects, He possesses in its fullness as cause. Hence we can say that by the analogy of causal attribution our notion of being extends to the whole range of being. We should bear in mind, however, that God is not simply the highest in the series of beings. Between the highest creature and God there is an infinite gap. All finite beings are effects; only God is being in Himself and by His nature, in no way an effect. By seeing God as the unique cause of being and all creatures as effects, the analogy of causal attribution emphasizes this "transcendence" of God.

Being and Participation

Sometimes this analogy is called the analogy of participation rather than the analogy of causal attribution. The difference, however, is one of names rather than of reality, for when we say that finite beings share in existence, and so in being, we are simply using the Anglo-Saxon derivative rather than the Latin derivative, "participate." Limited being at every level "participates" in the being which God has by His essence.

---

[14] There is some danger of confusion in speaking of "levels" of being with God on the highest level since it does not sufficiently emphasize the "transcendence" of God. God is not the highest as first in a series. He is outside the series, above and beyond it. As long as we remember that God is not the top rung of a ladder of being, but the transcendent creator and conserver of all finite reality, we can call Him the highest.

There are certain dangers to be avoided in the use of the phrase "participation in the being of God" which we have just used. We do not mean that creatures do not have their own being. They share in God's being by having *their own being.* We are not implying anything like a pantheistic identification of all beings with God as a part of God. Pantheism suppresses the true reality of creatures and contradicts the multiplicity and diversity of being which we experience. Pantheism also contradicts the infinity of God, for it denies to God the power to create finite beings distinct from Himself. Nor in talking about participation do we mean to imply that God is somehow divided up so that creatures would receive a part of God the way someone receives a piece of pie. God does not lose anything or any part of Himself when He gives being to creatures. We have alluded to this before when we said that the teacher can cause knowledge in the pupil without himself losing that knowledge. In a real sense there is more knowledge existing in the world when both the teacher and the student know a truth, but in another sense it is really the same knowledge, for the pupil does not know anything more than the teacher or anything different from what the teacher knows. We can make a kind of rough and ready comparison between the sharing of the teacher's knowledge by the pupil and our sharing of God's being. In both cases we have "something new" existing, and yet no reduction in the knowledge or being of the cause. Further, the participation we are considering does not imply that God and creatures share, analogously or otherwise, in a perfection which is common to both and prior to both. Our example of the teacher and the pupil does not work here. The teacher first must learn before he can teach the pupil and both teacher and pupil are dependent on the truth of being and the validity of their knowledge is measured by the truth of being. For St. Thomas, the creature is not said to be similar to God as though God participated in the same form which the creature shared.[15] God *is* wholly what every other being shares partially. Thus, God is not a participator of being; being is predicated of Him as He who is participated and of creatures as participants. To safeguard the profound meaning of participation it is helpful to remember that when it is used in this

[15] *De Veritate,* 2, 11 ad 4.

context it implies on the one hand a source which has all the perfection which we are discussing, and on the other, recipients or participants who have part of the perfection which the source possesses totally. It implies further that there is a continuing relationship of dependence of the participants on the source. To summarize, when we speak of the analogy of participation or sharing we might just as easily call it an analogy of causal attribution. We are not speaking of two categories of analogy but merely of two ways of stating the same understanding of the analogical unity of being.

CONCLUSION

The burden of this chapter has been to underline the unity in multiplicity which characterizes being and our understanding of it. We have discovered an analogical unity which we have expressed in two ways: the analogy of proper proportionality and the analogy of causal attribution or participation. We should emphasize that although these notions are valid, they are fraught with the limitations which hem in all our thinking about being. With our finite minds we can understand being only in a very limited way. We do not *comprehend* being or understand it fully. Only the infinite mind of God, which is commensurate with the infinity of being, can do that. But, as far as they go, our notions of being give us true insights into being. We do not penetrate the full mystery of being, but we speak whereof we have something to say, limited though our discourse be.

We have one more general topic to discuss before concluding our study of being. We have travelled the long and hard road from our first awareness of the beings of our experience to carefully elaborated notions of being. It remains for us to examine the most general modes of being, those strange predicates which cut through all levels and types of being, the *transcendentals.*

SUGGESTED READINGS

Clarke, W. Norris, "The Limitation of Act by Potency: Aristotelianism or Neoplatonism," *New Scholasticism,* XXVI (1952), 167–94. Considerations of the meaning of participation.

Clarke, W. Norris, "The Meaning of Participation in St. Thomas," *Proceedings of the American Catholic Philosophical Association,* XXVI (1952), 147–57.

Gilson, Etienne, *The Spirit of Medieval Philosophy,* trans. A. H. C. Downes, pp. 447–48, n. 14. New York: Charles Scribner's Sons, 1936. On analogy and participation.

Heidegger, Martin, *Being and Time,* trans. John Macquarrie and Edward Robinson, Introduction I. New York: Harper & Row, Publishers, Inc., 1962. On the meaning of being.

Johann, Robert O., "Community and Communion," in *The Meaning of Love,* Chapter 2. Westminster: The Newman Press, 1959. Bases understanding of love on understanding of participation.

Klubertanz, George P., *St. Thomas Aquinas on Analogy,* pp. 55–64. Chicago: Loyola University Press, 1960. On the meaning of participation in St. Thomas. Chapter 6: Systematic summary of the kinds of analogy used by St. Thomas and their relative importance in his theory.

Lonergan, Bernard J. F., *Insight,* Chapter 12. New York: Philosophical Library, 1956. On forming a notion of being.

Marcel, Gabriel, *The Mystery of Being,* I. *Reflection and Mystery,* pp. 35 f. Chicago: Henry Regnery Co., 1960. Gives expanded use of participation in referring to personal participation in Absolute Presence.

Maritain, Jacques, *The Degrees of Knowledge,* trans. Gerald B. Phelan, pp. 418–21. New York: Charles Scribner's Sons, 1959. On the notion of being.

———, *Existence and the Existent,* trans. L. Galantiere and Gerald Phelan, pp. 20–55. Garden City, New York: Doubleday & Company, Inc., 1956. On the notion of being.

Phelan, Gerald, *St. Thomas and Analogy.* Milwaukee: Marquette University Press, 1941.

St. Thomas Aquinas, *De Veritate,* 2, 11. On analogous predication.

———, *Summa Contra Gentiles,* I, 34. On the analogy between God and creatures.

———, *Summa Theologiae,* I, 35, 5. Shows that perfections cannot be predicated of God and creature univocally.

THE TRANSCENDENTAL FULLNESS OF BEING: I. UNITY AND TRUTH

INTRODUCTION

Man needs many words and many ideas to know and to express what, if his mind were greater and his understanding purer, he might know with a single idea and express in a single word. "Being" might be this word, for in a way it says everything; and yet all that it might say is not clear to us, for the limitations of human reason keep us from seeing all the fullness of being at once. However, as with other things, although we cannot see the fullness of being all at once, we can approach it in different ways and see different aspects of it at different times. As with a diamond, the whole beauty of which cannot be seen from one of its sides, but which can always be turned to see it better in all its dimensions, so being presents its different faces and each new vantage point gives a new revelation of the whole. Like a diamond, each view of which is an invitation to look at it from another angle, being demands of its viewer that he seek further insight into it. Every dimension of being speaks of itself and heralds yet another dimension beyond. If we could turn it over in our hands as we can a jewel, we might see at least every outer face it shows and resign ourselves to writing poetry about the mysteries of its depths within. But we, who are participants in being, are like one face of the diamond; we cannot turn it in our hands. Just as the facet of the diamond cannot stand back and look at the whole diamond, so we cannot stand outside of being and contemplate being.

This, however, does not mean that the meaning of being is so locked within it that we must surrender before its hiddenness. There are other ways in which it opens to our understanding, other faces in the vision of which we come closer—however short our advance—to seeing the whole of being. As a diamond flashes forth its visages, being as being gives rise to concepts which, like "being" itself, transcend any limitation to genus or species and speak of all reality. These, like "being," have been called "transcendentals."

Meaning of Transcendental

The transcendentals simply express other ways of understanding and saying "being." They are not synonymous with "being," but they refer to the same reality. Since that to which they refer is identical with being, all their meaning could be said to be contained implicitly in the concept of "being." But although they refer to the same reality, they render explicit an aspect of being which was before implicit, and so the different meaning. In this situation of referring to the same reality but with some difference of meaning the transcendentals are distinguished from each other by a minor mental distinction,[1] a distinction made by the mind in order to grasp what is not really distinct in reality. We must make such distinctions because our intellect cannot hold in one idea that which is too full for it to comprehend in one conception, so it must resort to many ideas all of which express or emphasize part of the fullness of what it knows.[2]

---

[1] See Chapter 3, note 17.

[2] St. Thomas, in speaking of the plurality of names all used to signify God, which are distinguished, like the transcendentals, by a minor mental distinction, says this: "The plurality of names comes from the fact that God is greater than our intellect. And the fact that God is greater than our intellect, on God's

There are four transcendentals which most consistently express man's insight into being: unity, truth, goodness, and beauty. But as we look at these and the way that metaphysicians have defined them, we cannot leave behind what we have already discovered of being —existence, Pure Existence, activity, Life. For whatever illumines being as being will shed light for our understanding of these new aspects of being which we are now discussing. If being is one and true and good and beautiful, it will be so ultimately by reason of that within it which makes it being—the act of existing. Further, if the act of existing and all else in finite reality is intelligible only in relation to its First Cause, to Pure Existence, the unity or truth or goodness or beauty of finite being will have its intelligibility only in relation to its First Cause precisely as Unity, Truth, Goodness, and Beauty. Finally, since existing being has an ordination or drive to activity, the transcendental aspects of being can be related to corresponding activities. Knowledge, love, and joy will be the activities corresponding to truth, goodness, and beauty. By studying these activities as a kind of fulfillment of these transcendentals, we may get a deeper insight into the nature of the transcendentals.[3] Consequently, in this and the next chapter we shall try to discover the transcendental aspects of being, understand them as they are in finite and infinite being, and unfold the activities which express them.

---

part, is because of the fullness of His perfection, and on our part, the intellect deficiently understands Him. So it is clear that the plurality of those intelligibilities arises not only from the side of our intellect, but also from the side of God, inasmuch as His perfection is greater than any conception of our intellect. Thus, to the plurality of intelligibilities there corresponds something from the side of God's reality—not indeed a real plurality, but a full perfection because of which all these conceptions are suited to Him. . . . On the side of our intellect, and also of the effects—from which we come to know God—[something corresponds] because our intellect cannot conceive the divine perfection with one concept only, but needs many. . . . Therefore, there is something in God which corresponds to all these concepts, namely, his full and every-sided perfection, according to which any name signifying any of these conceptions is truly and properly predicated of God." *In I Sententiarum,* d.2, q.1, a.3. What is true in the naming of God is also true in the forming of transcendentals which can be predicated of all being.

[3] Although there is activity which corresponds to unity, uniting activity, it is seen precisely under the other activities of knowledge, love, and joy.

Since there is an order in which the human mind develops its ideas of the transcendentals, it would be unwise to discuss them with no reference to our way of knowing them. We can become aware of this order if we realize that each transcendental makes explicit something about being. When we think of being we think of it first as unity, as being what it is and not something else. Secondly, we look at being in its relationship to mind, and so see its truth. Finally, the being we know is perceived to be good and beautiful. If we follow this order, it becomes clear that each succeeding transcendental includes the meaning of the one which precedes it and makes explicit something additional. Each, therefore, gives a further revelation of the fullness of being. In reality being is unity and unity is truth and truth is goodness and beauty—that which we are talking about is the same in all the transcendentals—and yet the meaning of each succeeding transcendental includes that of the others in a climactic order which ends in all-embracing beauty. Our later discussion will have to elucidate the full meaning of this statement.

Besides this order, which considers the transcendentals somewhat statically as "attributes" of being, there is a similar order among them based on the activities which correspond to what is indicated by the transcendentals as aspects of being. If instead of truth, goodness and beauty we take knowledge, love, and joy, it is clear again that each includes the meaning of that which precedes it and adds something more.

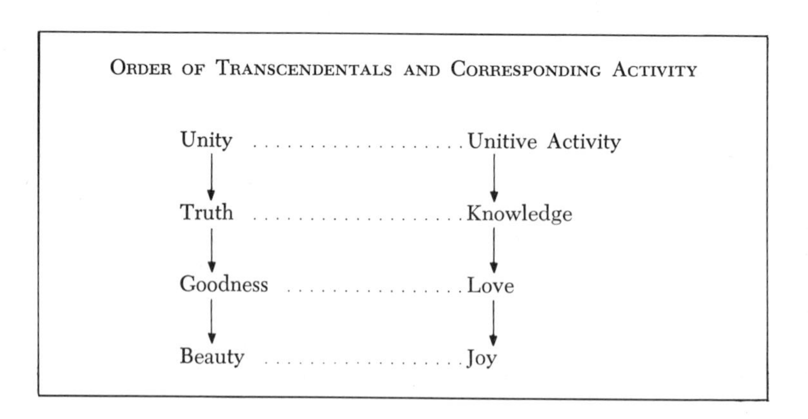

Transcendentals and the Names of God

As we consider each of the transcendentals, we will have to investigate how they apply to Absolute Being. We will find that when we study the affirmative absolute names of God with reference to the transcendentals, a new dimension will be added to our understanding of these names. We will take another look at God as Being and Life and go on to consider Him as absolute and infinite Truth and Wisdom, Goodness and Love, Beauty and Joy.[4] Again, as we considered the transcendentals in general somewhat statically and then dynamically, we can study the transcendentals with relation to God "substantially" and "operatively." As Pure Existence can be unfolded to mean absolute Truth, Goodness, and Beauty, so Life —infinite activity—can be unfolded to mean perfect Knowledge, Love, and Joy.

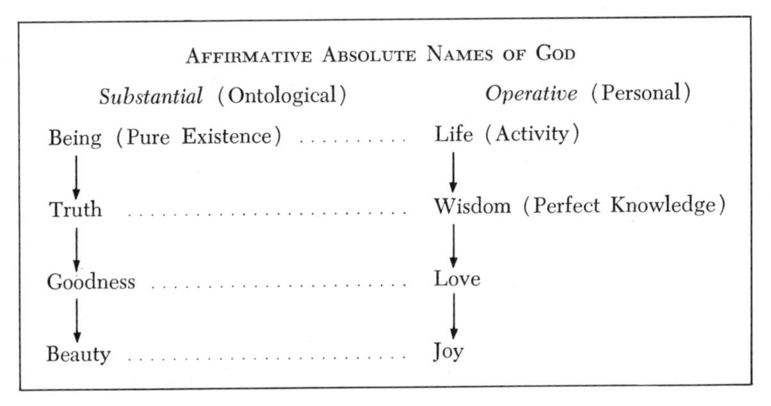

If each name which refers to a "substantial," or ontological, perfection in God is seen truly to correspond to a name which gives an operative perfection, it should become clear that God is a self-possessing reality, a personal reality. And as the transcendentals may

---

[4] Unity in its usual sense is not an affirmative absolute name but a negative absolute name. As we shall see, it negates division in being. Nevertheless, it should be kept in mind that every negative implies something positive.

be said to give an expanding revelation of being, so these names of God may be said to give an expanding revelation of Being, so that each name in each series, "substantial" and "operational," includes what is in the notion of the preceding name and adds something to that notion, culminating in our knowledge of God as Infinite Beauty and Perfect Joy.

Our procedure in naming these affirmative absolute perfections of God will be the same for each. As we discover the transcendentals, we will find perfections in the beings of experience. If these perfections are "mixed" perfections,[5] they are in God *virtually*,[6] and we can proceed no further in our argument. If they are pure perfections, they are in God *properly*, and can be so predicated of Him. They must, however, be purified by negation, a negation of all limitation—they cannot be caused, composed, spatial, changeable, temporal, multiple, or finite in any way. Our problem is not so much that of determining whether these perfections are in God, since we know that they are in Him because He is the cause of them in the beings of our experience. Our problem is to understand the *meaning* of the perfections—for even when we ask only of limited being, "What is truth?" or "What, after all, is love?" or "What is a beautiful being?" we stumble in our answers. And when we ask these things of Absolute Being, we move closer to the brilliant light of the mystery of God which so exceeds our power of knowing that it is for us darkness.

To round out our treatment of the transcendentals as we see them in the infinitely distant poles of reality—finite and infinite—we shall attempt to bring these two poles together as far as humanly possible by following our treatment of the transcendental perfections as they are seen in the beings of our experience and in our knowledge of God with a study of the relationship between God and creatures as it appears in the transcendentals. To do this we will have to consider the operational names of God not only as they name Him in Himself, apart from any relation to His effects, but as they name Him with relation to these effects. Thus, for example,

---

[5] See Chapter 6, note 16.

[6] "Virtually" here means the possession of these by God only insofar as he has the power to cause them in others.

while knowledge and love are to be understood as they are in God Himself, in His own Life, they will also be considered in the creative activity of God, naming Him once more according to what He is to His creatures.

TRANSCENDENTAL UNITY

Unity: Being as Undivided

There is an undividedness about every being, and this undividedness is its unity. To be somehow one in itself belongs to every being.[7]

Every being in our experience presents itself to us with this unity. A dog nuzzling the hand of its master is undivided. Everything within him goes to make him this dog. A tree outside the window, growing strong and whole, literally pulses with the forces of unification within it. If it should be cut down and dismembered, it will lose its unity and at the same stroke, will lose its being as a tree.

Being and undividedness, then, are the same reality. In no instance if a being is wholly disintegrated does it remain *a being;* in no case is it unified if it has not being. Of course, there will be as many kinds of unity as there are kinds of being. The unity of a nonliving being will not be the same as the unity of a living being. The unity of a spiritual being will not be that of a material being. The unity of Absolute Being cannot be identical with the unity of finite being.

Unity Within a Being

If we have understood what makes a being to be, we will see that it makes very great sense to say that every being has unity. If a single act of existing makes all that is in a being real, it is clear that the ultimate intrinsic principle of a being—the act of existing—is at one and the same time its ultimate unifying principle. Within a

[7] See *Summa Theologiae,* I, 11, 1. It is helpful in understanding the transcendental "one" to distinguish it from the mathematical "one." The latter is one in a series of numbers, a unit in counting. Transcendental oneness is the oneness of undividedess, being itself under the aspect of its unity, its absence of division. See also *Summa Theologiae,* I, 11, 2.

being of experience, each of the principles of being besides existence is united with the others precisely because it shares in the reality given by the one act of existing—so that substance and accident are distinct, yet one as principles of one being. Similarly accident is united with substance and power is united with activity, each distinct from the others yet made one by one source of actuality, the act of existing of the being. Where there is one act of existing all these principles constitute one and the same being. Where there is more than one act of existing, there is more than one being.

In the beings of our experience existence is always joined to essence, and it is essence which limits existence so that it is a certain kind of existence. By limiting existence in this way, essence determines the mode of being which a thing has and so determines the kind of unity which a thing has. Consequently, it is the essential mode of existence which a being exercises that determines its unity. Whether a being has many parts or few parts is not the important factor in this determination. Hence it is possible for more complex beings, such as living beings, to be more unified than beings with fewer parts, for instance nonliving beings. Living beings, with a higher mode of existence, are radically more unified than nonliving beings because the exigencies of life demand a more concentrated direction of activity than is found in nonliving beings.

One conclusion at least is clear from all this: regardless of the mode of existence in a given being, therefore regardless of the modifications of the unity of the being, every act of existing brings actuality and undividedness. Hence, there is unity throughout reality. It is for this reason that unity is known as a transcendental —for it applies to all being regardless of genus or species.

Imperfect being: imperfect undividedness Where the act of existing makes actual more than one principle in a being, the being is obviously composed of "parts." The unity which such a being has must be a "unity of composition."

Any composed being, as we have seen, is a limited being.[8] And a thing limited in its being will be limited in its unity. Although such a being, insofar as it is a being, is undivided, its undividedness is

[8] See Chapter 3, *passim*.

not absolute. Its act of existing makes it a being and makes it one. But a limited being is utterly contingent upon an outside efficient cause; it has of itself no necessary claim on existence and, thus, no necessary claim on unity. To be any being that is undivided by a "unity of composition" is indeed to be undivided but is not to be indivisible.[9] Where there are parts, there is always the possibility of disintegration and loss of both unity and being. If the parts should divide, the being must either return to nothingness, or become more than one being—the parts then having their separate acts of existing and forming thus new beings and new unities.

We have seen that all the beings of experience are composed. They all, therefore, have a "unity of composition," and there are as many kinds of unities of composition as there are kinds of composed beings.

Perfect being: perfect undividedness Although undividedness is a negative way of expressing being, it nevertheless signifies something positive. To say that a being is not divided, that there is in it an absence of division, is to imply that it is a whole from within, cohesive in whatever parts or lack of parts it may have, integral in itself. Since the unity of a being is its being—for unity and being differ only in meaning, not in reality—the more perfect a being's unity, the more perfect is its being. For this reason the degree of unity in any being is a sign of its perfection as a being.

It is quite evident in the beings of experience, whose unity is the "unity of composition," that the greater their unity the greater their perfection or actuality. As we have seen above, living beings are incomparably more unified than nonliving beings and incomparably greater in being. For example, the achievement of full personality for a man is decidedly an achievement of greater and greater unity within himself—the resolution of conflicts, the harmonization of the tendencies of all his powers, the unification of his love and so his

---

[9] This is true, therefore, not only of material beings, whose physical parts are divisible—or what we call corruptible. It is true even of beings who are not composed in the order of essence—for example, pure spirits. These are still composed of distinct principles in the order of existence, and hence they are still undivided but divisible. This divisibility, however, is not a *natural* divisibility because purely spiritual beings have no *intrinsic* principle of corruptibility.

life, the integration of what at first may have been experienced as being "torn apart" or "at loose ends," the "pulling together" of himself at the profound levels of his being.

If unity is a sign of perfection because it is identical with being, where there is limited being there will always be limited unity. This much we have seen. On the other hand, where there is perfect being there must be perfect unity. He Who is Absolute Being, must be Absolute One.

Unity in being comes from the act of existing. We have seen that God is His own pure act of existing, joined to no potency, unlimited, uncomposed, infinite. A being which has no composition at any level is utterly simple, utterly without parts.[10] He is identified with Himself in every respect. This unity is the "unity of simplicity." It alone is perfect unity, perfect integrity, perfect self-possession. It is dependent on no other being, sufficient unto itself. Unlike the "unity of composition," it is not only undividedness but indivisibility. Where there is no composition of parts, there is no possibility whatever of division.[11]

When even essence and existence are absolutely one, therefore, there can be no question of a particular mode of existence or modification of unity. To name God "Unity," or "One" is to negate of Him every kind of division.[12]

Unity Among Beings

Although the primary unity of being is the unity *within* each being, it is possible to speak of unity *between* beings. There, of course, we have more than one act of existing and so the unity will

---

[10] See Chapter 3.

[11] See *Summa Theologiae,* I, 11, 4 and I, 3, 4 and 7.

[12] There is sometimes a confusion between the name "One" as it refers to the absolute undividedness of God and to His uniqueness. In the first sense it carries the meaning of the transcendental one, and in the second it carries the meaning of "not many." There is a relationship between the two, however: It is because God is simple, with no composition, that He cannot be multiplied. There is and can be only one God, one infinite being. (Two infinite beings would entail a contradiction; if both were infinite, they would differ in nothing, and so be one.) Thus, depending on the meaning given to "One," it may negate a multiplicity of gods or a multiplicity—division—within God. St. Thomas speaks of it in both senses in *Summa Theologiae,* I, 11.

be a quite different unity from the unity within an individual being.[13]

Finite beings are united by their very participation in being, united to one another and to God as finite sharers in Pure Existence. To participate in being is to participate in unity. Although each being has its own existence and its own unity, it has both by participation. There is, therefore, not merely a unity in each being but a com-munity among beings.

Beings are united not only by their participation in existence, however, but also by participation in the same essence.[14] Beings with the same essence are united in the same species by their sharing in that essence. Since it is the same essence, there is a way in which we can say it is one essence, even though multiplied in many individuals. This is the foundation of, for example, the meaning we give to the natural "solidarity" of mankind—all men are united by reason of their share in human nature.

Beings are united even by sharing in the same accidental perfections. There is a oneness of all white beings, for instance, because they all share the same quality of whiteness. There is also a kind of accidental unity which is not based on sharing of an intrinsic perfection such as color, but because of some existential proximity, as in space and time. We have, for example, a certain unity when a number of things are together in what we call a pile. The unity of the pile is not the unity of a thing with one act of existence, but the unity of a certain accidental conjunction in space. We see the same in relation to time, as when we speak of a generation or a crop. In these cases we gather the things together because they occur at the same time or nearly the same time. Other unities can be based on participation in culture or belief or race. Since these do not affect the essential nature of the beings, they must be called accidental unities. The same is true when beings are united because they share the same activity or the same purpose, as, for example, when people work together as a team or on a committee. In these various ex-

---

[13] *Summa Theologiae,* I, 11, 1 ad 2.

[14] This participation is not the same as the participation of finite beings in Infinite Being. Here none of the beings *is* what the others participate. Rather, all share in a common perfection. The ultimate source of this perfection is, of course, God. See Chapter 6, *passim.*

tended meanings of unity we see greater or lesser unity depending on the closeness of the ties between the beings which are so united.

Because unity is a transcendental, applying to every being and to every aspect of being, it must, like being, be predicated analogously of beings. It means something the same and something different when it is used to refer to the different kinds of unity in different kinds of being.[15]

Summary

KINDS OF UNITY IN BEING

Unity Within Individual Beings

A. Unity of Composition
(among parts, undivided but divisible)

1a. one act of existing unifying one being
b. one essence determining one kind of unity
} = *Per Se* Unity *

2a. unity between substance and accidents in one being
b. unity between different accidents in one being
} = Unity *Per Accidens* *

B. Unity of Simplicity
(no parts, undivided and indivisible)

Unity Among Beings

By participation in
1. being (existence)—united as being
2. essence—united in same species
3. accidental form or relations—Accidental Unity *

N.B. Accidental Unity can be:
static (in terms of accidental relations other than those based on activity)
or
dynamic (in terms of activity)

* These are the traditional names given to identify these forms of unity. They are given here to facilitate relating our consideration of unity given here to similar considerations in other works.

[15] A fuller treatment of this would have to explain the analogy of unity as we explained the analogy of being in Chapter 9.

Undividedness and Activity

To conclude our discussion of unity, we must consider the relationship between unity and the activity which follows from it. Both the unity within a single being and the unity among many beings have their corresponding activities. Men and machines, individuals and groups operate in different ways and the variety of these operations stems from the different types of unity found in each. We can best understand these activities and their divergents in the context of existential dynamism. The dynamic drive of beings to seek and express fuller being is also a spur to seek and express fuller unity. Consequently, the activities of being are unifying activities. We can look on these activities as keeping the being together and so preserving its unity with its being or as relating the being to other beings and so developing a new unity. A few examples will make this clear.

A plant, for instance, which pushes out its roots to find the water it needs, seeks union with that water for the sake of union in itself. Without water to preserve and develop the plant's own being, that being and its unity slip away, because the plant's leaves will wither and the plant itself will eventually die and disintegrate. Its activities, therefore, hold the plant together and keep it in existence and so are directed toward its being and union. Again, a human being seeking his own fulfillment will want to be united with the food he needs, the clothing and shelter he requires, and the truth, goodness, and beauty which he desires. It is in union with these things that he will become united in himself—his powers will operate more fully in themselves and more harmoniously in concert. To the extent that this unification takes place, therefore, his life will be even more characterized by unified and unifying activities—and in particular the activities of knowledge and love. As his personal being grows in unity, he will stretch out for a broader unity with other people and other things in a conscious and loving affirmation of being. He will know his place in the world better and will love his fellow men not only well but wisely.

This quest for unity through knowledge and love is not some esoteric cult into which only saints and aesthetes can be initiated; it is not some Holy Grail which only an elite are permitted to pursue. It is, rather, an integral part of the pilgrimage of every man, part of the ordinary activities of our ordinary life in our ordinary world. The teacher strives for this union when he helps his students to be united with what they study. Here the union is knowledge. The doctor and nurse have as their whole preoccupation the holding together of other men's bodies so that they may continue to enjoy the union of body and spirit which we know as human life. The social worker bends every effort to promote unity or heal disunity in families, societies, and individual persons. The psychologist tries to help those who are mentally ill or weak to unify their lives once more, to heal the conflicts of their spirits, and to span the breach between reality and illusion. Mothers and fathers have as their whole task not only the unifying of their own lives, but of those of their children, educating and guiding them so that they may become firm and full in being and unity—with the internal unity of self-possession and the broader union of a healthy relation with the world of people and things about them. The artist unifies in himself reality through his unique vision, and invites others to unite with that vision of reality as expressed and communicated in his works of art. Since these activities are clearest in men, we have taken our examples from the area of human activity. However, the same sort of unifying activity exists at every level of being. And at all levels of being these unifying activities tend to unite the being of the agents as well as the being of those with whose activities they come in contact.

As the powers of a being are perfected through activity,[16] the being itself becomes more integrated within itself. This is the self-possession we referred to in the previous paragraph. As a being becomes more unified in its own being, it becomes increasingly itself —that is, increasingly actualized in the fullness of its own nature and mode of existence. And as a being becomes more and more itself, it is thereby united with other beings—in existence, in nature, in the various accidental ways. These unities are complexes of relations within itself or between itself and other beings.

As unity follows being, the highest unity and the source of all unity rests in the absolute being and absolute unity of God. Its unity in itself and in its relation with the First Cause is a participation in

---

[16] See pages 185–86.

the divine unity. Similarly, the unitive activity of a finite being participates in the infinitely unitive activity of Absolute Being, God's knowing and loving. It is ultimately in terms of this knowledge and love that the unity of finite beings can be understood.

Although knowledge and love, as the highest forms of unitive activity, are important in our discussion of unity, they are even more important for an understanding of two other transcendentals, truth and goodness. These two in turn, as we come to understand them better, will give us a fuller grasp of ontological unity and ontologically uniting activity, thus paving the way for a more profound vision of personal beings in the perfection of union which is communion.

TRANSCENDENTAL TRUTH

If human understanding of the transcendental aspects of reality can in any way be expected to grow, to deepen, to progress with succeeding generations—even as our understanding of particular areas within reality grows—we might expect to know more about the transcendental which is "truth." To survey the history of the meanings of truth, however, sometimes leads to little more than despair. The concept has been filled and emptied and filled again with meaning so many times and in so many ways that all that remains seems sometimes to be but the shards of human insight. Yet out of all this—out of the anchoring of truth in being and the rooting it out of being, out of the dying for the sake of truth and the prostituting of it under every tree, out of its affirmation and negation, its consequences and predictions, out of idealism and realism, optimism and skepticism, dynamism and nihilism—out of all this comes at least the possibility of still unfolding, and unfolding in a more profound way, the richness of being under the aspect of truth. The proving and harvesting of such a possibility may come in the study of the meaning of truth in many and varied philosophies. It may also come in a renewed philosophizing which turns again to being as being with an eye opened more widely by the discoveries of the insights of the ages. We will attempt this latter approach.

However we decide to determine the meaning of truth, we must admit that it is somehow associated with knowledge. We speak of knowing a truth, seeing the truth, making a true judgment. More than this, there seems to be something about being itself which we indicate in the word "truth." We speak of a true scientist, a true masterpiece, a true leader. What is there about knowledge and what is there about being which prompts us to call them "true"? What is the relationship between the truth of knowledge and the truth of being? Which of these is transcendentally true of all being?

The Truth of Knowledge

The Nature of Knowledge

To know is to be present to what is known, to oneself or something else, in a way which goes beyond mere spatial presence, even beyond the kind of presence which every being has to every other being by reason of participation in being. It is to be present by conscious awareness, by what seems like taking another within one's being or embracing oneself in conscious possession of one's being.

When we know something other than ourselves, it truly exists within us. We open our beings to enfold and affirm the being of this other. It is in our consciousness. Consciousness is a mode of being which implies both the openness to receive the forms of other beings and the active affirmation of the existence of other beings. Knowing beings are open in a way that nonknowing beings are not. A stone is closed within itself, informed only by its own form. It is a stone and nothing but a stone. An animal is more open, informed by the sensible forms of others. It has a sense awareness of other things, and so has them within it in some way. But no thing or animal is open as a person is open—capable of understanding the natures of other beings and of meeting through the act of judgment the very existence of other beings.

We spoke before of knowledge as a form of unity. The kind of union or presence which is knowledge is called "intentional" union. We experience knowledge as an "intentional" taking of another into our being. If we interpret this in the light of our discussions about ontological participation of beings in being by the very fact that they derive from Absolute Being, we can say that our union with being in knowledge is a union which reaches the level of conscious awareness and conscious affirmation.[17] Although the union we are speaking of here may sound to some more poetic than metaphysical, there is a real sense in which all beings are united to each other by reason of their participation in being. All share in being and so are united in this sharing. In knowledge something is added to this relationship, for we not only participate in the same being, but we know the being of various things. And we are united with them in this knowing. Furthermore there are many levels of knowledge—we can know many things or few things and we can know them superficially or intimately. Finally, knowledge is an expression of being and as such it signifies a mode of being, a way of existing, which is less limited than that which characterizes nonknowing beings. Nonknowing beings express only themselves; knowing beings express not only their own being but that of the things they know.

Sometimes this is explained in terms of formal perfection, that is, in terms of the possession of a given form or essence. Looking at beings in this way, we see that nonknowing beings possess only the perfection of their proper forms. A stone has the perfection only of a stone. A wild flower has only the perfection of a wild flower. But knowing beings possess not only the formal perfection of their own forms; they are not only what they are, but in a way which is called "intentional" they possess the forms of the beings they know. When we know the stone or the wild flower, we can say that in a certain sense we possess the perfection of the stone or the wild flower. Of course as knowing subjects we do not possess the form of stone in the way that a stone does or the perfection of a wild flower in the way that a wild flower does. However, we do, in the mysterious mode of being which we call knowledge, have within us the forms of the things we know. In some way, therefore, we are more than merely men; we "are" stones and flowers and so on. We therefore transcend the limitations of our essences and "exist" in a broader way.

Although all this may seem an unnecessarily detailed analysis of the nature of knowledge, it will be important both to the under-

---

[17] This would be true of all kinds of knowledge in the beings of experience, even sense knowledge in animals. However, the consideration here is pointed in terms of rational knowledge.

standing of the truth of knowledge and of the relationship between the truth of knowledge and the truth of being.

It will be helpful, too, to add that one who knows is not wholly passive in his knowledge. He is not merely a receiver, ready to have the form of another being imprinted upon his mind. All that we have said thus far would gainsay such a conclusion.[18] We have pointed out that the activity of knowing is the expression of being. It is dynamic with the dynamism of existence because it is an active reaffirmation, reliving, respeaking of the being of the object known both in terms of its essence and its existence. We know what a thing is and that it is. It is at one and the same time an active entering-into or embracing-of the reality of being in which it itself participates, and a recognition and affirmation of the limited share in the reality of being which constitutes individual beings all with their own act of existing and with their own individual share in their essence.[19]

Knowledge, even when it is specifically of oneself and not of another, is still a coming to consciousness of a profound ontological union—the union within one's own being. It is thereby the self-possession which is conscious awareness and affirmation of one's own being. This self-possession is, of course, an "intentional" and not a physical union.

Logical Truth in Human Knowledge

Whether we know ourselves or something else we have knowledge only when there is an affirmation which really does meet or relive or correspond to the being of the object known as it is in reality.[20] When knowledge does not meet the object as it is in reality, there is no intentional union, no affirmation of ontological union, no recognition of being, no possession or fulfillment. The difference between having something actually present in knowledge and miss-

[18] See also *Summa Theologiae,* I, 79, 3.

[19] This includes both affirmative and negative judgments.

[20] It would be interesting to consider Sartre's theory of nihilation through knowledge in light of this. It might thus be possible to establish that, although in knowing something—even something of myself—I thereby negate that I am that, nevertheless I do not thereby put what I know at a distance from me nor thereby nihilate the *pour soi.*

ing its actuality and thus its presence is the difference between truth and falsehood. It now becomes possible to grasp at least tentatively what is meant by truth in knowledge.

The truth which is in knowledge has traditionally been called "logical" truth. This truth is precisely the correspondence of what is in the mind to what is in reality. What we know is true when what is in our mind is in conformity with what is in reality outside of our mind. If the affirmation or negation we make in judgment corresponds with the ontological affirmation of the act of existing in what we know, we are said to possess the truth. Thus, for example, if a man judges that it is raining, he judges truly only if it really is raining. If he judges that the cause of a disease is a certain type of bacteria, his judgment is true only if that type of bacteria is indeed the cause of that disease. If he judges that a man is wise and good, there is truth in his judgment only if the man is in reality wise and good.

The measure of this kind of truth for the human mind, of logical truth, is reality itself. Man may be said to constitute his own truth only in the sense that he actively renders something present to himself in knowledge.[21] It is the role of human knowledge to "discover" truth, not to construct it.[22] Whether or not the human mind can arrive at truth depends on whether or not it is capable of truly being present to reality as it exists. The tests of this capability have been considered briefly in the Introduction, and are taken up in detail in the study of human nature, in the philosophy of man.

The kind of knowing being with which we are most familiar is, of course, ourself. Man exists in a way which allows him to open in consciousness to other beings—to other men, to all the universe, to God. He exists in a way which allows him to possess himself in consciousness, too. He, unlike any other being in the world, can turn to himself and know himself in knowing other beings, and

---

[21] The "constitution" theory of phenomenology is here pertinent. According to this, man does not construct his own truth in the sense that he is not measured by reality; rather, he constitutes something as true *for him* by making a thing intelligible in-act where before it was, for him, only intelligible in-potency. In this sense he constitutes a thing in intelligibility.

[22] Scientific theories which are based on mental constructs do not necessarily violate this, since they do not claim to be true, but only to be valid, or consistent.

know other beings in knowing himself. His knowledge is by no means perfect, and what perfection it has is hard won. Although he is an open being, a person, one capable of holding within himself in conscious affirmation an infinite number of beings, his openness is not such that the essences of these beings are bared directly to his gaze or that their acts of existing are directly experienced. Man is not even consciously aware of his own whole being, let alone of the being of others. His activity of knowing partakes of the complexity of his being, so that he must come to know as an incarnate spirit. This means that his knowledge is dependent upon what he first meets at the level of the senses, and although it is not tied to sense knowledge,[23] nevertheless it never loses the fundamental limitations imposed by the fact that man is a material being.[24] For this reason his truth will always be—at least as long as he exists with his present limitations and circumstances—partial truth. Thus man will never know the whole of finite reality nor will he know any one finite being wholly.

Because human knowledge is always partial in this way, the truths discovered by human reason have been challenged for their certitude, characterized as ultimately all relative, interpreted as having a meaning other than a correspondence to what is real outside the mind. We have already met some of these difficulties; [25] we will meet others when we attempt to understand the knowledge which is in God and the significance of the truth of being.

Knowledge in God

There is knowledge in god In our previous consideration of divine providence we have already seen that there is knowledge in God—that is, that God exists as a knowing being, a being in whom there is consciousness. It will nevertheless be helpful here to see again how it can be known that God has knowledge, and then to consider anything that can be known about His knowledge. We can

---

[23] That is, although for man all knowledge comes through the senses, the intellect can go beyond knowledge as sensible.
[24] *Summa Theologiae,* I, 14, 1.
[25] See pages 1–5.

use the same pattern of reasoning here which we used to find the pure perfections which we discovered in God earlier.

If knowledge is all that we have said that it is, it is clear that a being capable of knowing must be more fully a being—exist in a higher way—than beings who are incapable of the activity of knowing. Knowledge, in itself, and as expressive of a mode of existence, is a perfection. Although human knowledge as we experience it is always a limited knowledge, there is nothing in the nature of knowledge itself—considered apart from any limitation in the nature and the power of the being that knows—which implies imperfection. Every being in experience, and every perfection of every being in experience, has been seen to be totally the effect of the First Cause, of God. What is in an effect must be first in its cause; the perfection of knowledge, therefore, must belong first to God. And since knowledge is a pure perfection implying of itself no imperfection, it must belong to God properly, not just virtually. It can therefore be predicated of God properly, not just metaphorically.[26] God does know.

God's knowledge is perfect knowledge There are several ways in which the perfection of divine knowledge can be seen more clearly. One of them is to see that any activity of an unlimited being must be an unlimited activity. Another is to see from the nature of knowledge and from the nature of God that His knowledge must be perfect knowledge.

To know, the knower must have in himself the form of that which is known. We are speaking, of course, of "intentional" possession and presence. When we have a limited nature and hence a limited existence in the knower, there is a limitation on the forms which it can actuate by its existence. And as the existence is greater, the more forms it is able to actuate either physically-metaphysically or intentionally. As we have also seen, the limitation of existence is ascribed to essence or form, and the limitation of essence is ascribed to matter. Where there is no matter, we have the full perfection of the specific essence, and where there is no essence, we have the full perfection of existence. We know, too, that God is Pure Exist-

[26] See *Summa Theologiae,* I, 14, 1.

ence and so has no limitation. There is no limitation, therefore, on what God can actuate intentionally by His existence. This means that there is no limitation on God's knowledge.[27] The name for God which expresses His perfect knowledge is "Wisdom."

GOD'S KNOWLEDGE OF HIMSELF God's knowledge in all its perfection, His absolute openness and unrestricted consciousness, can be understood first of all as it is in Himself, apart from any relation to creatures. We can speak of absolute openness and unrestricted consciousness because, being infinite, God is open to the knowledge of all being and actually knows all being since He is the source of it. Limited beings share in this openness because through knowledge they transcend the restriction of their being to a single form or essence. They can know other beings and in knowing them acquire intentionally the forms of other beings, thus transcending their own proper forms. This is consonant with the mode of existence of limited beings wherein they are limited to their own share in being and yet partake intentionally of the fullness of the limited shares in being which other beings have. In God, unlike the situation in limited beings, His knowledge does not unite Him to other beings in a way that fulfills His own being. Rather, since as Pure Act God possesses the fullness of being, His knowledge will be the affirmation of His own infinite existence.[28]

God has no need to go outside Himself to find a perfectly intelligible object. In His own infinite being there is an infinity to be known which is infinitely knowable.[29] In Himself He is Pure Act with no potency at any level and hence no limitation to His ac-

[27] *Ibid.*

[28] There is a problem here for philosophy: How, since knowledge implies union —even in self-knowledge, to be oneself and to know oneself are different—can there be knowledge in God? Divine knowledge is cloaked in mystery, like divine being. Only the light of faith goes beyond the seeming dilemma offered by a being that is in no way dual: the Trinity reveals itself to faith as God in whom knowledge constitutes a Divine Person, the Word of God, which is a subsistent relation. This is not given in reason, though it may be pointed to by reason.

[29] God cannot know Himself at a distance through concepts, as a man must know himself—thus nihilating His being in knowledge, as Sartre holds. Rather, since in God there is no potency, His intellect is completely in act; hence it is not actualized by any kind of separate species, concepts or otherwise. See *Summa Theologiae,* I, 14, 2.

tivity.[30] His operation of knowing is therefore infinite. It might be said that since God's being is pure being, He is infinitely intelligible and infinitely intelligent. Hence, once again, we see that His knowledge is perfect knowledge.[31]

GOD'S KNOWLEDGE OF FINITE BEINGS For ancient philosophers God's knowledge of all other things posed an insoluble problem,[32] because they could only conclude that God had no knowledge of things other than Himself. Their reasons for such a conclusion were simply the seeming contradiction involved in having a being which knows in the highest way be somehow restricted in its knowledge to anything less than the highest object. If the perfection of an activity is determined in one way by its object, how indeed can God be said to know things other than Himself, which are objects limited and imperfect? Since His activity of knowing is the most perfect activity, they thought, His object of knowledge must be the most perfect object of knowledge, Himself alone.

We may resolve this difficulty by looking again at God's knowledge of Himself. If He knows Himself perfectly He will know Himself as imitable, as able to share existence with other beings in a way in which He Himself is not diminished in being. He will know Himself as the cause of every creature, and His knowledge will thus extend as far as His causality—that is, to every being and to every aspect of being.

God, therefore, not only knows all other things, but He knows

---

30 In God activity is not related to nature as act to potency; hence, His activity is not limited by nature. See *Summa Theologiae,* I, 14, 3.

31 Aware of the danger of anthropomorphism, we can nevertheless speak of the knowledge in God as analogous to the highest kind of knowledge in man, which is had in an I-Thou relation. Highest knowledge is knowledge in the most perfect manner, of a most perfect object, with the greatest intensity. The most perfect manner of knowledge which we understand is direct, experiential vision. The most perfect object is a personal object. The greatest intensity is had in I-Thou relation. The latter is characterized as knowledge of the Thou not as an object among objects, not as a thing. It is an active knowing, intensified, of course, by love, an addressing of the Thou with one's whole being. Even reason tells us that the knowledge which is God cannot be less than this, though it is infinitely more.

32 Aristotle, for example, considered the Prime Mover as a Thought Thinking Itself, a completely independent being who could not condescend to know anything less than Himself.

them perfectly, in minutest detail, individually, directly, totally, "even the thoughts and affections of hearts." [33] As the cause of the very existence of every other being, He knows each in its very existence—which is to know it in every aspect, actual or potential.

The Meeting of Infinite and Finite Knowledge in Logical Truth

God's knowledge, like true knowledge in man, will correspond to what is in reality. It will be a true and conscious affirmation of the being of what it knows. Unlike human knowledge, however, God's knowledge is not a discovery of the reality of what He knows. Unlike human knowledge, divine knowledge is not measured by the reality of limited beings. Rather, God's knowledge is creative of whatever reality there is outside Himself.[34] In the fullness of His own being, in infinitely perfect knowledge of Himself, in absolute conscious affirmation of His own being, He communicates from His fullness. In affirming His own being, He affirms the being of others, and they exist. In knowing Himself, He knows others, and they come into and are held in being. Creatures are related to His knowledge as finite expressions of His being, totally other—and yet portraying in their otherness the source of their being.

For man, to know is to hear the word of another's being. For God, to know is to speak the word of another's being. To be, for God—since all in Him is one—is to know. For man, to be is to be known by God. Creatures exist only because they are creatively thought—the end products of an act of knowledge—by God. Such is the relationship of all creation to God. Such is the foundation of the personal relationship of knowing beings to a knowing God.

Infinite knowledge pours forth to create beings that in turn may know. Infinite knowledge gives birth to finite knowledge. Objects

[33] *Summa Theologiae,* I, 14, 12c.

[34] Of course, as shall be seen, in one sense God must know a thing as existing before it does exist. He may know, therefore, beings that are merely possible and never become actual; the difference is that He knows them as possible and not as actual. What God knows creatively He executes through His will, though in God all is one. His knowledge, in this sense, can be said to be the cause of being.

in created reality receive their being in the light of infinite knowledge. They are, in a sense, words spoken by God, Whose speech is creative. Creatures capable of being joined to these objects through the light of finite knowledge respond to these creative words which come forth from God. Two intellects meet, the divine and the human; the one communicates, the other receives. Yet both intellects are active,[35] for not even the receiving intellect is totally passive. Man, or any created knower, must actively make intelligible for himself whatever he knows, must actively embrace the being he is joined to by knowledge. Thus it is that created knowing is truly a response to uncreated knowing. Objects which are words of God are taken as well as received, and creative and created knowers are both united in the known. And since beings of experience are images of the being of God and are existing subsistent images of what God knows in Himself, when man knows them, he knows that which they portray.[36]

In logical truth, therefore, there is true knowledge for man, true union, true presence, true affirmation, true correspondence to reality, true meeting through the creative knowledge of God. The truth of man's knowledge is the same as the truth of God's knowledge, though they differ as effect and cause.[37] This brings us long strides in our understanding of the truth of knowledge, but it becomes clear that it is not this truth which is transcendental truth. For although all beings can be taken up in the knowledge of a knowing being, not all beings can know. The truth of knowledge does not, therefore, belong to all being as being. It does not cut across every boundary of being, pervade every level and variety of being. Not transcending all these, it is not transcendental. We must therefore look to another truth, the truth of being, to see whether this is transcendental truth.

---

35 See pages 252–53.

36 This is why, ultimately, it is possible to know God through His effects, why each finite being is a glimpse-through to infinite being.

37 This difference, of course, is a radical one. As seen above, it is the difference between a measured and a measuring, a created and a creative, a finite and an infinite knowledge. Logical truth for man is at an infinite distance from truth in God, and yet it is a correspondence ultimately with the truth in the knowledge of God.

The Truth of Being

Truth of Being in Finite Beings

We have seen that in ordinary language we do use the word "truth" to indicate something in being itself—not just something in knowledge. Yet what is indicated in being has some relationship to knowledge. When we speak of a true father, we are indicating something in a person which is intrinsic to him. This truth is clearly not the same truth which we have in knowledge. It is a truth which is in the very being of someone or something. This is why the truth of being is called "ontological" truth. Even this truth is not without a relationship to knowledge, however, and the truth of knowledge is not without relationship to this truth. What we know is the truth of being, and the truth of being can be said to be being in relation to intellect, to knowledge.

Every being as being is capable of being known by an intellect. That is to say, every being as being is able to be in-another through intentional union, able to be present to a knowing being in conscious affirmation. Each being is knowable in this sense because it has what it requires in order to be and to be what it is.[38] What is given in the "explanation" of a being is what constitutes its being and its intelligibility. Thus, for example, the beings of experience have reality by their act of existing and they are knowable as real by their act of existing. They are the kinds of beings they are by their essences, and in addition they are knowable as the kinds of beings they are by their essences. Their essences are determined by substantial form and are limited by primary matter. Consequently, one knows and understands an individual by discovering these existential and essential principles. Everything in a being constitutes or modifies that being, and all that constitutes or modifies a being is what is able to be known of that being. Thus if one's power of knowing were great enough, everything about a being could be known. Each being unveils its being once it is placed under the unveiling light of a knowing being's activity of knowing.

---

[38] See page 22 for treatment of the Principle of Sufficient Reason in relation to intelligibility.

No being could be known unless it were knowable. This is to say that no being could be united to another being in the conscious affirmation of its existence by the other being unless there were about it something that allowed it so to exist in another. It is this aspect of being as being, that is, that which makes it able to be known, which gives it at least a potential relationship to a knowing being. This is part of what we mean by the truth of a being.

There is, however, something more than intelligibility involved in the truth of being. Or rather the very intelligibility of being demands that we see something further in ontological, transcendental truth. We can begin our search by noting that a limited being is a being by its act of existing, and is true by its act of existing. Furthermore, since the fullness of its existence depends on the fullness of the form which limits it, the fullness of its truth depends also on the fullness of the form which limits it. Thus the more perfect the share which a being has in its own nature or essence, the more it exists and the more true it is. This is what we try to express when we speak of a thing being "true." A true work of art is a work of art that corresponds to what a work of art should be, to the nature of a work of art. A true pencil is a pencil which is in conformity with the nature of a pencil. A true friend is a person who fulfills the requirements in being which make a friend a friend.

Our tendency to judge the "trueness" of a being in terms of its formal and existential perfection indicates that we place it against some measure. Something measures what a being should be, and we admit this when we impose that measure, at least implicitly, on every being. We seem almost unconsciously to assume a prior relation of being to knowledge, of each being to an intellectual measure of its being. The meaning we give to truth in this sense no longer implies a relationship in which reality is the measure of the intellect—as is the case with logical truth, the truth of knowledge—but rather a relationship in which intellect is the measure of reality. Whereas in logical truth what is in the mind must correspond to what is outside the mind, in ontological truth what is outside the mind must correspond to what is in the mind. In one case knowledge is measured; in the other, it is the measure.

The truth of being in this sense—that is, insofar as it corresponds to a certain standard of mind—could be considered as merely a relative truth, dependent only in its relation to a created intellect. Thus, for example, a true pencil could be a true pencil because it fits our idea of what a pencil should be. Similarly a certain type of justice could be called true justice because it corresponds to our idea of what justice should be. If this is the case, the truth of being has nothing absolute about it. It is wholly dependent upon ideas which men may develop or construct.[39] It neither corresponds to any absolute standard nor is its intelligibility a real intelligibility, for each man could make of a thing what he wanted it to be. If we understand being in this way we deny the possibility of the nature of a thing being something real, something given in its being. Nature would simply be imposed by the mind of man. But if this is so, certain consequences follow, one of which is that all that we have said of logical truth no longer holds—for there is nothing in reality to which man's mind must correspond. It becomes meaningless to speak of truth in man's knowledge.[40] It would even be meaningless to speak of truth in being—since the truth of every being could be different for every man. Fullness of being could mean nothing more than a sort of rough and ready conformity to the ideas of men.[41]

Were we to use this as our starting point to attempt to understand reality, if we began with human knowledge and with the relation of beings to human knowledge, we could very well question whether or not truth does not, after all, come down to being a truth which carries only the meaning of practical consequences or consistency and relativity. We could wonder whether true reality is indeed only in the mind, and whether there is any meaning other than what is imposed by the mind. But this has not been our start-

---

[39] In a restricted sense it is very legitimate to speak of the truth of being as something determined by the human intellect—as, for example, when we speak of the truth of a work of art, or of the truth in a man's actions, or of "truing" a beam. This, however, is a most restricted usage.

[40] That is, it would be meaningless except in a totally different sense, as for example, if truth were to mean simply the practical consequences of a thing.

[41] This involves a whole theory of knowledge, for if one were to accept such a meaning for truth and being, it would imply, first of all, a vicious circle in the acquisition of human knowledge through the senses. One would have to reverse the direction of coming-to-know for man, holding some position of innate ideas, and so forth.

ing point, and if all that we have seen has any validity, we must take into account the understanding of reality which we have already painstakingly gained. Being is that which is. What makes all the difference in the world is that a being exists. If it has an act of existing in its own right, it is real in its own right. If it is a limited reality, it has a real structure within its being and a real relation to its First Cause. If we are to accept the existence of reality—in its own right, apart from the mind of any creature—it is necessary to admit that there is something "there," regardless of what we may project upon it by our knowledge. The truth of a thing's being is therefore what is "there" insofar as it is able to be known. Whether or not it is able to be known by the human intellect is not precisely the question here, though all that has gone before does have bearing in this regard. If there is truth in being itself, and if that truth is perfected as a being is perfected, the measure of the truth of being is not the mind of man but another mind, a mind that does indeed determine the existence and perfection of a thing's being and truth.

The intellect and the knowledge which determines the nature of a thing, and thus its fullness of being and truth, is the intellect and knowledge of the First Cause, of God. The natures of created things are the effects of the knowledge of God. If ontological truth implies intelligibility and a measuring against some standard, it implies the conformity of created reality to the mind of God. When we speak of the truth of being we are speaking of being in relation to intellect, and to the intellect to which it is related primarily, that is, the intellect of God. A thing is and is what it is according to the knowledge of God. It is therefore true according to the knowledge of God.

This approach implies no frozen view of reality, of things petrified in a little box according to the knowledge of God. On the contrary, the infinitely creative knowledge of God encompasses all being in its actuality and its possibilities. God knows it as it is and may be, and this may mean knowing it as it is in its evolving fullness and even in its own created creative freedom.

The truth of being, therefore, is being itself in relation to intellect, to knowledge. In this sense of truth, every being as being is true. Truth adds to being the notion of a relationship to knowledge. It is being itself that is so related, but this aspect of being is explicitly unfolded in the transcendental name "truth."

The Truth of Being in God

If ontological truth in finite beings has its ultimate meaning from the relationship of these beings to God, what is the meaning of truth in God Himself? If truth is being in relation to knowledge, how is this to be understood of uncreated being? Created knowing beings possess logical truth, the truth of knowledge, because they know, and are ontologically true in their being because they exist. But in God, all is one. He is a pure act of existing. His act of existing is what He knows, and is absolutely identical with the object of His understanding. His act of existing is also identical with His power of knowing, His intellect. And further His act of existing is His activity of knowing. All these—object, intellect, activity—are entirely one and the same in God. They add nothing in reality to His pure act of existing. They are His act of existing and His act of existing is all of them. There is, therefore, in God a perfect unity of identity between absolute being and its own truth. God not only has truth in Him, in perfect knowledge; He not only is true by being known by His own knowledge; He *is* Truth, subsistent Truth.[42] As Saint Augustine says so beautifully, "Behold and see, O soul pressed down by the corruptible body, and weighed down by the multitude and variety of earthly thoughts; behold and see if you can, that God is truth. For it is written that 'God is light'; not in such way as the eyes see, but in such way as the heart sees, when it hears that He is truth. Ask not what is truth; for immediately the mists of corporeal images and the clouds of phantasms will put themselves in the way, and will disturb the calm which at the first moment shone forth to thee, when I said Truth; see what there remains, if you can, in that first moment in which you were dazzled as by a flash, when there was said, Truth."[43]

We could, like Augustine, refuse to ask further of what it means

---

[42] See *Summa Theologiae,* I, 16, 3 and 5.
[43] *De Trinitate,* VIII, ii, 3.

to say that God is Truth. But Augustine had a way of saying that no more should be asked and then going ahead to ask anyway. We shall do the same. How indeed are we to understand what it means to say that God is Truth? What do we mean when we name Him "Truth"? Whatever we mean, it falls infinitely far short of what God is as Truth. Nevertheless, our understanding of truth, gleaned from the beings of experience—chiefly ourselves—does give us analogous knowledge of the truth that is God. However far short we fall, we shall know that to say that God is Truth means infinitely more than it means for the highest beings of experience to be true. We go to the limit of our knowledge and point toward infinity.

In God logical and ontological truth come together. From every point of view, whether of knowledge or of being, God is Truth. His knowledge corresponds to reality because reality is the expression of His own being, first infinitely within Himself, and then as creatively pouring forth finite reality. His being corresponds with His knowledge because it *is* His knowledge, and every other being corresponds to His knowledge because insofar as each has being it has it from God's creative knowledge. Infinite consciousness, infinite openness, infinite communication, infinite affirmation, infinite presence—all say something, but not any of them enough—of what it means to say that God is Truth.

The Meeting of Infinite and Finite in Ontological Truth

All the truth of being is what it is by reason of its relation to God. Truth is being in relation to an intellect, and the intellect is ultimately the divine intellect. Just as each being is suspended from the causal activity of God, so the intrinsic truth of each being is suspended from the causal activity of God which we now see to be an activity of knowing. Created truth is what it is because it is a participation in uncreated truth. As absolute infinite being is infinitely intelligible, so finite beings are finitely intelligible insofar as they are. All being is knowable because God is knowable and knowing. The beings of experience share in the lucidity of God's pure existence. They partake of the manifestness of Absolute Being. Utterly open to the knowledge which creates them, they are open, too, to the created knowledge which discovers them—however opaque they may become behind the barriers which rise in our limited human knowledge.

From all that we have seen, the truth of being implies not only the intelligibility of being by participation in divine truth, not only an effect of which truth is the cause, but also the conformity of being to mind, the correspondence of forms and existents to the idea of them which is in the mind of God. The natures of things are as they are known by God. A thing exists as it is known by God. Hence, there is truth to be discovered by the human mind which is not merely relative to that mind. If things have their truth according to the knowledge of God, it is this truth which is to be discovered, in however partial a way, by human knowledge.

Man himself is true in his own being as he corresponds to the knowledge of God. He is true, and he possesses truth in knowledge as he consciously affirms his own truth and the truth of other beings. He does this as he makes the truth his own. And as he knows truth in knowledge, he is united to other beings and to himself, in a union in which he is united with God—Whose word created beings are. As he grows in the truth of knowledge, he grows also in the truth of being, for his being is fulfilled in the activity of knowing. He is himself first spoken by God, and so exists. But other things are spoken to him and for him, are made to be united with him in knowledge. And he affirms, speaks these words with his own being—for to know is to relive in the being of the knower the being of what is known.

We have said that as man grows in the truth of knowledge he grows in being and in unity with the true knowledge of God. Now we can see also that as he grows in the truth of being, he grows in unity with the being of God which is Truth. This occurs not only with man, but with every being.[44] To be thought into being by

[44] Man alone of all the beings of experience has the possibility of entering into the creative activity of God and creating, in a sense, his own truth—that is, the truth of his being. For if other beings are defective in their being—and to that extent not true, for to that extent they are not in conformity with God's idea of their nature, and to that extent do not have the full existence proper to them—they are not responsible for their failure, and insofar as they are, they are true. A dog without a leg is defective as a dog, but he is all that he ought to be as this dog. For a man without a leg the same would

God is to have an existential relationship to knowledge, and so to have the truth of being. To be thought into fuller being is to be more fully knowable and to have a greater truth of being. Every being in creation is thought into being by Truth. Being unfolds, therefore, to reveal itself not only as existing, but as true.

SUGGESTED READINGS

Black, Max, "The Semantic Definition of Truth," *Language and Philosophy,* Chapter 4. Ithaca, New York: Cornell University Press, 1949. General explanation of the meaning of "truth" in linguistic analysis, and relevance of this to the "philosophical problem of truth."

Desan, Wilfrid, *The Planetary Man,* Vol. I, Chapter 1. Washington, D.C.: Georgetown University Press, 1961. In a "phenomenology of survival," Desan considers the unity and totality of reality and of the human species.

Gilson, Etienne, *Elements of Christian Philosophy,* pp. 145–53. Garden City, N.Y.: Doubleday & Company, Inc., 1960. Concerning transcendental unity and truth in relation to God.

———, *The Spirit of Medieval Philosophy,* trans. A. H. C. Downes, Chapter 13. New York: Charles Scribner's Sons, 1936. On the intellect and its object.

Heidegger, Martin, "Dasein, Disclosedness, and Truth," *Being and Time,* trans. John Macquarrie and Edward Robinson, pp. 256–73. New York: Harper & Row, Publishers, Inc., 1962.

James, William, "Pragmatism's Conception of Truth," *Essays in Pragmatism,* ed. A. Castell, pp. 159–76. New York: Hafner Publishing Company, Inc., 1948.

Luijpen, William A., *Existential Phenomenology,* Chapter 2, pp. 74–79, 91–97, 112–17, 142–68. Pittsburgh: Duquesne University Press, 1960. On phenomenology of knowledge and truth.

---

be true. But for a man who is defective by some failure in his own freedom, there is responsibility for that lack of being and lack of truth. If, for example, he is too lazy to develop his talents or too selfish to choose a noble love, he fails of his being and so of his truth. The lucidity of his being is marred; he exists less and is less true—less in correspondence with the divine intellect and less intelligible in himself.

Pieper, Josef, *The Silence of St. Thomas,* trans. John Murray and Daniel O'Connor, Part II. New York: Pantheon Books, Inc., 1957. Shows relation of intelligibility in creatures to the fact that they are created by an act of knowledge.

St. Thomas Aquinas, *Summa Contra Gentiles,* I, 44 (God is intelligent); I, 50 (God knows things other than Himself).

———, *Summa Theologiae,* I, 11, 1 (on unity); I, 11, 4; I, 3, 4 and 7 (on unity in God); I, 14 (regarding God's knowledge); I, 16, 3 (the meaning of truth); I, 16, 5 (that God is Truth).

Tresmontant, Claude, *A Study of Hebrew Thought,* trans. M. F. Gibson, pp. 125–31. New York: Desclee Company, 1960. Considers emphasis in Hebrew tradition on understanding as action and life.

THE TRANSCENDENTAL FULLNESS OF BEING: II. GOODNESS AND BEAUTY

INTRODUCTION

We began our study of the transcendentals with the hope of studying being again in order to make explicit more of the richness of the meaning of being. So far we have seen that being is both undivided (one) and true. To understand being as true has meant to hold together within our understanding all that we saw of being and all that we saw of unity, and to add to this—not in reality, but in our minds[1]—the meaning of truth.

Being is rich enough to unfold itself still more. As we saw that it is one and true, so we may find that it is good and beautiful. But perhaps before we can talk directly about the goodness and beauty of every being, we shall have to discuss the most positive aspect of all that is in being as being, namely love.

---

[1] As we have noted, none of the transcendentals introduce a difference in reality, but only a difference in the understanding of reality. There is between goodness and being, therefore, only a minor mental distinction.

TRANSCENDENTAL GOODNESS

Goodness and love go together in the way truth and knowledge do. For as we have seen, to question the truth of being is to ask whether or not a being is knowable. When we spoke of things being knowable, we meant that they were able to be united to a knowing being, able to be taken within a being opened by consciousness, able to be affirmed by an act of knowledge, able to present themselves as luminous. When we question the goodness of being, we are asking first of all whether or not being as being is lovable—whether it is able to be united to a loving being, able to be affirmed by active love, able to be taken within a being capable of conscious love. Thus it is that as we came to understand truth through an investigation of knowledge, so we shall understand goodness through an investigation of love. Before we can know whether to exist means also to be good, we must know something of the meaning of love and something of what it means to be lovable.

The Meaning of Love

There are many ways of approaching the meaning of love, all of which have some value for a metaphysical understanding of reality. For centuries philosophers have asked about the nature of love, cosmic and human, created and uncreated. They have sought to know whether it is a principle or a movement, passive or active, free or determined, union or unitive, selfish or unselfish, fulfilling or outpouring. Contemporary philosophy, as well as theology, sociology, psychology, and biology, has concerned itself more and more with the questions of love, questions asked now in the context of human encounter, dialogue, communion, and friendship. Present emphases on the subjective approaches to being, on subjectivity and intersubjectivity, have tended to make love one of the principle avenues to being, and have tended to make human interpersonal love the principle avenue to love.

Love as Tendency

When we seek the meaning of love, we seek to understand affective activity. Our task is to discover and to unfold what is most fundamental in this affective activity.

Since love has often been identified as tendency, an inclination, a movement, it will be natural for us to approach love in terms of the dynamic aspects of being and existence which we have emphasized in previous chapters. It would be easy to equate love with the self-expansive tendency in finite being to attain, to preserve, and to communicate fullness of being. Thus, love would be the inclination of every being toward whatever will fulfill its being—the inclination of the plant for sun and water, the inclination of the dog for a bone, the inclination of a man for knowledge, for the completion of every power, for the completion of being in unity with every other being. Love would also be the drive to maintain being—love tending to whatever will contribute to the preservation of being. Finally, love would be the inclination to share being, the impulse or movement to give from fullness, to expand through communication.

This notion of love as tendency has appeared in countless and diverse philosophical theories. St. Augustine expresses it when he says, "A body tends to go of its own weight to its own place. . . . Fire tends to rise upward; a stone falls downward. Things are moved by their own weights and go toward their proper places. . . . My weight is my love; wherever I am carried, it is my love that carries me there." [2] Saint Thomas likewise implies a tendential character in love when he says that it is the "spontaneous movement of the lover toward the beloved," [3] or that "the movement of love has a twofold tendency: toward the good which a man wishes to someone—to himself or to another—and toward that to which he wishes some good." [4] From a quite different philosophical point of view, C. S. Peirce concurs: "In the emotional sphere this tendency toward union (like

---

[2] *Confessions,* XIII, 9; trans. R. Warner (New York: New American Library, 1963), 322.

[3] *Summa Theologiae,* II–II, 25, 2c.

[4] *Ibid.,* I–II, 26, 4c.

that of reason—logical analysis) appears as Love."[5] More recently and from another point of view Teilhard de Chardin speaks of love "in its natural dynamism and its evolutionary significance," as an "internal propensity to unite."[6] Other echoes of this are found in contemporary Catholic philosophers and theologians. For instance Gerard Gilleman, in an effort to reach the philosophical and theological depths of the meaning of love, declares that "all love must be an active tendency toward unity, more or less intense, according to the degree of being."[7] And Father Johann, in an attempt to push the meaning of love beyond the notion of desire, still identifies it with dynamic tendency: "The dynamism in man has two dimensions. One of them looks to the outside. . . . It consists in the quest of the potential for what it lacks, of nature for its completion. In virtue of this drive, man looks out upon the world that surrounds him and seeks to appropriate what he needs—first of all, what he needs for survival, but also, and hardly with less urgency, whatever may contribute to his natural perfection. He desires, therefore, not merely food and clothing and shelter, but, over and above these, all the fruits of civilized life—cultivation of mind, refinement of tastes, his basic share in the common patrimony of society, and, indeed, of the whole human achievement of reason and virtue. There is, nevertheless, another dimension, more profound. . . . Based on man's participation in the eternal presence of Being to Itself, and achieved through the inwardness of consciousness, it looks to the progressive fathoming by the finite self of the Unique Value, the Unique Self in whom he actually participates . . . a drive, not to possession or the appropriation of impersonal goods, but to communion. . . ."[8]

Despite the ease, however, with which we might equate love with tendency, the very nature of tendency points to a source beyond it

---

[5] *Values in a Universe of Chance, Selected Writings of C. S. Peirce,* edited by Philip P. Wiener. Copyright © 1958 by Philip P. Wiener. Reprinted by permission of Doubleday & Company, Inc.
[6] *The Phenomenon of Man,* trans. B. Wall (New York: Harper & Row, Publishers, Inc. [Torchbook ed.], 1961), p. 264.
[7] *The Primacy of Charity in Moral Theology,* trans. W. Ryan and A. Vachon (Westminster: The Newman Press, 1959), p. 131.
[8] R. Johann, *The Meaning of Love* (Westminster: The Newman Press, 1959), pp. 69–70.

in being, something which is more fundamental, which underlies and grounds tendency.[9] Tendential activity is affective activity, but if it rises from a more fundamental affective activity, this latter more fundamental activity is more properly called love. Tendency, therefore, will have love as its source and as its end. Tendency will be an expression of love, but will be love itself only in an extended sense.

Love as Affirmation

Deeper in being than tendency, love has been characterized as union with or affirmation of whatever is loved. But what can it mean to say that love is union or that it is affirmation?

We have seen that all finite beings are participants in being, united thus ontologically by their very share in existence. Unique existents, they nevertheless partake in and by their uniqueness in the community of being. "Only the community of beings in Being provides the basis upon which to build a theory of love." [10] There is a metaphysical union among beings—greater or less as they have greater or less being. This union is qualified by essential relationships, such as the relationship by which essence determines existence. This community of being is ordered to a certain kind of union even as one being is ordered to another being in countless different relation-

---

[9] This is seen not just because tendency, if it is to be intelligible at all, must rise from something more profound in being than itself, but because when tendency reaches its goal love does not cease. It is commonly recognized that—Plato's description of love in the *Symposium* notwithstanding—should every tendency toward perfection be perfectly fulfilled, and every tendency to preserve perfection be perfectly confirmed, and every tendency to communicate perfection be perfectly actualized, love, far from disappearing, would finally be full and perfect.

In perhaps all the theories whose statements have been cited above in favor of identifying love as tendency there is room for a more proper identification of love beyond tendency. For an interpretation of St. Thomas which seeks textual evidence of an understanding of love other than as tendency, see Frederick E. Crowe, "Complacency and Concern in the Thought of St. Thomas," *Theological Studies,* XX (March 1959), 1–39; (June 1959), 198–230; and (September 1959), 343–95.

[10] Johann, *The Meaning of Love,* p. 39.

ships of potency to act and act to potency and act to act.[11] This union, from the side of activity, can be called love.[12]

To understand the full meaning of love as union, however, we will have to uncover the reality of love as affirmation.[13] The affective affirmation which is love is an affirmation of being by being. What this means can be understood best in comparison with other kinds of affirmation—intellectual and entitative. An intellectual affirmation—which can be expressed in a verbal affirmation—is an affirmation by the mind whereby it affirms in a judgment that something is or is in a certain way. According to Father Toner, in this intellectual act the one affirming ratifies as true, makes firm, as it were, against denial in thought, that which he affirms. He backs up his proposition as true. His act, in some sense, establishes an intentional union with the reality of what he affirms; for his act of affirming is a sort of representational reliving of the object.[14]

There is another affirmation which is the affirmation of each existing being as a being and as a certain kind of being. The very act of existing in every being is an affirmation, an affirmation of the being's own self. Father Toner again suggests that to be is an act by which a being posits and holds itself in actuality. It is an entitative affirmation, therefore, of whatever the being is (including its potentiality and dynamism toward fuller actuality).[15] In union with and in total dependence on the creative affirmation of God, each

[11] Often it is said that love requires a certain proportion between the one loving and the one loved. Our understanding of proportion in this sense can be extended to include the proportion of one being to another by participation in being.

[12] Because love issues in tendency toward fuller union, it is easy to lose sight of the fact that it is itself union. The reality of affective union is often forgotten in the experience of unfulfilled tendency toward fuller union. St. Thomas distinguishes "a union which is essentially love itself. This union is according to a bond of affection, and is likened to substantial union, inasmuch as the lover stands to the object of his love, as to himself, if it be love of friendship; as to something belonging to himself if it be love of concupiscence." *Summa Theologiae*, I–II, 28, 1 ad 2.

[13] The analysis of love as affirmation given here is based on an unpublished manuscript of Jules Toner, S.J., of the University of Detroit and Bellarmine School of Theology. Father Toner, of course, though graciously consenting to read this section, is not responsible for our interpretation and use of his material.

[14] *Ibid.*

[15] *Ibid.*

being affirms itself not only in a proposition or a judgment, but also in existence, in actuality. Intellectual and verbal affirmation depend on this affirmation for their meaning.

The affirmation which is love is more like entitative affirmation than intellectual affirmation.[16] Furthermore, it is an affirmation of being by being—in the sense of the root meaning of affirmation, *ad-firmare*. The being of the one loving is placed by affection in affirmation of the being loved in such a way as to make the one loved firm and full in being. There is even a sense in which the act of entitative affirmation can itself be called love—love first of the being which exercises it for its own being, and love also of the other beings with which it exists in ontological union, a love which it exercises by existing in union with them.

If we hesitate to use the word "love" for entitative affirmation in every being, it is only because not all beings exist fully enough to give us clear evidence for including affectivity in our notion of their existence. There is, however, evidence in all beings of the existential dynamism, of the tendency which rises from a fundamental affirmation—which perhaps accounts for our usual equating of love with tendency. Or we can approach this from a different point of view and discover the basic entitative affirmation by a study of personal beings. In them we can find an affective activity which is more fundamental than tendency and which can be understood only in terms of entitative affirmation.

Human love, rational love, may be described as merely similar to entitative affirmation. It is possible, in terms of what we have said, to go even further and say that love is the act of being in its affirmative character risen into consciousness.[17] We can see this most clearly

---

[16] The affirmation which is love goes beyond the affirmation which is had in knowledge. It is not necessary to indicate this as J. de Finance does (*Etre et Agir*) as a difference between essential (in knowledge) and existential (in love) affirmation—for intellectual affirmation, too, in some sense is an affirmation of existence. The distinction is expressed, however, when we speak of intellectual affirmation as an intentional affirmation, "You are"; and of loving affirmation as affirmation-by-*being*, "I want you to be." The latter, when in regard to love of something that is not yet full in being, issues in concern, in an act of inclining toward the deeds of love, and finally in the deeds of love themselves—insofar as they are possible.

[17] Based on Toner, unpublished manuscript.

in the case of self-love,[18] in which love is an active, conscious, self-affirmation, the act of being expressing itself consciously to a greater or lesser degree.[19] Love of another is the act of being of the one loving consciously uniting itself in coaffirmation of and with the act of being of the one loved.[20]

Love, and indeed being, is most translucent for us in human being. Efforts at a phenomenology of human love tell us something by analogy of what can be called love in impersonal being, and whatever we know of human personal love will tell us better than knowledge of any other love what the perfection of love is as it must be without limit in God.

William Luijpen, attempting a phenomenological description of human love, speaks of love as an "active leaning." In finite personal beings love goes forth in response to a "call" from being, from other beings. It is an "invitation to transcend myself." [21] This call is possible because of the participation of being in being, because of the prior ontological union which can develop into union at the level of consciousness. But the response is not merely tendency. It is an awakening to conscious affirmation, the will to "be 'for' the other," to "will his subjectivity, to offer him the possibility to exist, to consent to his freedom, to accept, support and share in it. My affirmative reply to his appeal is known as affection." [22]

Summary

We have indicated three possible meanings of love: tendency or inclination, entitative affirmation at a preconscious level, and conscious affective affirmation. The word "love" can be applied to all. We have preferred to apply it properly to affirmation, and only in

---

[18] That is, *true* self-love, not love of self in the pejorative sense sometimes given it, which must be understood only as it relates to true self-love.

[19] The fact that conscious love has degrees of expression is due to the various conditions under which it rises—as, for example, the condition of knowledge.

[20] Marcel is open to an ontological meaning of love in this way, too, when he speaks of love as communion. Cf. *The Mystery of Being: II, Faith and Reality* (Chicago: Henry Regnery Co., 1960), p. 170.

[21] *Existential Phenomenology* (Pittsburgh: Duquesne University Press, 1960), p. 215.

[22] *Ibid.*, p. 218.

an extended sense to tendency. We can narrow its proper application still more by restricting it to conscious affirmation. It is sufficient to have seen both aspects of the reality of affirmation. Our further discussion will consider transcendental goodness primarily from the focus of conscious affective affirmation—that is, primarily in terms of personal love.

The Meaning of Goodness

We began this chapter by asking whether being as being is lovable—whether it is able to be united to a loving being, able to be affirmed by active love, able to be taken within a being capable of conscious love. The answer to this question is already implied in what we have seen of love. Nevertheless it will be helpful to unfold it explicitly in terms of goodness, for "good" designates whatever is in some way the object of love. If all being is related to love—that is, is lovable—then being as being is indeed good.

Being as the Object of Tendency

Some beings are recognized as lovable because they are the goal of a tendential act. Thus, while our primary focus in understanding goodness will be on the object of conscious affective affirmation, we shall still learn something of goodness by seeing it in relation to tendency. In this sense, we speak of one being as good—that is, as lovable—because it is perfective of another being, as medicine is good for a patient or the sun is good for crops or consoling words from a friend are good for a suffering man. We speak also of something within a being as good relative to the being, as strong limbs are good for a tree or insight is good for a scholar. In all these examples, being is good insofar as it is the end or goal of a tendency to grow in full being or to preserve full being. All that is perfective is lovable for what it perfects.

We can speak, too, of being as good when it is the end of a tendency to communicate being. The end or goal of such a tendency can be a product, such as the fruit which a tree tends to produce or the painting which the artist yearns to create.

From all of this we can see that being may be defined as good inasmuch as it is the end or object of the threefold tendency which expresses the dynamic nature of existence, the tendency to attainment, preservation, and communication. For being is good, insofar as it is lovable or desirable as something (1) to be attained; (2) to be preserved; or (3) to be shared, given, or communicated.

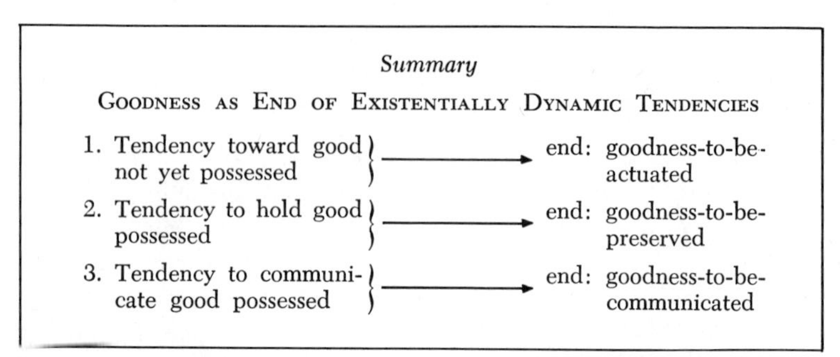
Summary

GOODNESS AS END OF EXISTENTIALLY DYNAMIC TENDENCIES

1. Tendency toward good not yet possessed	→	end: goodness-to-be-actuated
2. Tendency to hold good possessed	→	end: goodness-to-be-preserved
3. Tendency to communicate good possessed	→	end: goodness-to-be-communicated

When St. Thomas asks whether goodness is transcendental—whether every being as being is good—he most often considers it within this context, that is, he considers it as the object of a tendency. He begins with the notion of goodness as what is desirable [23] and maintains that a thing is desirable because it is perfect—with the implication that it is perfective. Since a thing is perfect insofar as it is actual, and to be actual is, of course, to exist, goodness is therefore the same as being, but under the aspect of desirableness. This for St. Thomas means not only that every good is being, but that every being is good.[24] The necessary implication is that all being is able to be the object of desire, of tendency. This does not mean that it is actually desired, but only that it is desirable.

There is a difficulty here, perhaps more apparent than real, but nevertheless a difficulty. What is there about being, or what have we discovered about being, that allows it simply as being to be the object of desire, of tendency? What allows St. Thomas to imply that every good is good precisely because and only because it is being, and hence that every being is good? Could one not as easily imply that every red being is red only because it is being, and therefore every being should be red? To focus on the question we can point

[23] *Summa Theologiae,* I, 5, 1 and 3.
[24] *Ibid.,* I, 5, 3.

out that in the sense in which we speak of good here—that is, as the object of tendency—every being can be good only if every being is somehow able to be desired, either as perfective or as expressive of perfection. Unless we see that this is so, we would conclude too quickly to the desirability of all being.

The key to understanding that being as the object of tendency is good lies in an understanding of personal being. Persons are persons, and not things, because they are capable of opening in knowledge and love to receive other beings than themselves into their own being. Since they are "open" beings in this way with a kind of "infinite" capacity for knowing and loving, their very perfection and completion can come through conscious affective union with all other beings. Moreover, they tend to communicate their being to all other beings, *tend* finally to affirm all other beings.[25] Thus, whether or not in the world of things there is an interrelatedness of beings sufficient to imply that each is in some way able to be the object of tendency for another, the existence of personal beings shows that by their activity conscious tendency may extend to every being.

We need not, and indeed cannot, conclude here our consideration of transcendental goodness. Being is lovable not merely as the object of tendency, but as affirmed, and as able to be coaffirmed, in its own being—just because it is. We can see this if we see that as a more fundamental affective act underlies tendency, so a more fundamental goodness underlies goodness which is the object of tendency.

Being as Object of Affective Affirmation

To be loved, to be the object of the fundamental love which underlies and grounds every other form of love, is to be affectively affirmed in being, to be by an affirmation of one's being. We have seen enough to know that every being is so affirmed—by a self-affirmation affirmed within the creative affirmation of the First Cause. From this fact alone we could justify the conclusion that all

[25] It is possible to see that in a world comprised of impersonal and personal beings, all impersonal beings must somehow exist for the sake of persons. All persons can be the object of tendency for all other persons, as perfect or perfective.

being, just because it exists, is good. It is not only lovable, able-to-be-affirmed, it is loved—at least by God.

And yet to see and to say this is somehow inadequate. It is true and even wondrous. But it falls short of the full understanding of love and of being-loved which can associate only with personal conscious love. We can, of course, speak of the goodness of each being in terms of its participation in being since it exercises its act of existing in affirmation of its own being and in union with all other beings, loving and being-loved. However, it is only when we reach again to the realm of personal being that all that we say of love begins to have full meaning. Only personal beings are able consciously to affirm their own goodness and only personal beings are able—if they break out of the forces of egocentric gravity in their being—to place their own act of existing in conscious affirmation of the existence of another, coaffirming in the union of love the being of the other as good.

If in relation to personal being we ask why every being is lovable, we can point again to the community, the ontological union, of all being in being. What a person affirms in himself is the same value which is to be met in another to a greater or lesser degree, whether in a person or in a thing. Preserving the uniqueness of the individual being, persons are yet able to enter into the being of another and consciously, even freely, to affirm the being of the other even as they affirm their own, in love. We must relate this understanding of goodness to the goodness of God, for apart from infinite goodness, it is impossible to understand finite goodness and hence to understand the transcendental goodness of being. "What I love in myself or another is a subsistent likeness of God. The ultimate oneness of value is assured. God the Creator, present in all, is loved in all and above all. But this unique Value, as *participated,* is indistinguishable from that core of reality most proper to each creature, its own subsistence. It is the presence of this Value in the creature that is the creature. Hence each creature is a unique value, yet communing in its uniqueness with every other creature in *the* Unique Value. Since, therefore, what I love in being is the presence of the Absolute, I can love it in the other as well as in myself. And since as in myself it is myself, and in the other it is himself, so my own proper good, loved in myself, can be found by likeness in the other in the very trait that irreducibly distinguishes him from me, his proper subsistence."[26]

This leads us to look finally at goodness and love in God.

God: Infinite Love and Lovableness

It would be easy to conclude immediately the fact of both goodness and love in God. We would have only to reason once again from a perfection which is a pure perfection in the effects of God to that same perfection analogously but properly in God. We could say, also, that if to be is to love, and if being is good and goodness being, He who is Absolute Being is Absolute Love and Absolute Goodness.[27]

In God love can only be infinite loving affirmation. He not only loves, but He is love. He who is His own being is His own love. He is Himself an act of conscious affirmation; He affirms His own being, embracing it in total affirmation of being by being.[28] The human mind stumbles in the light which is darkness when it tries to understand anything more of what it means to say that God is Love. Lover and loved are one in a love which is infinite, open, self-possessed, personal, subsistent love.

If in God love is infinite, its primary object must also be infinite: infinitely lovable, infinite goodness. Otherwise there would be no proportion between the love and its primary object. But since God alone is infinite, the primary object of His love can only be His own being. This means that not only is there goodness in God—not only is He good—but He must be subsistent goodness. A thing is good by

---

[26] Johann, *The Meaning of Love,* p. 30.

[27] See *Summa Theologiae,* I, 6, 1; I, 20; and *Summa Contra Gentiles,* I, 37, n. 2. Goodness and love, like the other affirmative absolute names of God, must be purified by negation in our understanding. Thus, God as Goodness and Love is not limited to space, but is eternal, utterly one, unchangeable, infinite.

[28] One of the difficulties we meet in trying to understand anything of the love God has for Himself is that it is almost impossible for us to see it as something totally different from what we consider selfishness in human love. We would understand it better if we thought of it in terms of the noblest forms of unselfish love that we know. In what is analogous to our experience of unselfish love, God affirms His pure existence, and this affirmation is His existence.

its act of existing, and all that is actual through that act. Hence God who is His own act of existing and is infinite actuality is His own goodness.

Moreover, to love and to be lovable are one and the same in God. His love is His goodness, and His goodness is His love, and both are one with His being.

It remains to see briefly the relation of created beings to the goodness of God, the meeting of participated and participating goodness, and participated and participating love.

The Meeting of Finite and Infinite in Goodness and Love

The ultimate reason why every being is good is that it is loved into being by God. The ultimate reason why every being loves is because it partakes of existence through existential and affective affirmation. Created love begins from union with God in being and through the dynamic tendencies of existence ends in fuller and fuller union with God. Furthermore, the central tendency of conscious personal love in human beings is toward communion with God.

When we attempt to understand God's love of beings other than Himself, the same difficulties arise as did in our attempt to understand His knowledge of things other than Himself. Objections have been raised which deny His love for anything but Himself, objections which center around the fact that once again His activity would be limited if terminated in a limited object. We are infinitely less than God, so the objection goes, therefore He could not possibly love us.

And yet the first reason why we know that God does indeed love His creatures is because they—we—are.[29] We have already seen that the creative causality of God involves knowledge. It is now possible to see that it must also be an activity of love. What is known by the intellect is executed by the will. God therefore has willed that we exist. And this willing must flow from love. Of course, as we have said, in God all is one—so that the activity whereby He creates other beings is a loving knowledge and a knowing love. Creatures are the effects of an act of love on God's part, even as they are effects of an act of knowledge. Because God loves us, we are.

---

[29] *Summa Theologiae,* I, 19, 6; I, 20, 2.

We have seen that love is an affirmation of the existence of the one loved by the very affirmation of the existence of the one loving. We can therefore see that the creative causality which reaches to the depths of every being and holds it in being in every respect is a causal act of love. "Love directs itself toward the other according to the latter's own proper existence; it takes up on its own account and prolongs within itself the act by which the other inserts itself in the order of existence. Let us now suppose a love which would not be a spiritual participation in the existence of another, but of which this existence would rather be the expression. This is what we mean by that communication of act, raised to its highest degree, which is Creation." [30]

Thus as in knowing Himself God knows all other beings, so in loving Himself He loves all other beings—loves them into being and into fullness of being. Since each finite being comes forth from the creative love of God, it is for this reason lovable in its very existence. It is goodness that God diffuses, and insofar as any being exists, it is lovable and therefore good. This means that the love of God for each created being is not the kind of love which finds goodness present and then responds to it. Rather it is the kind of love which makes the goodness to be present. Because He loves His own goodness and wills to diffuse it, God creatively causes by the causality of love beings who participate in His goodness.[31] All that we have said of love thus applies to God's love for the beings He creates: in loving them He affirms their being, relates Himself to them as their ultimate good. As they grow in being, they grow in participation in His goodness; they are thus affirmed in greater and greater union with God.

On the other hand, as created beings are placed in being, as they exercise their own existence in coaffirmation of being, so do they, too, begin to love. Beings who exercise a personal existence are able consciously to affirm their own being in God, consciously to affirm God by their own being. Such beings have been described as exist-

---

[30] J. de Finance, "Being and Subjectivity," trans. W. N. Clarke, *Cross Currents,* VI (Spring 1956), 175–76.

[31] Nevertheless, it must not be supposed that God is necessitated to create. The diffusiveness of His goodness is not dependent for its communicativeness on creatures.

ing at the "turning point" of God's activity—coming forth from infinite love, returning to infinite goodness, meeting in a union which is conscious communion. In relation to God, their love is not a love which creates goodness; it is wholly a love which responds to goodness. The goodness of God is a call to their love. Created participants in God's goodness participate in the call of His being to their being for the awakened affirmation and transcendent coaffirmation which is love.

Summary

Being, then, is itself good. It is, as being, lovable. It is desirable as the object of tendency, and more profoundly, lovable and loved in the very affirmation of its being by being. Absolute Being is subsistent goodness and all other being as being is good by participation. For God, to be is to love; for every other being, to be is to be loved by God—to be loved into the fullness of being which is characterized in turn by its own love. Subsistent Goodness, which is the source for all other goodness, creates beings that are not only lovable but, because they are, also love.

There is, however, a serious difficulty which comes to the fore at this point. It is by no means a new difficulty, for we have met it more than once before and in particular, we have met it in our consideration of divine providence. When we saw that God, through his providential care, leads all beings to fullness, to good, the problem of evil in the world became immediately apparent. It becomes even more acute now in the face of the conclusions which seem to have been reached in regard to God's goodness and love.

The Problem of Evil

Introduction

Before meeting the problem which evil presents, it will be well to place it in context by gathering together what we now know of God's activity. We see Him now to be Truth and Wisdom, Goodness and Love. This means that we see Him now as a Person—for it is the prerogative of persons to know and to love. He can no longer be considered by us as an impersonal, almost anonymous force, remote from the beings of experience and causing them as any cosmic force might cause them. Rather, He can only be considered as infinitely personal—more, not less personal than any person known in experience. He is, therefore, personally present to everything as its cause, present as a free and knowing cause. Every being is present to Him by reason of His knowledge and love.[32] To be, for finite beings, is to be known and loved by God—and this, in a sense, sums up all metaphysics, though always there are the inevitable new questions which keep us in the pursuit of understanding.

All this means that the knowledge, the Wisdom of God is the cause of things, for He whose being is His act of understanding causes by His intellect.[33] Moreover, God causes through willing, through loving, since the will is the cause of things as the act of executing what is conceived by the intellect. In God, both are one. It might also be added that, since there is no limitation to God's activity, the will of God is always fulfilled.

If, then, the causality of God and His providential care of all His creatures is the causality and providence of a Person, and of a Person who is infinitely wise and good, how is it that there is evil in the world—and such evil that it sometimes covers the horizon of man's consciousness with darkness and despair? How do we explain disruption in the physical universe, jungles of beings preying on other beings, savage disorder in the face of order, human suffering in bodies ravaged and spirits torn, the destruction of man by man, the self-destruction of moral evil? St. Thomas points up the question, "A wise provider excludes any defect of evil, as far as he can, from those over whom he has a care. But we see many evils existing in things. Either, then, God cannot hinder these, and thus is not omnipotent; or else He does not have care for everything." [34]

This is the age-old objection of the spirit of man in the face of evil and suffering. If God were all-powerful and all-good, He would both want to take away all evil and be able to. Since there is, however, evil in the world, God must either be not all-powerful or not

---

[32] This is the meaning of "presence" properly so called, which we considered in anticipation above, pages 160–64.
[33] See *Summa Theologiae,* I, 14, 8.
[34] *Ibid.,* I, 22, 2, obj. 2.

all-good. In either case He would not be God. It is for reasons like this that some have denied the very existence of God.[35]

The problem does not admit of an easy answer. In the end, there is left the mystery of suffering. Faith can shed a light which reason cannot give; and yet reason can approach in preparation for the light of faith, and it can work within the light given by faith—not, of course, basing its conclusions on revelation. In any case, it is hardly possible for man simply to shrug his shoulders in the face of such a question, as if it makes no difference to him whether he says anything at all in answer. Suffering, especially human suffering, is of such a kind in experience that it demands that a man, from time to time, grapple with the very mystery it presents. Being is itself ultimately a mystery; so is activity. So are truth and knowledge and love. Just as the mind of man in the presence of these mysteries must go as far as it can and then admit the mystery, so it must do in regard to the problem of evil.

The problem of evil is as old as thinking man, but it seems to be at least as intense, if not more intense, for contemporary man as for any other man in any other time. Whether it appears in his preoccupation with anguish or guilt or nothingness or absurdity or despair, it takes center stage more than once in the concern of philosophical, literary, psychological, and theological questionings. For this reason, we shall consider it now in some detail.

Once again, before attempting to see what possible way there may be to solve the problem, it is necessary to understand the problem itself accurately. Since we have already demonstrated that God does have providence over everything, and that He is infinitely good and powerful, these truths cannot be called into question except by questioning the arguments by which they have been established, by questioning the procedures through which they have been discovered. We are not, therefore, asking whether or not God does have providence over everything, or whether He is good and wise and powerful. The problem is, rather, how God can be both provident of all things, good and omnipotent, and at the same time permit evil in creation. It is a problem of reconciling all these estab-

---

[35] For example, the character of Ivan Karamazov in Dostoievsky's *The Brothers Karamazov,* or such writers as J.-P. Sartre.

lished facts, of seeing how they fit together without contradiction.

In order to see whatever may be seen in answer to the problem it is necessary to understand how evil is caused; and to know this, it is necessary to understand what evil is. We shall, then, discuss the problem of evil by considering three questions: (1) What is evil? (2) How is evil caused? (3) How can the existence of evil be reconciled with an omnipotent, loving, and providential First Cause?

The Meaning of Evil

Evil is not foreign to anyone's experience. It presents itself at every level of being. Natural catastrophes mar the face of the world; animals survive at the expense of other animals; men suffer sickness and death; human beings sin against other human beings and against God. What is it, in all of these instances, that is evil?

The common factor in all these is that something is missing in the reality involved in each of these instances. Order is lacking in the conflicting forces of nature; an animal loses its life; a man is without physical health; an action lacks direction or wholeness. Evil is an absence of good, an absence of being or actuality. Yet not every absence of being is an evil. A bean plant lacks the power of seeing, but it does not thereby suffer evil. If, on the other hand, a man lacks the power of seeing, he is indeed the subject of an evil. Evil, therefore, is not just any lack of being, but an absence of being which should be present. Another word for the absence of something that should be there is "privation." Every evil is a privation.[36]

If this is what evil is, nothing can be totally evil. Evil must exist in some subject that is good. Total privation would mean nothingness.[37] We have seen that every being, insofar as it has being, is good. Insofar as it lacks an aspect of being that it should have—a fullness or good—it is evil.

There are those who have rejected the definition of evil as a privation. They say that evil cannot be explained away by saying that it is unreal, that it is not there. Evil is intensely real in experience. Indeed so. But to say that evil is a privation is not to take away the

---

[36] See *Summa Theologiae,* I, 48, 1 and 3.
[37] *Ibid.,* I, 48, 4.

reality of the experience of evil. The being that is deprived of a good is in some way a defective being, and to have a defective being is to have a very real state in which to be.

In order to understand the cause of evil and finally to attempt a resolution of the problem of evil, it will be helpful to speak of three kinds of evil, or three classes of evil which include the myriad kinds of evil. These are: physical evil in the universe, physical evil in man, and moral evil in man or any personal being.[38]

The Cause of Evil

The nature of evil demands a certain kind of cause. Since evil is a privation, it cannot be caused *per se*, that is, the efficient cause of any evil cannot be a *per se* cause.[39] Evil can have only an accidental cause. We saw in Chapter 4 that the characteristics of a *per se* cause are that it (1) acts for an end, (2) produces its like, and (3) is causing here and now. The cause of any evil fails of the first characteristic, that is, no cause directly intends evil for its own sake as its effect. Evil cannot be an end in itself. It can be only indirectly intended for the sake of some good. For a cause to intend evil directly would be to contradict the very nature of intention—which is directed to some good. What this means, practically speaking, is that every cause has for its end a good.[40] If that good cannot be brought about without an accompanying evil—evil as a condition, result, occasion, or means—then the evil is intended along with the good, but it is the good that is willed directly and the evil only indirectly for the sake of the good. This indirect intending of evil makes it always the effect of accidental causality. Thus, for example, what the bird causes directly when it eats the worm is its own nourishment; this also happens to entail the destruction of the worm. The nourishment of the bird is caused *per se*, and the destruction of the worm accidentally. If a man wishes to build a house, he may have to build it out of the wood from growing trees. The good which he wills directly and so causes *per se* is the house. But he cannot have

---

[38] In other terminologies moral evil is known simply as sin.

[39] For the distinction of the kinds of causes, see pages 89–92.

[40] Or an end which appears desirable—that is, good—from some point of view. It is not necessary that it appear morally good.

the house without cutting down the trees. He therefore also truly wills the trees to be cut down—not for the sake of cutting down the trees but for the sake of building the house. He thus causes the trees to be cut down accidentally. Even if a cause apparently intends an evil for its own sake, there is still always a good that is directly intended. Thus, if a man directly intends to take another man's life, he intends something that appears at least to him as good —the other man's money, his own satisfaction in revenge, and so forth. So that even here he is the cause of evil only accidentally. He is, nevertheless, the cause.

Evil is, therefore, always the effect of accidental causality. An agent may intend evil, cause it, by reason of some defect in itself as agent or in the patient. Thus an artist may paint a poor picture because he is a poor artist or because he does not have the right materials. On the other hand, an agent may cause evil by reason of some perfection in itself as agent. If a piano student plays a piece on the piano and makes a mistake, he probably makes the mistake because of some defect in his skill. If, however, his teacher, wishing to show him his mistake, replays the same piece and makes the same mistake, he may do so precisely because of his skill in piano playing.[41]

All this may help us to understand God's causality of evil. His causality is not the same with regard to physical evil and moral evil. In regard to physical evil, whether in the universe or in man, He is its cause; and because evil can only have an accidental cause, He is its cause accidentally. He is, moreover, the accidental cause of evil by reason of the perfection of His power, not by reason of any defect. As the piano teacher wills a defect in his playing for the sake of the greater good of instructing his pupil, so God wills physical evils for the sake of the greater good. This means that He causes some goods which are necessarily connected with some evil. He wills the good directly, and the evil only insofar as it is connected with the good. If the good which is willed directly were not more desired than the good of which the accompanying evil is the privation, the first good would not be willed at all—and of course the evil would not follow.[42]

---

[41] See *Summa Theologiae,* I, 49, 1.
[42] *Ibid.,* I, 19, 9.

In regard to moral evil, God does not will it at all. He is not even the accidental cause of moral evil. This becomes clear when we understand that moral evil is contrary to the order of things, contrary to God's goodness, and that it is not possible for God to intend anything which is in contradiction to His goodness. For as we have seen, His goodness is the primary object of his will and it is in relation to this that He wills all other things. To say that God does not cause moral evil is not merely a glib way of excusing the presence of moral evil in the world. Our reasons are established as conclusions from our study of the nature of being, the nature of reality. Whatever persuasion they have will depend upon the validity of these conclusions and their appeal to us as metaphysicians.

The only sense in which God's causality can be said to have any bearing on moral evil is that He causes the kind of beings who are capable of sinning. He may be said to permit moral evil in that He causes an order of things in which there is the possibility of sin.[43]

To see the relationship of evil to the causality of God is not yet to reconcile evil with an omnipotent and provident First Cause. It does, however, provide the foundation for a beginning reconciliation.

Reconciling Evil with the Providence of God

Obviously, the reconciliation which we will attempt will go only as far as our understanding can penetrate. It in no way denies a fuller and more complete reconciliation in reality itself. It is for us to see what we can see, to understand what we can understand, to find what light we can discover. If the light we find is not all the light in reality, whatever light it is will serve as a harbinger of greater light to come.

The key to reconciliation is to see that evil can be caused by God only for the sake of a greater good. This must be so, for God is infinitely good and powerful, and it is not in spite of His goodness and power but because of it that He causes evil. In every instance of evil, it must be true that it is caused or permitted by the First

[43] To speak of God's "permission" of evil in the case of moral evil is not the same as to speak of his "permission" in the case of physical evil. In the latter, it is only another way of saying that He does cause, but accidentally; in the former, it is a way of saying that He does not cause—but does not prevent.

Cause only because out of it He can bring a greater good—a greater good, from every point of view, than the good which is lost in the accompanying evil, and a good in the creation of which evil, or privation, has a real role. The problem, then, will be one of seeing the greater good to which every evil can contribute.

If we look merely to physical evil in the universe, the problem is not so difficult. This universe is quite obviously a universe of hierarchically ordered beings. The good of the whole universe is a greater good than that of any individual beings within it—excepting for the moment personal beings. Thus, physical evil in an individual being in the universe is for the sake of the good of the whole. The destruction of a plant for the nourishment of an animal, or even the destruction of one animal for the nourishment of another animal, is simply an expression of the order in the universe whereby nothing exists for its own sake alone, but for the sake of a higher order of beings and ultimately, for the sake of the good of the whole universe.

When a wolf eats a lamb, it is the good of the wolf which is directly caused. It is easy to see how the evil which befalls the lamb is for the good of the wolf, but not so easy to see how it is for the good of the lamb. One might have to conclude simply that it is not in any way for the good of the lamb, that the lamb suffers evil, purely and simply, for the sake of the whole universe. But we may be able to find some light in the situation which points even to a good for the lamb. If the lamb exists for the good of the whole; if, in particular, it exists for the good of the wolf, in providing food for the wolf it somehow fulfills its own *raison d'être.* In other words if the meaning of its being is in terms of its place in the universal order of things, then the only unintelligible evil which might befall it would be for it to be destroyed in this very meaning. But if, as a matter of fact, it finally serves the very purpose which lies at the root of its existence, it can hardly be said to have undergone evil and nothing else. To deny the place of a being in the universal order of things is not to preserve its good, but ultimately to destroy it. Thus, for example, if a man were to give to his cat a meaning which the cat does not have, if, for example, he were to see and treat the cat as a human person, giving to it what should be given to other men—what may perhaps result in the deprivation of other men—he destroys the meaning of the cat. If he bequeaths his entire fortune to the cat, he does not affirm the real good of the cat any more than he affirms the real good of his sons who might be in need of that fortune. No self-respecting cat would wish to be treated so.

All that recent studies have told us about the continuing progression of the universe, a universe which is still to evolve in all its perfection, throws added light on this specific question. The meaning of each thing in the universe must be understood in the light of its role in the evolutive creation of the world. This is a main theme in Chardin's thought: "In a universe where every created being formed a small self-contained whole, willed for its own sake, and theoretically transposable at will, we should find some difficulty in justifying in our own minds the presence of individuals painfully cut short in their possibility and their upward flight. Why this pointless inequality, these meaningless restrictions? In contrast, if the world really represents a conquest still under way, if at our birth we are really thrown into the thick of the battle, then we can well understand that, for the success of the universal effort, in which we are at the same time the partners and the stake, pain is inevitable. The world, looked at empirically on our scale, is an immense groping, an immense search, an immense attack; it can only progress at the cost of many failures and many casualties." [44]

It is more difficult to see always the greater good involved when one is concerned with physical evil in personal being. There is a serious difference in the meaning of evil in persons and the meaning of evil in things. Although it may be said of things that none of them exist for their own sake, but for the good of the whole, this may not be said of persons in the same sense.[45] Persons do exist, in a sense, for their own sake—as ends in themselves, having eternal value in an eternal destiny. Thus, no person may be sacrificed for the good of the whole in the sense that the total good of the person as a person is destroyed. This does not mean that the partial good of individual persons may not be sacrificed for the good of the whole

---

[44] Teilhard de Chardin, "The Meaning and Constructive Value of Suffering," trans. N. Lindsay, *Jubilee*, X (June 1962), 22.

[45] In the passage given above from de Chardin, he is speaking more specifically of human suffering—in a sense in which it serves the whole, but in a sense also where it serves the whole good of the person. See also, Wilfrid Desan, *The Planetary Man* (Washington: Georgetown University Press, 1961), Chapter 1, pp. 11–22.

—the good of the community or the good of all mankind. But even this partial loss of individual good must ultimately serve the greater good of the person as well as the community. Physical evil in persons, therefore, may indeed serve the good of the whole, or the good of other persons, but it must somehow also serve the good of that whole person.[46] To see that this must be so is not the same as seeing in every instance how it is so. We can try to see the necessity of its truth, and we can try to see it in reality in enough instances to know that it is true even in the instances where we cannot see.

Human suffering is ultimately a mystery, but there is enough light for us to know that where there is darkness it is because the light is too great. Everyone can see some instances where from suffering comes greater good. Sometimes it is only suffering which will awaken a man to himself and to all reality. Some things can be seen only in the cleansing fire of pain. Without suffering, what some have thought the most beautiful thing in all creation, a courageous love, would be impossible. If there were no sorrow, where would comfort be? As Leon Bloy has said, "Man has places in his heart that as yet have no existence; pain has to enter before they can *be*." [47]

To see that a greater good can come from evil is by no means to imply that evil is never to be opposed. That a man may grow strong through sickness is by no means an excuse for not trying to make him well. Indeed, the greater good which is to come from evil may be directly involved with the facing of evil and the effort to alleviate it. Evil cannot be desired for its own sake; all that we have said of it gainsays this. It is to be opposed wherever it can be, and to the extent that it can be. The greatest good which may come from evil may be final surrender in the face of it—to God, not to evil—but such a surrender must not be made too soon.

Moral evil in personal beings is the greatest mystery of all. Once again, however, even moral evil can make the philosopher look to his proofs. It cannot itself refute his proofs. Once again, too, the

---

[46] Human freedom may be the determining factor in deciding whether or not it does serve the good of the person as a whole.

[47] Quoted by L. Halin, *A l'ombre de la mort,* Cahiers de la Revue Nouvelle (Paris, Tournai: Casterman, 1947), p. 183. See Y. Congar, "The Problem of Evil," in *God, Man and the Universe,* ed. J. de Bivort de la Saudée (New York: P. J. Kenedy & Sons, 1953), p. 401.

key to reconciling moral evil with the goodness and power of God is to see that it can be allowed by God only because a greater good can come out of it. What that good is may be seen in a few instances —the goods of freedom or forgiveness, a forgiven love, repentance, understanding, the possibility of entering into the struggle of life and so creating one's being in the exercise of freedom. In any case, whether we see the greater good or not—and we do see it in enough instances to provide hope for more—the fact that a greater good can come from the presence of evil in the world is the *sine qua non* for understanding how evil is reconciled with the providence of God. If we can see that the two at least need not be contradictory, it is enough for now. God is still Subsistent Goodness and Love, and the very presence of evil may attest to the embrace of Providence.

We have seen, therefore, that being is good and this vision of the fullness of being includes the vision of unity and of truth and now, of lovableness and love, of value in itself and value for every other being. Absolute Being is Goodness itself, and beings utterly dependent upon Him for their existence are thus utterly dependent upon His love which, pouring forth from His goodness, constitutes them and holds them in being.

TRANSCENDENTAL BEAUTY

Introduction

Being may unfold to yet one more aspect, one more face of reality. There is something else about being which hints at transcendence of limitation to any particular kind of being. We receive our greatest revelations of being from things that flash forth to us in what we know as beauty. Even though we usually reserve our notion of beauty to things that have some degree of excellence, or to a particular kind of beauty which is aesthetic beauty, there is something in our recognition of the beautiful that resounds through all of reality. The gifted moments of quiet ringing beauty may be fleeting, but if what we see as beautiful does indeed tell us something of being itself, there may be in a meeting with even one being a rare revelation of what there is in all being—a manifestation through one of what is hidden in all.

The Meaning of Beauty

But what is beauty? What is a beautiful thing? What do we mean when we call something "beautiful" that we do not mean when we call something "good"? Every man has known beauty in something, and it is perhaps easier for him to speak of his reaction to the beautiful than to say what it is that calls forth this response. In the experience of the beautiful there seems always to be joy—fullness, completion, even peace. These are the characteristics of the activity which corresponds to beauty, even as love corresponds to goodness and knowledge to truth. Yet just as there is something in being itself which calls forth the response of love to goodness, and something in being itself that allows it to be known, so there is something in being which awakens the activity of joy.

This much begins to be clear: being is beautiful insofar as it can, when intellectually apprehended, give joy.[48] Nothing is beautiful merely by relation to a sense power and the pleasure it can afford sensibly. Beauty is, therefore, in a way the same as truth—it is being in relation to intellect. Yet not every grasp of truth gives joy, even though every being may be beautiful. The knower has not grasped the beauty of the being unless his knowledge is such as to give joy. This would indicate that there is something more to the beautiful than is included in the notion of truth. Being as beautiful is somehow logically distinct from being as true. Etienne Gilson says that beauty is not like reading a book and then not having any need to read it again. With beauty there is always the desire to repeat the experience.[49]

Being is beautiful insofar as it can call forth joy. Joy is an affective activity of the rational appetite or will. It is love of a good possessed. Beauty is, therefore, in a way the same as the good—it is being in relation to love. Yet not every affective response is to a good pos-

---

[48] This is what St. Thomas means when he defines the beautiful as "that which upon being seen pleases," *quod visum placet*. "Seen" refers to human knowledge and means any kind of perception at the sense level—though the primary reference is to visual perception—along with intellectual apprehension. It implies disinterested—that is, a nongrasping—pleasure in a rational perceiver.

[49] E. Gilson, *Painting and Reality* (New York: Pantheon Books, Inc., 1957), pp. 177–78.

sessed.[50] Similarly not every good possessed is possessed primarily by knowledge and love alone. And finally, not every affective response is a joy. Being as beautiful is somehow logically distinct from being as good.

If the beautiful is both intellectually apprehended and gives joy, it must somehow be related to both intellect and affective power. Beauty is the object of both intellect and will. It is therefore at one and the same time knowable and lovable. The beautiful differs from the true in that it adds the notion of the relation to love, and it differs from the good in that it adds the notion of relation to knowledge. Beauty is therefore the splendor of the true, the good of the intellect, the object of both knowledge and love.[51]

Beauty does not imply a relation to intellect in one sense and a relation to will in another. It does not call forth intellectual affirmation and loving affirmation as two activities merely juxtaposed. Rather, somehow it unites the activity of intellect and will, so that each qualifies the other. The apprehension of beauty is affective apprehension and the affection for the beautiful is an intellectual good. What is involved here is a profound union of activities in a knowing love and a loving knowledge.

Since every being has been seen to be both knowable and lovable, every being as being is beautiful. The treasured manifestations of beauty which are a special flashing forth to us of a being bear witness to what is in the depths of every being.

But what is it in being that allows it to call forth the unified response of knowledge and love? We should be able to find the key to this somewhere in the possession which is implied in the union of a beautiful object with the subject that apprehends it. Joy is love for a good possessed. Beauty brings joy just in the knowing of it. Vision is itself possession in such a case. What must it be in a being that allows it to be affectively possessed in the union of knowledge?

---

[50] As we have seen, the activity of an appetite may take the form of desire for what is not possessed, sorrow at an evil possessed, and so forth.

[51] ". . . beauty adds to goodness a relation to the cognitive faculty: so that good means that which simply pleases the appetite; while the beautiful is something pleasant to apprehend." *Summa Theologiae,* I–II, 27, 1 ad 3. "Beauty relates to a cognitive power, for those things are said to be beautiful which please when seen." *Summa Theologiae,* I, 5, 4 ad 1. See also *Summa Theologiae,* I, 16, 4 ad 1.

The mind stumbles again when it tries to go further in attempting to unveil the reality of being in its beauty. Philosophers have pointed to the intrinsic ontological characteristics of integrity, harmony, splendor, and the other transcendental aspects of being—unity, truth, and goodness. Being as beautiful does in a way imply all the transcendental aspects seen thus far. It is in a way a climax to the metaphysical revelation of being. It includes all that has been included in the others, and adds something more. It adds the unification of truth and goodness; and it adds whatever may be meant by integrity and harmony and splendor. But these last three perhaps are just another way of saying the transcendentals over again, for integrity harks back to unity, implying as it does the wholeness of perfection, a completeness and undividedness. Splendor is the mysterious element of brightness, clarity, brilliance, luminosity, the opening of the radiance which is truth. Harmony points to the proportion in being—of one part to another, of unity in variety, of deep fullness reminiscent of goodness, unity, and truth. If beauty contains within itself all the perfection of the other aspects of being, it is undivided in itself, whole. It is manifest, flashing forth. It is source and end of unified affirmation. It awakens joy because it is an end. It gives forth beautifully because it is a source.

If beauty is being in relation to intellect and will, there are as many kinds of beauty as there are kinds of being. Like being and one and true and good, the beautiful must be understood analogously of all the kinds of being. There is beauty in a mathematical equation, in a rose, in a diamond, in a painting, in a deed of love, in a person. In none of these is beauty exactly the same, but in none of them is it totally different. It means something the same and something different in all.[52]

God: Perfect Beauty and Perfect Joy

It will not be surprising to come at last to the necessary conclusion that as all else in being is rendered intelligible ultimately in

[52] If all being insofar as it exists is beautiful, ontologically there is no such thing as ugliness. We use the term to refer to beauty that is lacking, even as evil refers to goodness that is lacking. Most often, however, ugliness as a positive term refers to aesthetic ugliness—which is an entirely different thing.

relation to Absolute Being, so beauty, too, has the source and end of its meaning in reality in the First Cause of all being and all beauty. Plato wanted to know centuries ago if there was an absolute standard of beauty, pure beauty in which all beautiful things participate. For us there can be only the affirmation that there is. We have seen again and again that every perfection in being, every pure perfection, is first in its cause. And in its cause it is one with a pure act of existing. God, who is the perfect object of knowledge and the perfect object of love, and in whom these two—Truth and Goodness—are perfectly united, is perfectly beautiful. God, whose activity, object, and existence are one, is Perfect Beauty.

As all creatures participate in God's being so they participate in His beauty. Insofar as they exist, they are beautiful. Insofar as they are whatever they are, they are beautiful. If being as being is beautiful, every being and every aspect of being is beautiful. Men, who have an infinite need for being, have an infinite need for beauty. And this beauty is to be found at least partially in conscious and loving union with all the beings of experience. The rare flashes of beauty which touch our lives and leave them beautified carry with them all the beauty of all being. Each beautiful thing is a glimpse-through to Absolute Beauty. Every aspect of life, therefore, opens and offers its beauty. Even the mundane details connected with food, clothing, and shelter have their beauty. And the sacred revelation of personal being, the highest object to be known and to be loved, is the most beautiful revelation of all.

As beauty takes up within itself all the aspects of being, so the activity of joy which corresponds to beauty takes up within itself all the aspects of activity. Sometimes its meaning is restricted to an activity of the will, but here it might better refer to that activity which is the combined affirmation of knowledge and love. St. Thomas distinguishes between joy and happiness, meaning by joy the result in the will of happiness in the intellect, and by happiness the perfect good of an intellectual being. There is, however, perhaps a sense in which joy and happiness come together. For joy is the response to a good possessed, so that perfect joy should be the perfect response to the perfect good possessed perfectly. The perfect good is the beautiful, and the beautiful is the object of both intellect and will, so that the perfect good of the intellect is the perfect good of the will. In any case, God, Who is one with His activity, is not merely joyous or merely happy—He is subsistent Joy, subsistent Happiness. In the affirmation of His own infinite Beauty, He rejoices in infinite peace.

Infinite Beauty pours forth, so that what is found in God is participated by creatures. At the turning point of beautiful activity, lies creation—brought forth from Beauty, from a First Cause which is one and true and good. Created beings are led forth by Providence, a present, merciful, creative providence, to beauty, the subsistent Beauty who is for them, too, the perfect object of knowledge and love, their happiness and joy.

Our vision of reality, therefore, comes full circle. Our desire to understand the beings of our experience led us to an affirmation of God. In God we see the fullness of meaning of the transcendental aspects of being. In God we understand more fully the beings from which we learned to know of God.

SUGGESTED READINGS

Aristotle, *Nichomachean Ethics,* Books VIII and IX. On love and friendship.

Camus, Albert, *The Rebel,* trans. A. Bower, pp. 302–6. New York: Vintage Books, 1956. Rejection of nihilism and absurdity as responses to the problem of evil, without an embracing of theism.

Congar, Yves, "The Problem of Evil," *God, Man and the Universe,* ed. J. de Bivort de la Saudée. New York: P. J. Kenedy & Sons, 1953.

Crowe, F. E., "Complacency and Concern in the Thought of St. Thomas," *Theological Studies,* XX (March 1959), 1–39, XX (June 1959), 198–230. An attempt to understand love as something other than tendency.

Dubay, Thomas, "An Investigation into the Thomistic Concept of Pleasure," *The New Scholasticism,* XXXVI (January 1962), 76–99.

Gilleman, Gerard, *The Primacy of Charity in Moral Theology,* trans. W. F. Ryan and Andre Vachon, pp. 100–60. Westminster: The Newman Press, 1959. Metaphysical analysis of love as tendency.

Gilson, Etienne, *Elements of Christian Philosophy,* pp. 159–63. Garden City, New York: Doubleday & Company, Inc., 1960. Concerning transcendental beauty.

———, *Painting and Reality,* pp. 187–95. New York: Pantheon Books, Inc., 1957. Discussion on being and beauty.

———, *The Spirit of Medieval Philosophy,* trans. A. H. C. Downes, Chapter 14. New York: Charles Scribner's Sons, 1936. On goodness and love.

Johann, Robert O., *The Meaning of Love.* Westminster: The Newman Press, 1959.

Luijpen, William A., *Existential Phenomenology,* pp. 214–31. Pittsburgh: Duquesne University Press, 1960. On a phenomenology of love.

Marcel, Gabriel, *Royce's Metaphysics,* trans. Virginia and Gordon Ringer. Chicago: Henry Regnery Co., 1956. Chapter 5 on the problem of evil and its relation to human freedom.

Plato, *Symposium.* Concerned with the meaning of love.

St. Thomas Aquinas, *Summa Contra Gentiles,* 1, 91 (on God's love); I, 90 (regarding joy in God); I, 100–102 (divine happiness).

———, *Summa Theologiae,* I, 5, 1 and 3 (on the nature of goodness); I, 6, 1 (that God is good); I, 20 (concerning beauty); I, 26, 1 and 2 (on happiness in God); I, 19, 9; 48, 1; 49, 2 (on the problem of evil).

CONCLUSION 12

Now that we have completed our survey of the main lines of metaphysics, it is time for us to recapitulate and show how our discussion has given us some insight into the problems which we raised in the first chapter. The basic problem posed there, it will be remembered, was the problem of the meaningfulness of the universe. Our whole treatment of "being" has been an attempt to solve this problem, even though we were not able at every step to stop and show how the insights we achieved did help in its solution. Some of the questions we asked in the first chapter were: Is there more to the universe than appears at first glance? Does it have any sort of unity? Where did the universe come from and where is it going? Who are we and where are we going? All these questions about the meaning of the universe ultimately find their answer in our affirmation of God as the source of all being and as the guiding force in its development. Once we understand that God is Absolute Being, Pure Act, and Pure Existence, we realize that there is more to the universe than appears in our experience. We see, too, that there is a fundamental unity of being because all finite being derives from God as its creator and participates in His being. Our answer to the first question includes the answer to the question about the source and destination of the universe. God as Creator is the source of the universe and His Providence guides the world to the end He has in store for it. Finally, we are finite, intelligent beings who share in being in a special way through knowledge, who can be united to God and to all being in knowledge and love.

These insights give us a hierarchical view of the universe. Seeing God as the source and destiny of being, we can understand where we fit into the structure of being. Our lives will have to be an affirmation of the truth of being as it derives from God, and a love of being in keeping with God's plan. Our lives are not the blind gropings of hopeless creatures in an absurd world. Nor can they be tales told by an idiot signifying nothing. We are pilgrims on our way to a fuller union with God. In another discipline, moral philosophy, we will have to investigate the full significance of the fact that we are pilgrims. Since we are such, we cannot act as though we were not; as though we were not created by God and completely dependent on Him. Presumption is just as wrong as despair. Our lives can be meaningful, but we do not have within us their full meaning. We are finite beings and we must accept our finitude. This means that our lives have meaning because we are children of God and we must admit this source of meaning in our lives.

While insisting on these positive insights, however, we must never overlook the other side of the picture. What we know is very important, but it is very little compared to what we do not know. For instance, although we have uncovered the structure of being so we know that potency is the source of limitation, we do not know the detailed structure of very many beings. Man, whom we know best because we are men, is still a subject of metaphysical inquiry. For instance, just how are we to understand matter and spirit in man? How do the forms of things below man compare and contrast with the form of man, the human soul? These are but two of the countless questions which are still unanswered.

Similarly, we know that causes are at work and that every modification in being must be explained in terms of efficient and final causes. We have taken one big step toward understanding this problem by seeing that God in His Providence is the source of all being, and that He directs all being and every phase of being to the proximate and final goals which He decides for them. Again, this tells us something very important, but it tells us nothing about these goals except that in a general sense they must be compatible with God's being. We have emphasized these limitations on our knowledge in our discussions of the problem of evil and in our rejection of the "clock theory" of the universe as a proof for the existence of God. When we talk about causes, we can draw only the sketchiest of outlines. We know very little of how to fill in the rest.

Finally, although we can show that God exists and although in our human way we can get some idea of what God is, we must be very careful not to overestimate the depth of our insight. We have to realize that we have no direct, positive knowledge of God. All our ideas of God are derived ultimately from our human experience of finite being. We extrapolate from this and purify it of all limitation, and raise it to infinity. But in doing this we get so far away from the original meaning of the terms which we use that there is little real positive content in our ideas. We must strain our minds to the breaking point to get behind the words to the meaning they bear. And when we do this, we find how little we do understand.

The little we do understand, however, is most important. It tells us where we stand in the world and it gives us that tiny toehold on the truth about God which makes it reasonable for us to expect and accept His revelation. It gives us a world in which there is room for acceptance of God. This is perhaps a strange way to put it, but this is precisely the problem for many of our contemporaries. Without a valid metaphysics, they have a world view which makes any rational affirmation of God impossible. If they are to have faith in God, it must be a completely irrational faith, a leap into the absurd.

It is important to emphasize the value of the metaphysical view of the world which we have presented. It does give us a world view compatible with the divine revelation which is at the heart of the Judaeo-Christian religious tradition. Philosophy, of course, is no substitute for revelation—we have been careful to keep the two separate—and consequently philosophy cannot give the full basis for a way of life. Man does not live by philosophy alone. At the same time, if we are to avoid a kind of intellectual schizophrenia, we must have a philosophy and especially a metaphysics which does not contradict or undermine our total world outlook. We maintained that the metaphysical view of the world which we have outlined in this book helps us to avoid this intellectual schizophrenia. And this is one of its important values.

In choosing the particular issues which we have discussed rather than some others we have had to make decisions. Were this a monograph rather than a textbook we would have had to go more fully into many issues which we treated briefly and would have had to discuss several things which we omitted. For instance, we have not discussed relations or the predicaments generally, and we have limited our discussion of the proofs for the existence of God to one proof, leaving the treatment of the traditional five ways to an appendix. Our purpose, as we stated at the beginning, has been pedagogical. We have made no attempt to present a complete metaphysics and natural theology. We have, instead, constructed a course which we believe will give the student a solid introduction into the philosophy of being and God without overloading him with more than he can manage. Those who go on to major in philosophy will certainly need more than we have given here.

The approach we have taken, the problems we have studied, the arguments we have used, have all been chosen with one goal in mind, to help students to a fuller *understanding* of the meaning of being. To do this, even in an introductory text, has meant that we have had to push to the borderlines of human knowledge. This is especially clear in our discussions of causality, God, and the transcendentals. In handling these topics we found ourselves continually straining at the limits of human knowledge.

This straining was most acute, of course, when we talked about God and about the transcendentals with reference to God. We found ourselves looking out beyond what it is humanly possible to know into the area in which faith alone can tell us what we want to know. Divine revelation fills in our picture of God and tells us things about God of which the human mind could never dream. Philosophy does not enter this new country. It can only stand at the borders and point toward it. This we did especially in our discussion of the names of God.

Perhaps this is the point at which to conclude our treatment of metaphysics. We have gone as far as human reason will lead us in giving the general lines of a metaphysical world view. We recognize the limits we have reached, but we do not let them frighten us or keep us from seeing that we have achieved real insights into being and that we have come to a solid understanding of the *meaning of being*.

INDEX